The Need
To Question

THE NEED
TO QUESTION

An Introduction to Philosophy

Malcolm Clark

LOYOLA COLLEGE
Baltimore, Maryland

Prentice-Hall, Inc., Englewood Cliffs, New Jersey

Library of Congress Cataloging in Publication Data

CLARK, MALCOLM.
   The need to question.

   Includes bibliographical references.
      1.   Philosophy—Introductions.   2.   Questioning.
I.   Title.
BD21.59   100   72-5579
ISBN 0-13-610857-1

BD
21.59
.C5

© 1973 Malcolm Clark
   Englewood Cliffs, New Jersey

Printed in the United States of America

10   9   8   7   6   5   4   3   2   1

Prentice-Hall International, Inc., *London*
Prentice-Hall of Australia, Pty. Ltd., *Sydney*
Prentice-Hall of Canada, Ltd., *Toronto*
Prentice-Hall of India Private Limited, *New Delhi*
Prentice-Hall of Japan, Inc., *Tokyo*

To Edith
and Christopher

Table
of Contents

Preface

Philosophy was said by Kant to be like a lover with whom one repeatedly quarrels and yet to whom one always returns. It is difficult, maddening, fascinating, and all-absorbing.

Introductions are not completed at first meeting. If the relationship is a deep one, we find ourselves constantly being reintroduced. All starts afresh and is seen anew. So, in philosophy, even those who have already gone far need regularly to start again. Questioning foundations, which may contribute little in other disciplines, is the business of philosophers. It is their own questions they put in question.

If this is the reader's first encounter with philosophy, all he need bring is a questioning mind. Readily or reluctantly, he is caught up in questioning and cannot escape. What this book tries to show is that the traditional questions of philosophy are contained in any question we ask. The journey may seem to take us through strange lands, but its aim at each step is a renewed familiarity with what we already have and are.

The philosopher's task is to put himself in question. The discipline might be expected to reveal a remarkable unity. This, however, is far from apparent. Works of the classical philosophers are now easily available, and the beginner can have the primary sources on his desk at no great expense. But whether he reads them is another matter. Most are maddening without being fascinating. They are too difficult for the uninitiated to follow with appreciation, let alone with any feel of engaging in questions that are his.

Anthologies are a help. There are many today of high quality; selections are carefully made and introductory notes informative. But the array of topics, styles, and purposes is forbidding. Even the reflexes of the expert may not be sharp enough for the sudden change from a few pages of Plato and Aristotle to Descartes, Spinoza, Hume, Kant, Sartre, and Strawson.

This book is intended to lead a reader to the classical texts, rather than to replace them. It was written because some such preparation was found necessary in the effort to teach through the original works. Before he can explore the philosophical library with interest and with understanding, the beginner needs some grasp of the unity of the venture and some sense of its origins in his own experience as a questioner.

It is with this experience that the present book starts, and it is with this that it ends. The reader is invited to experiment with his own questioning and gradually to discover what is already involved in it. If our age stands out for its uncertainty, its lack of common purpose and accepted values, its questioning of where we are or where we should be going, then this introduction will be at home. The philosophy to which it introduces or reintroduces comes through a shaking of the foundations, from perplexity about our own perplexity.

The book owes its origins to a ''team-taught'' course. This project has strengthened two convictions. One is that philosophy grows out of disagreement and open discussion of differences; the student learns to think for himself by seeing other minds at work and at variance. But the second belief is that a consistent, comprehensive yet open position must be presented as a basis for such disagreement; and that is why I was asked to write this book. If its readers follow the argument with as critical a mind as my colleagues, the purpose of the book will have been met. Philosophical questioning is under way.

Philosophy, more than any other subject, comes from thinking for oneself. However, no discipline is so dependent on its history. Each philosopher finds his own questions by entering into those of others. Where have I found mine? A glance through the pages will indicate a debt to most of the important names in Western philosophy. But that of Kant occurs most frequently. There is much to be said for Karl Jaspers' view that each age of philosophy has its ''seminal thinker,'' on whom the subsequent ''creative orderers'' and ''great disturbers'' are alike dependent. For Jaspers, Kant is the seminal thinker for modern philosophy, as Plato and Augustine are for ancient and medieval.

Other historians may disagree. But at least the questions that troubled

Kant are still with us and serve as a common ground on which most contemporary schools of philosophy can find some way of expressing their differences. I have myself read Kant with eyes that may have been affected by Hegelian studies and influenced by certain recent writers, such as Ernst Cassirer, Emerich Coreth, and Bernard Lonergan. Yet there is no view without a viewpoint. To claim strict neutrality is to admit that one is not doing philosophy.[1] And those who have won a position in the history of philosophy did so, not by shopping in a supermarket of ideas, but by questioning a strongly defended line of questioning.

My main debt is clearly to my colleagues in the philosophy department of Loyola College, Baltimore: notably the chairman, Bernard Nachbahr, and the others who have been with the enterprise throughout, Frank Cunningham, James McAndrews, and John K. McCormack. Their own lectures in a common course supplied the starting point for many of the chapters. Their discussion and criticism in department meetings gave stimulus and shape for my writing. Their cooperation, rare enough among philosophers, provided a climate in which scattered notes could grow into a book.

I should also like to thank Stephen McNierney, the academic vice president, for his aid and encouragement, and Mrs. Genevieve Rafferty for her unfailing patience and good will in typing the many versions that led to the final manuscript.[2]

Malcolm Clark
Baltimore, Maryland

---

[1] I have tried to justify my philosophical position and historical interpretations in *Perplexity and Knowledge: An Inquiry into the Structures of Questioning* (The Hague: Martinus Nijhoff, 1972). In the present book, however, documentation has been kept at a minimum.

[2] One comment on terminology may avoid confusion. The word ''section'' is frequently used in the text; it refers to the primary divisions of each chapter, as shown in the table of contents.

1

What Do
Philosophers Do?

Everyone knows what it is to question. Or, if you do not, just ask and you will find out.

But what makes a question "philosophical"? How does it differ from those that are scientific or historical or religious? Reading various books and articles which are classified as philosophical will give you some idea of the distinction. You learn what sort of problems philosophers discuss. You see the way they put their questions, the type of answers for which they are looking.

The advice to explore and then reflect is sound. We do arithmetic and biology and art before asking what precisely they are. There must be grist for the mill before it starts grinding.

However, problems of method and scope are more intimate to philosophy than they are to physics or history or even to sociology. Philosophers disagree strongly among themselves about what philosophy is, and most beginners do not even know in which direction to look, let alone how to start walking. A gentle introduction is needed. This chapter will take three preliminary steps. The first section will look at the types of questions we normally ask and at those which are commonly, if not always in academic circles, called philosophical; the second section will indicate some of the tasks which professional philosophers regard as their business; and the third section will suggest what approach to philosophy this book adopts and what advice can be given to those who make their way through it.

Questions
Most People Ask

We spend a great deal of our time questioning. Sometimes our questions are explicit. We think them to ourselves or speak them to others. If we write them down we set a question mark at the end of each. But the question is not so easily ended—implicit questioning underlies all we think and say. We are problematic creatures, puzzled, hesitant, perplexed, doubting, wondering. Even when we feel most sure of ourselves and most certain of our statements, these come as answers to questions we have somehow posed or felt. You could never know or believe that the earth goes round the sun, or that pollution of the atmosphere is wrong, or that you will or will not survive death, unless you had somehow, however confusedly, put astronomical questions or moral questions or questions about life and death. Or could you?

The Range
of Questions

What sort of questions do you ask spontaneously? It would be an interesting experiment to carry a notebook and jot down the questions that come to mind throughout the day. Perhaps the first, as the alarm goes off, is what is the time? Or even, where am I? Then, as the needs of the day arise, a multitude of "how" questions come flooding in, technical questions of finding the means to goals: how to get work done, deal with people, enjoy life, cope with its many problems. Any grammar that gives a list of interrogative pronouns will help with the recognition of the questions that make up our everyday experience. For instance, scarcely an activity goes by without counting items, measuring things, or estimating distance. Can you eat a meal, drive a car, or even sit down without some questions beginning with a "how many," "how much," or "how far"?

These everyday practical questions may be easy or difficult to answer. But the method of answering is fairly straightforward. We take a look. We count or measure. We experiment. We see what happens.

There may be no great difference when we come to a second class of questions, which we call "scientific." What is the cause of cancer? Where is the center of gravity? When was the last ice age? How many electrons in an oxygen atom? How far from the earth to the sun? How can we help a manic-depressive? We cannot count electrons with a finger or pace off the distance to the sun. But the answers we expect for our scientific questions come from experimenting and taking a look. The fact that we count electrons by examining sophisticated instruments rather than "baby billiard balls" needs careful explanation but falls under the same sort of procedure as counting our toes.

The above practical and scientific questions may all be classified as questions of fact. What is meant by a "fact" is far from easy to state, and the following chapters will say much to question our confidence that the notion of a fact is clear and free of problems. But for the moment let us assume we know what we mean by saying it is or is not a fact that I have ten toes and an oxygen atom has eight electrons.

We may then go on to a third class of questions, ones that do not seem to be answered by any simple or sophisticated appeal to facts. The "how," "what," and "when" questions of my daily life are from time to time interrupted by "why" questions. Why should I carry on with distasteful work or put up with irritating people? Instead of an "is" question, answered by a fact, I have a "should" or "ought" question, answered by a "reason" for acting in a certain way.[1] Facts are involved, for example the fact that the unemployment rate is high and I may not easily get another job, or the fact that most jobs involve irritating people. But such facts merely postpone the appearance of a non-factual element, such as that I ought to work, or to live, or to respect people.

Such reasons are not disclosed by a scientist. He tells us what napalm does, not whether we ought or ought not to use it in warfare. Nevertheless, there is a sense in which we often, or even usually, treat moral situations much as purely factual ones. Work can become so much a part of our life that we simply take it for granted that we should work—unless an unexpected legacy comes our way, and even then we retire from work with a conscience made uneasy by force of habit. We accept what custom tells us much as we accept what the astronomer says. All too easily, we rely on the newspaper for values as well as for facts.

Still, there may be times—whether of revolt or of insight—when we recognize a class of questions beyond questions of fact and those of merely "accepted" values. Granted that custom or feeling or law or even God tells me I should work, or keep promises, or be courageous, ought I to follow such dictates, whatever authority lies behind them? The question is not what I am in fact told to do but what I ought to do for reasons that

---

[1] The following discussion could have been broadened by considering "value" questions in general, but for the sake of simplicity attention has been confined to moral questions.

are not reducible to any such fact of authority or to any mere fact of inclination on my part.

Going any further in this discussion would land us in difficult questions about the reality and nature of genuinely moral reasons or imperatives. We can safely postpone this to later chapters. The suggestion here can be left in conditional form. *If* there are value questions which cannot be reduced to questions of fact, then anyone acting for moral reasons will somehow or other be aware that he is acting for such reasons and not merely because he is in fact told to act this way or is in fact led to do so by custom or whim. This awareness may be confused and far from explicit. You do not have to study moral philosophy in order to act morally. But such awareness as there is will involve some recognition of moral reasons as distinct from mere facts.

That is, any genuinely moral action will require more than knowledge that the specific action does or does not fall under a given command or prohibition. It involves some knowledge of what it means to act for an "ought" rather than from an "is." Such knowledge, clear or confused, is an answer to a question about a question: namely, what is an "ought" question so far as it is not reducible to an "is" question?

Thus, in surveying the range of questions we commonly ask, we started with the ordinary factual questions of everyday life and the more sophisticated factual questions of science. Turning to moral questions we have distinguished between a factual element (What does custom, authority, or inclination say?) and a strictly non-factual element (Why ought I to follow what is "said"?). The latter, clearly or confusedly, involves a question about a question (What is an "ought" question as distinguished from an "is" question?).

Since this book will be largely concerned with questions about questions, we need a label for them. We may refer to them as *reflexive* questions and oppose them to *direct* questions. Whereas in the latter I take my question for granted and go directly in search of an answer (e.g., What does the law state?), in the former I reflect on problems contained in the question itself (e.g., What is law and am I bound to follow it?). Reflexive questions may seem esoteric and a discussion of them far removed from practical concerns. However, it will be argued later that some reflection on, and responsibility for, the way we put our questions is present at least implicitly in all our questioning.

Though not limited to the moral realm, reflexive questions come home to us here in a most personal manner. That is why they have been introduced in this way. Unless I at least vaguely ask myself whether I am acting morally and what it is to act morally, it is difficult to see that I could be acting morally rather than simply conforming. Nevertheless, the question is still open whether distinctively moral activity does exist.

Perhaps all our supposedly moral actions do come from hidden social pressures.

So we may turn to questions about questions as they arise in the first two classes, in our everyday problems of fact and in our science. As well as asking how many electrons a certain atom has, I may turn back on the problematic character of my question and inquire what it means to ask about the number of electrons. Are electrons really "things," like billiard balls, which can be counted, or do they merely belong to a "model of explanation," an imaginative scheme for talking about events we observe? That is, instead of asking a further scientific question, I ask a reflexive question about the meaning of my scientific questions. Similarly, instead of contenting myself with such direct questions as when a certain star exploded or what the time is now, I may ask what is meant by time, by events happening at the "same" time, by measurement in general. Instead of asking what causes cancer or what caused my sleepless night, I may ask what is meant by saying that anything is the "cause" of another thing. Or what is a "thing," or a "person," or a "fact"? Indeed, what is a "question"?

With such questions we are obviously in deep water. The suggestion is that it is philosophical water. The second section of this chapter will try to make reflexive questions a little less mysterious by looking at the various jobs they do. But first we may glance at a few of the ways people commonly use the word "philosophy," and we shall ask what these have to do with putting our questions into question.

Questions Thought To Be "Philosophical"

Many of us claim, or even boast, that we are practical-minded and have little use for theory. What this often means is that we are wild theorists who confront each problem with a different theory and make little effort to fit our theories together. To act without any theory at all is to act on sheer impulse—and this is by no means so easy as it sounds.

The word "philosophical" is commonly used in a variety of senses that seem to be linked to each other, and to the academic discipline, by the way in which different theories are united in some more comprehensive theory.

"MY PHILOSOPHY OF LIFE"

We all have attitudes and convictions with which we go ready-armed into the problems of each day. Life would be too complex if every question had to be thought out afresh, so we incline to answers which anyone who knows us well could probably predict.

Such attitudes have usually been picked up from our parents and peers, from television, newspapers, and casual reading. It is when they are in some way formulated and more or less unified that we speak of a man's "philosophy" in politics or business or personal relations. His "philosophy of life" draws together the convictions he has formed or inherited in various fields into a synoptic view.

This may offer both less and more than we get from the reflexive questioning described above. A philosophy of life is commonly built up piecemeal from largely unexamined opinions formed on little evidence. However, those philosophers who have gained a place in histories of the subject usually began by putting into question the beliefs that were handed down to them as "obvious." By such critical appraisal they have added coherence, clarity, and justification, and hence a certain stability and endurance, to the beliefs they have reformulated. Criticism is not here to be taken in a negative sense; convictions and ideals can be supported and extended by it. The philosophy of Plato is still with us. The "philosophies" of those politicians with whom he early became disillusioned passed away with them.

However, a philosophy one can defend through critical questioning will normally be less rich in detail than a set of beliefs coming from intense persuasion and scattered experience. This remark should serve as a warning at the beginning of a book on philosophy. False anticipations may be present that academic philosophy will reveal the "meaning of life" or give ready answers to pressing problems. What philosophy has to do with personal, social, and political questions must be asked repeatedly. But the philosopher is neither prophet nor oracle. He is a reflective person who puts into question all that originates elsewhere, even his own inherited questions. Reflection may come with age, and philosophers are often to be looked for when the convictions of a culture have begun to weaken. In Hegel's famous words: "When philosophy paints in colors of gray, life is already grown old; gray upon gray does not rejuvenate but at best helps us to understand. The owl of Minerva takes to flight only as the shades of dusk begin to fall." (from the preface to his *Philosophy of Law*)

"TAKING IT PHILOSOPHICALLY"

The more a person achieves a synoptic view, the less he is likely to be overwhelmed by changing events and current fads. The older we get the more we expect the depreciation and obsolescence of ideas. Perhaps it is not so surprising that, in an age when all is so open to sudden change, philosophy flourishes as an academic discipline. It is thought to offer a basis for calm and relaxed assessment. We learn to take upsets "philosophically."

Again, popular anticipations may be misleading. Professors of philosophy do not stand out from others for their equanimity. Concerned as they are with ideas and possibilities rather than with the details of "hard realities," philosophers are seldom found among the conservatives and may fall as easily as others for passing fancies. They are not notably successful at managing their personal lives and have usually been disasters when given political power.

Still, there may be an element of truth in the ancient search for the "consolations of philosophy." At least, the discipline is more explicitly concerned with questions about values than are most other subjects. Foolishness may sometimes be magnified rather than cured by a course of philosophy, but an already sound temperament can profit from the reflective habits of philosophizing. Questions must often be clarified before they can be answered, and putting old questions into question is sometimes the only way out of an impasse. Critical thinking is more likely than burning conviction to be dispassionate—and this is not the same as being passionless.

"ULTIMATE QUESTIONS"

Perhaps the commonest expectation people have in picking up a book of philosophy is neither to unify their various beliefs nor to acquire a calm detachment but to find a discussion of certain "great" questions: whether there is a God, what man's place is in the universe, whether he has an immortal soul. Today people are more likely to be disappointed in this expectation than in the previous two. Such questions are usually branded as "metaphysical," and the brand is read as saying they are meaningless or at best dependent on faith rather than reason.

To explain, let alone answer, this problem would take us far beyond these introductory remarks. The following section may offer some indications of what is involved, and the question will remain with us throughout the book.

Questions
Philosophers Ask

The chapter heading is relaxed. It asks what philosophers do. It does not claim that this is of more value than what others do, nor that we should all do it, at least in any academic way.

In the spirit of the title, this section will try to indicate the range of questions that philosophers ask today. Not all philosophers would agree that all questions in this list are valid or important, but to ignore any of them would be to omit, through prejudgment, something of the variety of tasks philosophers still claim even after abandoning many of the once great pretensions of the subject.

Tasks Left
by the Sciences

The senior university degree is still normally called a "doctorate in philosophy," though many get it who have read scarcely a word of any of the recognized philosophers. This is a survival of days when the term "philosophy" covered all knowledge. If you wanted to learn about the movement of planets or the fall of apples you studied "natural philosophy." If you wanted to learn about human behavior or emotions, you studied "philosophy of mind."

However, with the rise of the sciences, the imperial role of philosophy was reduced dramatically. Each of the special disciplines which now make up the departments of a university gained its independence. Each established a field and a method of its own and rejected dictation from the philosophers. To find out about the planets, men turned from the books of Aristotle and began looking through telescopes, recording their observations and founding the science of astronomy. Natural philosophy turned into the sciences of nature. Philosophy of mind became psychology. Philosophy was left an imperial capital without an empire.

The suggestion may be that philosophers have been playing a losing game, that their subject is the residue of mere talk when a precise way has been found of doing the work. However, the game is far from over. It seems that what has taken place is a clarification of the philosopher's role rather than a rejection. He may still feel a problem of identity, but there are at least some questions which the sciences leave to the reflective work of philosophy. Following are half a dozen such questions: they overlap, for they are all questions about questions.

QUESTIONS ABOUT METHODS

Problems arising within the special disciplines have made us realize that no mere declaration of independence could lead to an adequate understanding of their field and method. Physicists began to worry whether the things they talk about really exist, and whether the results of observations are dependent on the "interference" of the observer. Biologists wonder whether their study involves basic principles foreign to physics, whether it is right to speak in terms of "purpose." Historians wonder whether the situation of the historian introduces "subjectivity" or "objectivity" to his work and what these terms mean.

Now these are all reflexive questions. Questions about the status of a discipline and the meaning of its questions are not to be solved from within the discipline (though they suppose a competent knowledge of it). Here a genuine task remains which may still be called philosophical. The philosopher is required, and has contributed much, as a student of the methodology of the various special disciplines. He asks what each is doing and how they are related one to another. The philosophy of science has become a serious subject. So have the philosophy of history, of religion, of art, of language, of mathematics, of education. Philosophy reflects critically on all other disciplines, whereas they do not reflect critically on philosophy. To reverse each of the above titles produces some interesting results, but not ones that reverse the critical role.

QUESTIONS ABOUT ASSUMPTIONS

One of the earliest tasks of philosophy was the criticism of religion. The assumption that the gods existed and acted "literally" as described could not stand. And each reinterpretation of "god-talk" was shown to be based on certain assumptions which were open to criticism. So the task of sorting out what religion is telling us has continued till today. Whether the person who does this is believer or nonbeliever, theologian, scientist or historian, the task and its achievements are philosophical. The question is not about the details of particular religious problems but about the status of any such questions.

The same applies in political life. Revolution and evolution are both the product of a realization that systems stand on particular assumptions which can be brought to light and are criticized in the process.

It has been said that the most important point to notice in studying any thinker is not the explicit questions he poses but the ideas and beliefs he takes for granted. He thinks he has "solved" a problem or "explained" an event when he has reduced it to terms with which he feels completely at home and which strike him and his contemporaries so clearly as to need no further account. Thus he rests in an appeal to "God," or "matter," or "nature," or "law," or "experience," or "reason." Such explanation may perhaps be analyzed as a restatement of something in terms of current interests and assumptions.

However, it is precisely the problematic nature of these assumptions to which we need to be awakened. And it is in "stirring us from our dogmatic slumbers" that the questioner becomes philosophical. He cannot expect a happy reception from the sleeper, but the work has proceeded from Socrates to the present and may be listed among the continuing tasks of philosophy.

QUESTIONS ABOUT CONCEPTS

Closely allied to the above is the task of repeatedly clarifying the words that roll most easily off our tongue. We all know how the politician trades on the unexamined acceptance of key words and slogans, though they change from age to age: democracy, communism, liberty, equality, rights, peace, law and order. We are grateful to any critic or commentator who helps us to see the diverse applications of such terms, the many different ways in which they are used.

Yet multi-colored words make up·our life far beyond the political realm. We live in a world of words. They pass like coins from hand to hand till their outline becomes obscure and their cash value uncertain. Such obscurity allows for the development of language. But none of our problems can go far toward solution without a keen analysis of the diversity of meanings.

In any attempt to be clear, we are all engaged in this task. Yet philosophers, by temperament and by training, may be specially fitted for it. Some, notably today, hold that the philosopher's main work is that of "linguistic therapy." Perplexity comes from muddle in the way we state problems, and the most important contribution we can make is to help untie the knots. According to a famous saying of Wittgenstein, the philosopher's aim is "to show the fly the way out of the fly-bottle." It might even be said that the whole story of philosophy is a commentary on some of our key notions, such as "idea," "form," "real," "subject," "good," "free," "cause," "meaning." Though the cynic may comment that philosophers have contributed their share of mystification, this work of reflecting critically on basic concepts represents a remarkable achievement and a continuing task.

QUESTIONS ABOUT ALTERNATIVES

The depositions of Plato, Aristotle, Thomas Aquinas, Descartes, Spinoza, Leibniz, Locke, Berkeley, Hume, Kant, Hegel, merely mean that ideas which these men introduced into the philosophic tradition must be construed with limitations, adaptations, and inversions, either unknown to them or even explicitly repudiated by them. A new idea introduces a new alternative, and we are not less indebted to a thinker when we adopt the alternative which he discarded. Philosophy never reverts to its old position after the shock of a great philosopher.[2]

---

[2] Alfred North Whitehead, *Process and Reality* (copyright 1929, by The Macmillan Company, New York; renewed 1957, by Evelyn Whitehead), p. 16.

Philosophers, old and new, are exposed to the charge that they make no progress. Putting the commonly accepted ground of discussion into question may yield the satisfaction of shocking but appears to lead nowhere. Surely progress in knowledge consists in standing on the firm shoulders of our predecessors and making our own contribution to the store of facts?

Now if we are certain that we are in full command of our question, then progress can consist only in the discovery of an answer. However, the suggestion may have come across in these pages that all questions are themselves questionable. Even scientists today feel less confident than before that they know exactly what they are asking and what scientific explanations achieve. In all fields, particularly the more practical ones, we are familiar with questions that seem to yield no answer. Neither "yes" nor "no" will work. There is no way out of the impasse but to return to the question and ask if it cannot be reformulated in a more fruitful way.

That is, alternatives are not fixed. We do not stand at the junction of two roads already laid out before us; the "roads" are projected in terms of the way we put our question. The apparently obvious choice between theism and atheism may not be so rigid as many take it to be. The scientist no longer allows himself to be forced into choosing between a particle theory and a wave theory of light. The more we put our questions into question, the less happy we become with stereotyped debating on problems of freedom and determinism, relativism and absolutism, capitalism and socialism.

This art of seeing old problems in a new light, of revealing possibilities unrecognized by our predecessors, may be one of the more valuable results of a philosophical training. To disclose a fresh alternative is liberating, whether in politics or religion, in labor disputes or in our personal life. It is a creativity that goes beyond the mere rearrangement of old pieces in a new pattern. Such originality is certainly not shown only by professional philosophers. But this is the sort of progress in knowledge for which they look in "reformulating questions."

QUESTIONS ABOUT
WHAT MUST BE SO FOR ALL

All philosophers would probably agree that the four tasks above, if seen as calmly analytic and descriptive, do belong to their subject. Since Socrates, philosophers have been engaged in the critical questioning of assumptions, concepts, and methods, and this work has borne fruit in a renewal of the alternatives we face. Two further tasks will now be considered. Philosophers today are not all agreed that these are valid, though they would admit that the effort has been made in one form or another throughout Western philosophy. It is with these two tasks that we come to the ambiguous and difficult notion of "metaphysics."

The first claim to be considered here is that philosophers disclose what is necessary in the strongest sense, what must belong to anything that exists. The claim is a remarkable one and distinguishes the philosopher (as metaphysician) from all other scholars. To ignore it is to miss much of the fascination of philosophy.

Terms that convey necessity are used in a variety of ways. Let us consider several uses of the word "impossible."

a) It is impossible for me to come tomorrow morning because I have an appointment with the dentist.

Here the impossibility is clearly conditional or hypothetical. *If* I set a higher priority on my dental appointment, then I cannot come. But I can choose to come with a toothache.

b) It is impossible for parallel lines ever to meet.

As mathematicians now tell us gladly, this impossibility is also conditional. The parallel postulate is only a postulate. We may choose to accept it, as in Euclidean geometry, or to deny it, as in other geometries. So, every system of mathematics begins with a series of axioms. These are not absolutely necessary truths but are defined to hold, or not, as we choose. The necessary truths of mathematics are only hypothetically necessary.

c) It is impossible to dissolve gold in hydrochloric acid.

What happens in a chemical experiment is obviously not the mere result of a choice I make. However, the necessity which science reveals comes only from the way things have been observed to behave. The scientist organizes his observations in a most comprehensive way and predicts results with great confidence. Yet no scientist claims to have proved that things must happen as they do, that the world could not possibly have revealed different laws or the same laws with different numerical values. Hence the necessities of science are still only hypothetical. They depend on a variety of *if*'s: "if things continue to behave as we have observed them up to now," "if we agree to classify and relate things in this way rather than that." Indeed, during this century we have come to realize acutely the extent to which science is conventional. The principle of inertia, for example, has proved immensely valuable, but recent astronomical discoveries may make it advisable to change the conventions and develop a physics that allows the principle to be broken.

d) It is impossible for an event to happen without a cause.

If my car breaks down, I may not be able to do anything about it because I am not much of a mechanic. But if I do nothing because I say there was no cause for its breaking down, then you may think it is more than mechanics I lack. Is the necessity that every event has a cause also merely conditional or hypothetical? Could anything "just happen"? Could we change our conventions and develop a system of thought that allowed the principle of causality to be broken? Most philosophers have replied to these questions in the negative. Some have tried to justify their reply. If you think they are wrong, then you have learned opinion on your side. But at least since the time of Plato there have been philosophers to make the claim that they can disclose features of reality which are absolutely necessary and hence completely universal. If an event *must* have a cause, then *every* event has a cause.

The four tasks of philosophy mentioned above have not taken us beyond science in any very dramatic way. Scientists spend much of their time questioning assumptions and clarifying concepts, though in philosophy the analysis may go a bit deeper. But the fifth task, if valid, takes us clearly beyond the pretensions of any record of what we happen to find. This is one meaning that has been read into the word *metaphysics*: "beyond physics or science."[3]

QUESTIONS "BEYOND" . . .?

The title of the final task has been left incomplete and a question mark added. To be more definite would involve taking a position at this early stage on one of the most basic and most acute problems of philosophy.

As mentioned at the end of the first section of this chapter, a frequent anticipation is that philosophers spend their time on "ultimate" questions, topics such as those of the soul and God. However, it is recognized that such topics—if valid—take us beyond the procedure we find in the sciences and other special disciplines. A physiologist who tells us of the functions of the brain starts with the data of observation and presents conclusions which are meaningful only so far as they represent other particular facts we can see or somehow record. A historian likewise begins with items given in documents or elsewhere and draws conclusions

---

[3] The origin of the term was accidental. The ancient editors of Aristotle's works happened to set after his "physics" a collection of writings which discuss what must belong to anything that is. Lacking a better title, they referred to these as *ta meta ta phusika,* the writings after the "physics."

which, if less directly "verifiable" than those of a scientist, are at least accounts of what we could have observed if we had been living at that time. But talk of God or of the soul is quite different. Though we may also start with particular facts (e.g., change in nature, language in man), it is normally assumed that reasoning here takes us to conclusions that are beyond the need or possibility of verification in any similar observations. People who believe in the existence of God do not usually suppose that their belief will be proved by a happy turn of events or disproved by a disaster. Those who believe in the immortality of the soul do not in most cases submit their conclusions to the evidence of voices they hear or ghostly figures they see.

Terminology may help to state the problem. The experience of particular facts or data to which the scientist refers at each stage of his work may be called "empirical." He reasons from the empirical to the empirical. But this notion of metaphysics seems to involve the claim that we can reason to realities that are beyond empirical experience. The traditional, though perhaps over-simple, interpretation of Plato is that this is precisely what he was doing. And Aristotle seems to have held that the discovery of what must belong to any being in the world involves the disclosure of truths about "spiritual" beings "separated" from the world.[4]

Many philosophers, however, even in allowing for metaphysics as an investigation of what must belong to anything we can know in this world, deny that we can reason to any reality "beyond." How could we even talk of such realities, since our language is constructed for expressing a world of particular objects in observable relations? Are we sure it is meaningful to apply the plural to "soul" or to ask how the soul is related to the body or the world to God?

Possibly such problems can be reformulated in terms of basic ambiguities in the notion of "experience," a word we take all too much for granted. Can we go beyond empirical experience without going beyond experience as such? Can metaphysics take us beyond the experience of particular beings observable in the manner of the sciences and yet avoid the claim to take us beyond any aspect of human experience and hence beyond any meaningful discussion? Such questions will demand a good deal of tortuous thinking, but anyone who sets up a program which shirks them is turning his back on tasks most philosophers have regarded as central.

---

[4] Terms to be explained later may simply be mentioned here. The study discussed under the fifth heading has been called "general" metaphysics or "transcendental" philosophy. What has been indicated under this sixth heading has been called "special" or "transcendent" metaphysics.

Example of a Philosopher
at Work: Descartes

This chapter has already run a good distance talking in very general terms about what philosophers do. An example is overdue. As philosophers need to be taken in large doses, no brief example would be fair. But, at risk of injustice, some quotations will be given from one of the more readable philosophers. At the beginning of his *Discourse on Method*, René Descartes (1596–1650) describes how he happened to turn to philosophy and explains the first steps in his method :[5]

I was brought up on letters from my childhood; and since it was urged on me that by means of them one could acquire clear and assured knowledge of all that is useful in life, I was extremely eager to learn them. But as soon as I had finished the whole course of studies at the end of which one is normally admitted among the ranks of the learned, I completely altered my opinion. For I found myself embarrassed by so many doubts and errors, that it seemed to me that the only profit I had had from my efforts to acquire knowledge was the progressive discovery of my own ignorance. (p. 9)

[He then discusses the problems he found with literature, history, mathematics, theology, and he continues :]

I will say nothing of philosophy but this: seeing that it has been cultivated by the most outstanding minds of several centuries, and that nevertheless up to now there is no point but is disputed and consequently doubtful, I had not enough presumption to hope to fare better there than others had; and considering how many different opinions on a given matter may be upheld by instructed persons, whereas there can at most be only one that is true, I almost regarded as false whatever was no more than plausible.

As for the other sciences, inasmuch as they borrow their first principles from philosophy, I judged that no solid building could have been made on such shaky foundations. . . .

That was why, as soon as my age allowed me to pass from under the control of my instructors, I entirely abandoned the study of letters, and resolved not to seek after any science but what might be found within myself or in the great book of the world. (pp. 12–13)

[He explains how, having set aside all his academic learning, he de-

---

[5] The best translation of this work is by Elizabeth Anscombe and Peter Geach (London: Thomas Nelson and Sons Limited, 1954). The following quotations and page numbers are from this edition.

veloped principles for acquiring knowledge from his own resources. After applying these with success to certain problems in mathematics and science, he turned to his first "metaphysical meditations":]

I had noticed long before, as I said just now, that in conduct one sometimes has to follow opinions that one knows to be most uncertain just as if they were indubitable; but since my present aim was to give myself up to the pursuit of truth alone, I thought I must do the very opposite, and reject as if absolutely false anything as to which I could imagine the least doubt, in order to see if I should not be left at the end believing something that was absolutely indubitable. So, because our senses sometimes deceive us, I chose to suppose that nothing was such as they lead us to imagine. Because there are men who make mistakes in reasoning even as regards the simplest points of geometry and perpetrate fallacies, and seeing that I was as liable to error as anyone else, I rejected as false all the arguments I had so far taken for demonstrations. Finally, considering that the very same experiences (*pensées*) as we have in waking life may occur also while we sleep, without there being at that time any truth in them, I decided to feign that everything that had entered my mind hitherto was no more true than the illusions of dreams. But immediately upon this I noticed that while I was trying to think everything false, it must needs be that I, who was thinking this (*qui le pensais*), was something. And observing that this truth "I am thinking (*je pense*), therefore I exist" was so solid and secure that the most extravagant suppositions of the sceptics could not overthrow it, I judged that I need not scruple to accept it as the first principle of philosophy that I was seeking.

I then considered attentively what I was; and I saw that while I could feign that I had no body, that there was no world, and no place existed for me to be in, I could not feign that I was not; on the contrary, from the mere fact that I thought of doubting (*je pensais à douter*) about other truths it evidently and certainly followed that I existed. On the other hand, if I had merely ceased to be conscious (*de penser*), even if everything else that I had ever imagined had been true, I had no reason to believe that I should still have existed. From this I recognized that I was a substance whose whole essence or nature is to be conscious (*de penser*) and whose being requires no place and depends on no material thing. Thus this self (*moi*), that is to say, the soul, by which I am what I am, is entirely distinct from the body, and is even more easily known; and even if the body were not there at all, the soul would be just what it is. (pp. 31–32)

[He then goes on to a proof of God's existence and adds his version of the famous "ontological argument":]

Going back to an examination of my idea of a perfect Being, I found that this included the existence of such a Being, in the same way as the idea of a triangle includes the equality of its three angles to two right angles. . . .

Consequently it is at least as certain that God, the perfect Being in question, is or exists, as any proof in geometry can be.

The reason why many people are convinced that there is difficulty in knowing God, and even in knowing what their soul is, is that they never raise their mind above sensible objects. . . . If there are still men not sufficiently convinced of the existence of God and of their soul by the reasons I have brought forward, I would have them know that everything else that seems to them more sure—that they have a body, that there are stars and an earth, and so on—is really less certain. (pp. 34–35)

Before this book has gone very far, it will be clear that the position it adopts is at some distance from that of Descartes. But the quotation has been given at length because it illustrates many of the aspects of philosophical questioning listed above.

One can see in Descartes the philosopher's dissatisfaction with piecemeal approaches to knowledge resting on no secure basis, and his own desire for a synoptic vision and unshakable foundations. His method begins with reflexive questioning, the attempt to doubt every assumption he had previously held, even his belief in the reality of his own body. In the absolute impossibility of doubting his own existence, Descartes finds a foundation that is necessary in the strong sense demanded by metaphysics. Then he slips easily over to the further sense of metaphysics in concluding to the existence of God and the soul as beings altogether separable from the material world.

A further reason for giving this quotation from Descartes is that he offers a striking argument which is open to criticism at all stages. We are supplied with a model on which we can try out our own philosophical analysis. This leads to the final section of this chapter.

Questions This Book Will Ask

This section is brief. It will mention some of the difficulties confronting any student of philosophy. Then the policy of this book will be considered, the options made and the attendant dangers. Finally, a few hints will be given on reading philosophy.

The Difficulty of Philosophy

Everyone can have a "philosophy of life." Most can express their convictions simply and strikingly. But few can read Aristotle or Kant or Whitehead without great effort and much help.

A writer who is needlessly obscure deserves not to be read. Perhaps most philosophers merit the accusation and receive the penalty. Yet much of their obscurity of expression comes from the fact that what they are trying to express is obscure. In passing from a philosophy of life to academic philosophy, one becomes involved in the most general and most fundamental of all subjects. The words we find at hand were not designed for this.

The words and grammar we use were fashioned in an attempt to pose everyday practical questions. Needing to hit things sharply, man developed a hammer and a word for this instrument. The extension of language to cover scientific questions created no great difficulty. We may not be able to point out a nucleus the way we can a hammer, but a nucleus still fits readily into a language of particular things in relation to each other. Yet when the metaphysician tries to talk or think of what must belong to everything that is, he is no longer talking of particular things or particular properties of things. He has to invent or radically adapt words (e.g., "form," "category," "structure"). If he then speaks of "forms" in the plural, or of form "and" matter, he is straining language beyond its normal uses and perhaps creating false problems. We have already met some of the difficulties given to the philosopher by the little word "beyond."

Even if we had an adequate language, philosophy would still present more basic problems than all other subjects. These can say, by and large, what sort of things they will investigate and what method they will follow. A geologist will study a rock by various types of measurement; he will not attend to the empty beer can nearby or make moral judgments about the person who left it. But a philosopher can simply exclude nothing from his concern. He does not measure but must ask what measurement is. Whether or not he is called upon to make aesthetic and moral judgments, he must at least ask what these are.

Now clarity and precision come very largely from delimiting the object and method of one's questions. This is how each of the sciences established itself and broke away from philosophy. And it may seem that the philosopher is left in complete confusion, not knowing where to start, what to look for, or by what method to proceed.

Hence the suspicion that philosophy is the most subjective of disciplines, indeed that it altogether lacks "discipline." If there is no agreement on where to go, then surely "anything goes." And the influence of the phrase "philosophy of life" does lead many to expect that a philosopher will give us his "credo" or "insights," his highly particular way of seeing and evaluating things. Are not all philosophies relative, expressions of individual temperament or at best the "ideological superstructure" of a certain age, of a society and its way of making a living? (Karl Marx)

This book will later examine the word "subjective" and suggest senses quite contrary to "particular" or "capricious." But does not the history of philosophy reveal a chaos of conflicting opinions that would not be tolerable in any of the sciences or even in history, that battleground of heated scholarship?

If we limit the scope of philosophy to clarifying questions, concepts, and assumptions, then this task remains difficult but respectable. It is when we turn to metaphysics that the difficulty of method casts serious doubts on the validity of the discipline. Immanuel Kant (1724–1804) saw his main work as asking:

> . . . whether such a thing as metaphysics is possible at all. If it is a science, how does it come about that it cannot establish itself, like other sciences, in universal and lasting esteem? If it is not, how does it happen that under the semblance of a science it ceaselessly gives itself airs and keeps the human understanding in suspense with hopes that never fade and are never fulfilled? Whether we demonstrate our knowledge or our ignorance, something certain must at last be settled about the nature of this would-be science; for things cannot possibly go on any longer on their present footing. It seems almost ridiculous, while every other science makes ceaseless progress, to be constantly turning round on the same spot without moving a step forward in the one that claims to be wisdom itself and whose oracle everyone consults. Also it has lost a great many of its supporters, and we do not see those who feel themselves strong enough to shine in other sciences wanting to risk their reputation in this one, in which everyone who is ignorant in all other things arrogates to himself a decisive judgement; for there is in fact no sure weight and measure as yet in this territory with which to distinguish soundness from shallow chatter.[6]

Nevertheless it is a safe prediction that the chatter will continue. The imperative to question to the limit and to question the limit itself lies deep in the structure of reason. Whatever we decide about the status of this would-be science, we have a "natural disposition" to ask metaphysical questions. No resolution of the affair has kept them from returning. Or, to borrow another image from Kant, we are seafarers who find ourselves already embarked on a voyage with a goal we can never reach yet never abandon.

[6] From the preface to his *Prolegomena to any Future Metaphysics*, trans. Peter G. Lucas (Manchester University Press, 1953, 3rd. imp. 1962), pp. 3–4.

Options,
Gain and Loss

If such is the voyage, it would be futile to try to plot an exact course in advance. We shall ask questions and see where we are taken. Yet some decisions have been made at the beginning, and it is only honest to mention them and warn of the loss which any decision entails.

Some introductions to philosophy are historical. They start with Thales and proceed step by step to the present. This procedure is respectable but has been rejected here. Even if attention is limited to the major figures, any such survey of man's most difficult thoughts appears all too easily as a rapid tour through what Hegel described whimsically as "a museum of the aberrations of the human mind." If it took Plato, Kant, and Heidegger each a lifetime to work out a never complete version of what he thought, how can a beginner repeat the task for these and many others in a few months?

So this approach will be "problematic" rather than historical. As the chapter headings suggest, each will tackle some general question. The same objection could be posed, that no one question can be solved in a few pages. But philosophical questions are not "solved" as others are. And each leads on easily to the next. Devoting twenty pages to the problem whether machines can think may take a beginner further on the way toward his own philosophical thinking than a like chapter which summarizes what various philosophers have said about thought.

The danger with such a method is that the student could complete it without ever hearing the names of the classical philosophers. So the main figures of Western philosophy will be introduced at points where their questions are relevant to the discussion. For instance, the first half of Chapter Five consists in an exposition of the approach made to metaphysics by Aristotle, Descartes, and Kant. This is no substitute for a history of philosophy or for first hand acquaintance, but it is hoped that the bait may occasionally be swallowed. The more readable philosophical works have been made amply available today.

There is a related choice that any introduction to philosophy must make. Many authors of such books feel bound to cultivate a detachment that commits them to none of the views they present. However, the result is likely to resemble a shopwindow. Also, such detachment is usually specious. The way in which an author selects and organizes opinions, especially the way in which he expounds them, will either reveal his own position or will be so superficial as to be useless. The present author agrees with R.G. Collingwood that if asked (1) to describe Plato's theory of Forms and (2) to explain whether it is true or not, he has been asked only one question.

Hence this book will unashamedly work its way toward a coherent philosophical position. In an approach based on the experiment of questioning, the fear of uncritical acceptance by the reader is not great. It is more easy to form opponents than disciples. Indeed, philosophizing starts through opposition and argument. It is the shop window that produces both skepticism and dogmatism.

Finally, an option has to be made between depth and breadth. Perhaps it was a mistake to try to cover so many topics in one book. Twice as many pages per chapter and half as many chapters might have been better. However, the attempt at a coherent approach lessens the danger of a butterfly study. It could even be that the reader is helped to go more deeply into one problem by trying his wits at another. In philosophy, fecundity may not be irrelevant to truth. There is wisdom in Hegel's remark that ''just as superficiality is vain, so there is a depth of thought which is empty. . . . The power of mind is only as great as its expansion, its depth only as true as its daring to expose and give itself in its expressions.'' (from the preface to the *Phenomenology of Mind*)

Hints on
Doing Philosophy

. . . The universities send more addle-heads into the world than any other institution. . . . The youngster is sprung on them from schools where he was accustomed to learn. So now, thinks he, I'll "learn" philosophy. But that is ridiculous. What he should be learning is *to philosophize*. Let me explain. It is possible strictly to "learn" only where [as in history, languages or law] . . . we can be presented with an already accomplished discipline. So before we could learn philosophy this way, we should need to have it right there before us. We should have to be able to point at some book and say, "Here it is, here is true wisdom and insight!" (Kant's announcement of his lectures for 1765–66)

Philosophy is like the measles. It must be caught from someone who is already infected. To learn to philosophize, you must try your luck arguing with a live philosopher.[7]

Sharp words, and they put this book in its place. It does not consist of thoughts to be learned. Instead it offers questions and arguments which the reader must question if he is to take the first steps toward his own philosophizing.

Paper does not easily spread the measles, and the need for discussion

---

[7] Elmer Sprague, *What is Philosophy?* (New York: Oxford University Press, 1961), p. 3.

—equally with philosophers and peers—is gladly admitted. Yet some groundwork and prompting are required for any "yes" and "no" to begin. These pages propose to make a start.

How are they, and more serious philosophical works, to be read? Descartes offers the following advice to the reader of his longest work:

> I should desire that it may first of all be run through in its entirety like a novel, without forcing the attention unduly upon it or stopping at difficulties. . . . After that it may be read a second time in order to notice the sequence of my reasoning. . . . It is only necessary to mark with a pen the places where difficulty is found and continue to read without interruption to the end. Then if the book is taken up for a third time, I venture to say that [the reader] will discover the solution of the greater part of the difficulties which have formerly been marked. . . .[8]

The last sentence is over-optimistic. But the advice to try several readings of each chapter, with progressive attention to arguments and criticism of them, is very sound. One's first need is to discover what the question is, and this is more difficult in philosophy than in other subjects. At this stage, sympathy with the writer must be at its greatest. Assume his problem is genuine and he knows what he means. Where his question and his reply remain obscure, experiment with various interpretations as you go along, until one begins to fit. But do not delay over details on a first reading.

Approach the second reading as a test for whatever interpretation seems to hold best. Underline key words and sentences. Put marks or comments in the margin at sections which seem most critical or most open to criticism. Then with a third reading you may know your way around and can identify the lines of argument and the points at which you wish to direct your own questions.

Your job is to ask: What does the writer mean? Is it true? What would I say? That is: understanding, criticism, reconstruction. It was suggested above that the three may, in the end, turn out to be one. But the beginner is advised to try at first to keep them as distinct as possible.

In learning to philosophize, the problem is largely one of locating ambiguity in words and in arguments. For example, in the long quotation given from *The Discourse on Method,* Descartes finds he can doubt the reality of all particular material things, even his own body, but cannot doubt the reality of his own self (soul) as a thinking being. From this he concludes that he is only a soul which could be just as it is even

---

[8] *Principles of Philosophy,* Author's Letter, from *The Philosophical Works of Descartes,* trans. E.S. Haldane and G.R.T. Ross (copyright Cambridge University Press, 1911; reprinted by Dover Publications, Inc., 1955), I, 209–10.

without his body. Is he right? Has he proved that he is *only* a thinking being? Or has he *only* proved that he is at least a thinking being, leaving open the question whether he could continue to be such with the death of his body? The two conclusions, differing in the place of the word *only*, are in marked contrast. Is Descartes mistakenly drawing the stronger conclusion when merely the weaker one follows from his argument?

Again, in his ''ontological proof'' of God, Descartes argues that the idea of a perfect Being includes the existence of such a Being with the same logical necessity that the idea of a triangle includes the equality of its three angles to two right angles. But, he claims, we do have the idea of a perfect Being. Hence, he concludes, God must exist. Is this a valid argument? Has he rightly concluded that God exists, or only that anyone who has an idea of God must have an *idea* of God as existing?

Such, at least, are the sort of questions the reader can try to locate and clarify in studying this or any other philosophical book. Then, for the measles, turn to a live philosopher.

2 | Can the Machine Take Over?

The opening chapter distinguished between the convictions of a personal philosophy of life and the study of academic philosophy. It suggested that the distinction is no chasm. We can indeed spend our whole life asking what is its meaning, and what we ought to do, without ever sitting down to thrash out the question what is meant by "ought" questions and by "meaning" itself. However, such questions about questions do lie at the heart of our spontaneous problems and will sooner or later be asked explicitly by someone. Concern about the meaning of suffering may be quite different from inquiry into the meaning of sun spots. When Job asked why he was born, he would probably not have been satisfied by an explanation of the facts of life. Confusion coming from failure to question our own questions can be an obstacle to the clarification and solution of our most personal and spontaneous questions.

Philosophers have been led to reflective questioning along many different paths. Plato found his way to philosophy from practical concerns about politics, morality, and pedagogy and from an interest in mathematics. Aristotle began with the questions of a biologist, and the medievals came with those of a theologian; most of the seventeenth- and eighteenth-century philosophers can be understood only in the light of the newly developed natural sciences.

Where are we to begin? This could be largely a matter of individual preference. If you take any question and push it far enough, soon it will lead you into the traditional concerns of philosophy. But it must be *your* question, not someone else's puzzle.

However, every book must propose a common starting point for its readers, some concern which they can make their own. So the first section of this chapter will indicate the difficulties we face in an age that is increasingly dominated by the spread of technology. The following sections will invite the reader to draw from this a personal question, one that is directed at his own existence as a person. What am I that cannot eventually be taken over by "the machine," whether this be electronic or bureaucratic? Am I more than a complex series of functions, destined sooner or later to be replaced in all my "human" activities by the advance of technology? If humanity does represent something "more," what is this?

The problem is real, the question most intimate. Threats once posed through the possibility of invasion by intelligent beings from outer space have now taken a more terrestrial form. Our struggle is to save ourselves from our inventions. Automation is not merely a problem of loss of jobs; more fundamentally the loss is of self-respect. And our embarrassment leads us quickly to the heart of philosophical questions, which may still in their odd way reformulate the ancient imperative of Socrates: "know thyself."

The Threat of Technology

Broad generalizations must be excused in the rapid survey of this section. People clamor to tell us "what's wrong with us today." At least, the conviction seems common that there is something radically wrong. This may itself be a mark of our century as contrasted with its predecessor. Then there was a sense of confidence, a complacency in the power of science and industry to solve all our problems, a belief that progress was inevitable. Today we are by no means so sure. We have seen wars more widespread and destructive than any before. In this century more men have been engaged in killing each other than in any other five centuries together. And the conflicts between races, between classes, between generations, between political ideologies, have never been so keenly recognized or have threatened such grave consequences.

The brave hopes men once had that the means for solving their major problems were within their grasp have now faded. We may vote for our leaders, broadcast our opinions freely, travel widely; but we realize all the more painfully how powerless we are. Perhaps never before have so many been so much at the mercy of the decisions of so few. And never before have even these few been so helpless before growing problems that seem to escape solution.

It would be far beyond present purposes to investigate any such questions. What is proposed here is that we reflect on our sense of powerlessness in the midst of plenty. For this sense is acute. Even if some unexpected twist of history could unite east and west, white and black, young and old, developed and underdeveloped countries, still the threat of alien forces would remain. The very technology which held out such hopes of giving control now seems to be taking control. To solve problems of production and distribution would only set in focus our insecure hold on the quality of human life.

The term "alienation" is frequently heard today. It will form one of the principal themes running through this book. Briefly, it means becoming a stranger to oneself, no longer feeling "at home," losing one's "self-identity." I am alienated when I become unsure of what I am and can expect to be, when I fail to express and find myself in what I do.

The word is commonly associated with the economic and philosophical theories of Karl Marx, and connected most clearly with the rise of industrial society. The worker may once have owned the instruments of his trade. He expressed his ability and personality in what he produced, and he disposed of his products as he chose. But with the rise of industry, the means of production became concentrated in the hands of a few. The worker lost control. He became separated from his work, could no longer find himself in it, and could overcome this alienation only through a revolution in which the expropriated recover control.

All too crudely, this is the account Marx offered of alienation and its solution. But whatever the value of his theories for his own time, it could be that his problems are no longer ours. To apply labels, we may say that he lived in an industrial society whereas we live in a technological one. And the resulting problem of alienation may go far deeper.

What is the difference? Perhaps a look at the word "technology" will be suggestive. It comes from the Greek *technē,* meaning a skill, a craft, a regular method of making something. However, we sometimes speak rather disparagingly of a man as "a mere technician." We mean that he is skilled at following the rules of a job, but without fully understanding why they apply. The television repairman can indeed mend your set by carrying out the instructions of his manual without knowing the theory of television or of electricity. This usage is faithful to the Greek. Plato assigned *technē* to *doxa* (mere opinion) and distinguished it from *epistēmē* (adequate knowledge). He would say that the technician is like the pupil who simply follows the rules for bisecting an angle without knowing enough geometry to see why the two angles he forms must be equal. He may work efficiently but does not see into his work or "possess" it. He is an alienated worker.

Now this is the threat that technological society poses. It represents a more radical alienation than the industrial society which Marx wrote about. The factory worker may not have had legal ownership of the machinery or the articles he helped to produce. His work may have been monotonous, offering little scope for the expression of his individuality. But he did at least understand his work and in this sense possess it. For the lathe simply does more quickly and powerfully what human hands can do. The principle is the same and is understood by the operator.

However, science and industry introduced a qualitative difference with the invention of the computer, and it is this which we may look upon as the mark and symbol of technological society. For as computers become increasingly complex and take over more and more of our tasks, we find ourselves slipping steadily into the position of mere technicians. Of course we still program and operate such machines. But very few of us have the scientific knowledge· to understand what the computer does with the facts we feed it. And the threat now seems genuine that computers will take over even the "non-mechanical" tasks that seemed to be the prerogative of the human mind. The machinery of industrial society may have done the drudgery, but it was left to men to make the decisions, to "work out" how many articles of which sort should be produced for optimum sales. Now, however, even such "work" seems to have become mechanical. Computers can excel over minds in making decisions, just as lathes excel over hands in making axles.

The full threat of technology lies in the future. But cybernetics (the science of "thinking machines") seems to have as its goal the complete replacement of men with machines. So far as human minds are still required at various stages of a task, they are regarded as inefficient, erratic, fallible survivals of a pre-technological age. The aim is to analyze the thought processes involved and design a machine to take over the performance from the bungling novice. With the achievement of this goal, man would be radically alienated, dispossessed of the work of his mind as well as of his hands.

We may still be far from recognizing this distant threat as a personal problem. Yet if we do not see the computer as a present concern, we can at least take it as a symbol for worries we do feel about the growing depersonalization of life. "The machine" has already taken over large areas of our experience in the form of "the system." We may look upon this as primarily economic or political. Or we may simply say that as society gets increasingly complex, administrative tentacles spread and the bureaucratic spirit multiplies. The individual feels himself lost in an impersonal mechanism, unable to make his way through the system to find himself in what is arranged for him. Alien forces seem in control. We are technicians working at machines we no longer understand.

Perhaps the picture seems too strongly painted. But with the surrender of human functions to nonhuman forces, problems arise which lead us to traditional philosophical questions. If so much that once seemed our prerogative has been turned over to the machine, can we draw the line anywhere? Is there anything which is "inalienably" human? Is there some part of "mind" or "will" which can never be translated into a mechanical process? If so, what precisely is it, how can we talk about it, and how can we best educate this while calmly allowing machines to take over all in us that is purely technical?

This attempt to identify our humanity is basic to more practical questions about leading "the good life" in a technological age. We shall approach the problem, in the following sections, by considering what computers do and how some philosophers have effectively reduced man to a model of this sort; then we shall ask whether such a reduction does not refute itself, and what provisional conclusions about man can be drawn for further investigation in the chapters to come.

What Computers Can Do

In discussing what "thinking machines" can do, and what they may eventually do, we must keep a sense of proportion. Computers can already manage some of the tasks of thinking better than we can, but others which we take for granted still give them surprising difficulty, like recognizing shapes at various angles. The previous section may have implied that there is no limit to the possible complexity and efficiency of a computer. However, there are some practical limits, for example the speed of electricity. The amount of information a computer can store is much less than the human brain can. Even taking the lowest estimate for the brain and the most optimistic prediction for computers, these will still be able to hold considerably less facts than the brain at the close of the century.

Nevertheless, ours may not be the final century, and even the present development of computers is sufficient to rob us of our confidence in pointing at any human work and saying, "no machine could have done that." Computers are already able to defeat their designers at simple games. They can analyze literary style and have been used to determine whether certain writings (e.g., the Pauline Epistles of the New Testament) do or do not come from the same author. They break codes with speed and efficiency. They write some form of music and their taste may improve. Their influence on our daily life is likely to increase dramatically. The politician is already affected, for computers take part in forecasting the vagaries of public opinion; the day may come when we witness an all too literal battle of the political machines. And computers may soon play an important role in medical diagnosis; by remembering more details about each patient and seeing more complex relationships, they could be able to render a more "personal" service than the busy doctor.

Those of us who are intent on defending our prerogatives against computers may be skeptical about the "music" they produce and may stress that the tasks they perform all consist in following out "logical" relationships. Even with the complexity of sickness to which a doctor attends, there is presumably a finite number of ills and of the symptoms they cause. Diagnosis consists in following the relations from the latter to the former and can perhaps be left eventually to machines. But surely no computer could ever take over the specifically human art of healing? It is not always the most analytic mind that makes the best doctor.

The objection may have some ground. Again, a sense of proportion should be kept in our predictions. A bedside manner is not irrelevant to healing. Yet this is a matter of custom, and tastes change. Just as I prefer the company of a dog on a walk to that of some two-legged acquaintances, so I am prepared to engage in conversation, certainly to play chess, with a machine. It could prove more witty and entertaining than some people.

This may be facetious. But are we so sure that the "human" qualities of which we boast are not complex behavioral patterns that can in principle be reduced to logical relations and simulated by machines? Could it not be that the "humanity" of a good doctor consists in a more subtle recognition of the patient's full state and a more apt rendering of the appropriate response: greater input and more fitting ("logical") output?

Behavior as Input and Output

These questions can be generalized. Cannot all human behavior be set into an input-output scheme which, however complex, is finally logical or mechanical? It has been said that those whose jobs are most threatened by computers belong to the managerial class. They are the people who make decisions, and it is in the making of right decisions that computers will excel most dramatically. For what is a decision but the process of converting information into action? And are not machines likely to prove superior at both the gathering of information (input) and its conversion into the best course of action (output)? Let us look at both sides of the equation.

We are surrounded by facts, so many of them that we could never hope to take them all in. We do not need to be cynics to realize that the doctor sees only a minute fraction of the facts of our physical state. The president of a company or of a nation sees scarcely enough of the facts of business or society to make his decisions even intelligent guesses. But a machine can scan a range of discrete facts exhaustively and systematically. Radar picks up everything of a certain size and material that is within its range. The human eye misses a surprising amount even where it happens to look.

What about the output side, the realm of policy where decisions are made how information should be converted into action? Surely words like "decision" and "should" save something that is inalienably human? But do they? A dilemma may be posed. Policy is either rational or not. If rational, a course of action follows from information according to precise criteria. From the information of a sub-zero thermometer reading outside the window, it follows that if you are going out you should put on your heavy clothes and not your swimming suit. But where the relation of fact to action is "logical," the computer is completely at home and will soon take over. Some businesses already leave policy decisions to a well informed computer. If, on the other hand, policy is said not to be rational, this may mean either that the facts and norms are too complex for us to have a clear grasp of them or that we act blindly, without troubling to get an adequate knowledge of facts or prediction of consequences. But it would be an odd gambit to identify our humanity with blindness. And the more we stress the complexity of decisions, the more we play into the hands of the machines. It is precisely because of their "superhuman" ability to hold together a complex knot of relations that we prefer computers to the slow mind that wanders painfully through the network and forgets the first steps before coming to the last.

The Extent of Mechanism

The question whether machines can think has provoked a vast literature. Here we need only touch the problem sufficiently to introduce a few philosophical considerations. We shall look at three "common sense" proposals to set a limit to what machines can do and thus to protect ourselves from a purely mechanical account of human thinking. In each case doubts will be expressed that the proposal, if made from the viewpoint of an observer of men and machines, can reveal any phenomenon which could not in principle belong to both.

PROGRESS AS FEEDBACK

It may be proposed that a machine is basically static or repetitive, doing the same task in the same way, whereas human action is under constant revision and shows genuine progress. The facts to be gathered change with the decisions we make about them. The very presence of the doctor can affect the state of the patient.

Much will be said later about the dependence of facts on minds. But it is rash to remain content with the simple claim that machines are distinguished from minds by being repetitive rather than progressive. Take an ordinary thermostat. It makes a decision about the need for more heat, sets the furnace going, asks about the correctness of its decision, discovers it has overestimated, revises its decision, shuts the furnace off, and so on. This is the simplest possible example of an "equilibrium machine," based on the principle of "negative feedback." The governor of a steam engine is·another obvious illustration.

The suggestion is that the "constant revision and progress" of which we boast may eventually be reduced to the workings of a highly complex equilibrium mechanism. Cannot all the most brilliant scientist does be explained as a series of renewed approximations (answers) to solving a disequilibrium (question or need·)? Success achieves some form of equilibrium which may remain, with very simple questions, or become a renewed tension leading to further tentative answers. The process may be random (consisting of "hunches") or systematic. A personal example. This is not the first draft of this paragraph. If time and patience were adequate, many further attempts would be made at resolving the remaining disequilibrium.

Conclusion: The notion of "revision and progress" needs far more analysis, and perhaps a different viewpoint, if it is to reveal anything that no sophisticated computer could eventually exhibit.

ORIGINALITY
AS REARRANGEMENT

A similar claim often made is that humans show an "originality" or "creativity" that is simply absent from machines. In terms of our scheme, there is output without corresponding input. Now if this represents sheer blind activity, it is a strange quality with which to salvage our humanity, as just remarked. And if this sort of capricious behavior is wanted in machines, a "probability device" can be introduced that admits of erratic working.

Just as "progress" needs careful examination if it is to distinguish minds from machines, so the simple appeal to originality is far from conclusive. Is it so certain that man, for all his claim to creativity, does ever reveal anything new under the sun? What passes for originality may be no more than a rearrangement of elements that are already there. Does the rising star in the political sky have original ideas, or is he not merely giving a novel twist to old solutions? We all have our gimmicks and rearrange the pieces of the puzzle, but can anyone draw out pieces that are not already there? To say complacently that a computer can do only what it was programmed to do is much like saying that Euclid could derive only what his axioms contained or that Newton could get out of the falling apple only what was in it.

A variation of the claim to originality is that machines will always lack the "personality" and "feelings" we see in humans. Yet if someone spent as much care for as long a time on the education of his computer as he does on his child, we might well be able to speak of it having a character, preferences and prejudices that reflect those of its "father." We are perhaps too ready to identify being human with having idiosyncrasies.

THE APPEAL
TO CONSCIOUSNESS

The third proposal is in some ways the reverse of the second. Do not minds differ from machines in having input without any corresponding output? A machine always produces. Push down one side of a lever and the other goes up. Even "storage" in a computer can be classified as output; the law of the conservation of energy is not broken. However, minds have "consciousness." Whatever sounds and sights strike me, I may know them by having an "idea" of them and without reacting or doing anything about it. The mental world is radically different from the physical world. Machines simply respond to stimuli; they are not conscious of what strikes them or of what they are doing.

Again, as with "progress" and "originality," the appeal to consciousness needs careful treatment if it is to serve as a way of identifying humanity. The discussion of "subjectivity" in the following chapters could be interpreted as such an attempt. But this will be conducted from a viewpoint that allows no division of reality into two "worlds," a public physical world of bodies in space and a private mental world of ideas which somehow come from bodies and "represent" them. Whatever "ideas" mean, they are not objects which I know in my mind and relate to other objects which I know outside my mind. How, for instance, can I compare the former with the latter, for I know a thing only through my idea of it? But the philosophical difficulties of such a theory need not be explored here, since the theory gives me no help in distinguishing your thinking from that of a computer. If your mental world is really private, I cannot take it into account and am left with your observable behavior and that of the machine.

The following section may clarify these remarks. It will suggest that an account of thinking in terms of ideas which are privately observed stands on much the same footing as an account that reduces all thinking to what is publicly observable. If humanity is to be identified, it is from some viewpoint other than that of an observer.

Interpretations of Man as a Computer

The title may be misleading. Two philosophical accounts of human thinking will be presented. Both appeared before the age of computers. So if they are introduced here as forms of ''reductionism,'' attempts to reduce all that goes on in minds to what machines can in principle do, then an interpretation is involved which may go beyond the intention of the theories' authors.

The first theory to be mentioned originated in the United States at the beginning of this century and is particularly associated with the psychologist, J. B. Watson. It is called ''behaviorism'' and tries to take all we attribute to the mind and give an exhaustive account of it in terms of physical behavior, of observable stimuli producing observable responses. The sight of an approaching car strikes me and I respond by shouting, jumping, running. My shout is a stimulus that produces alarm-responses in you, and so on. All talk of ''knowing,'' ''thinking,'' ''meaning,'' far from requiring a distinct mental world of private ideas, is irrelevant. ''Ideas'' are a confusing way of talking about the output which comes from input. Both are physical, observable. You know what my cry of ''look out'' means. But your knowledge is no ghostly idea locked up in a world of its own. It consists precisely in your own reactions, in the way you respond. If you misunderstood me and ''thought'' I was joking, your knowledge would have consisted in annoyance or some other response than alarm.

This is an over-simple account of behaviorism. A little ingenuity can extend it in many ways. For example the ''hidden'' nature of thinking comes from a learned suppression of overt responses which is a form of storage, still perfectly physical, a delaying of immediate responses in favor of later ones of greater complexity and efficiency. I learn to discriminate between loud noises. I remain relatively calm at most of the street sounds, conserving my energy for a good jump when one of them is that of screeching brakes bearing down on me. But enough has been said to suggest the plausibility of reducing all ''mental'' terms to a stimulus-response scheme which would fit a computer well.

The other theory to be considered is an older one that may not at first seem reducible to a computer-like account of knowledge. It is the theory that physical stimuli produce not physical responses but mental ideas which "represent" what caused them. So the theory may be called "representationalism." It is close to the account most people might give of knowledge. In its simplest philosophical form it is shown clearly by the English philosopher John Locke (1632–1704).

Locke holds that the physical world is composed of a multiplicity of facts (he calls them "qualities") which are there independently of human knowing—though an important qualification of his will be mentioned in the next chapter. Some of these facts strike me and "impress" themselves on my mind, producing "ideas." Locke insists strongly that the process is one in which the mind is passive to its impressions, for any activity could only be a distortion of the facts rather than a reliable reception of things as they are. He speaks of the mind as a mirror. A camera would offer a good contemporary model. Ideas thus are like photos which correspond point by point to the things they represent. And that, basically, is it. We can then do things with photos, sort them, classify them, make composite photos. But similar activity with ideas is subsequent to the moment of knowledge, which is a simple reception of ideas from impressions.

Such a theory was developed by Locke at length and with subtlety. But we have seen enough of it for the present to recognize what may well be the lines along which we should be inclined to develop our own account of what goes on in minds. Is this a good defense against the machine? It may seem to be by removing ideas from the physical world of observable stimulus and response. But the account is by no means so different from behaviorism as it appears. Ideas are treated as things in a world much as physical responses are. I may see ideas by introspection rather than perception, but in both cases I am taking a look at an object. And the problems Locke poses, of how ideas are caused by qualities and correspond to them, are basically the same as problems about the relation of responses to stimuli or of any one thing to another in the same world.

Kant refers disparagingly to Locke's theory as "a physiology of the human understanding." Both Locke and the behaviorists offer a theory of the mind which, whatever they may have intended, establishes nothing that is irreducible to the sort of account which a physiologist would give of the body or an engineer of a computer. The following section will consider some difficulties into which an exhaustively physiological or observational account of the mind runs.

Hesitations about Such Theories

This chapter is intended as an introduction to the sort of questions philosophers ask. Facing the threat of finding our life taken over increasingly by the machine offers only one way of raising philosophical problems, and, perhaps, of making them seem less remotely academic. But a number of questions have been stirred up which will remain topics of discussion throughout the book. This section will consider three of them: the possibility of alternative viewpoints in giving an account of man, the supposed independence of facts from the knowing subject, and the self-contradiction involved in any consistent project to exclude the subject altogether from a philosophical account.

Spectator and Participant

The attempt any philosopher may make to reduce everything to one sort of thing was called above "reductionism." It is shown by the behaviorist's effort to give an exhaustive theory of human activity in terms of the physiological model of stimulus and response. The suggestion above was that Locke's account of human understanding is similar in its basic features. However, it may be well to try and clarify what they are reducing to what.

The behaviorists and Locke differ in many respects. The former present a one-world theory, whereas the latter, in the tradition of Descartes, holds for a distinction between physical and mental worlds. Where the theories agree completely is on the viewpoint of the theorist. He is a spectator of things and events before his gaze. He tells us what's what in the world he views, whether it be a physical world or a mental world or a combination of the two. Thus, he informs us about stimuli causing responses, or he measures the correspondence of ideas to qualities, much as a boxing commentator tells how a punch causes a cut eye or a cartographer measures the correspondence of his map to the terrain. That is, the theories of the behaviorists and of Locke are reductionist in their claim or assumption that man, minds, thinking, and knowing can be explained without loss through a spectator account, given from the point of view of an uninvolved observer.

If this is what they reduce man to, from what do they reduce him? What other type of "account" is there? A simple illustration may help. As I come to the station on my way to work I notice the train is already beginning to move. Two statements may be made: "The train is running ahead of time;" "I am running to catch the train." Grammatically, the word "running" is used in the same way in each. But logically there is a difference, and it goes with a difference in my viewpoint. In making the first statement I am a spectator of an event in the world before me; I could go on to say how the fuel is moving the driving shafts and these are turning the wheels. In making the second statement I could presumably step outside myself and report how my breakfast is moving my legs. But that is not quite what I said. I spoke in terms of my purpose, why I am running. I should elaborate this by trying to convey what it is to *be* a worried person late for work rather than by relating the speed of my legs to that of the train, which relation could be the same even if I had other purposes in mind.

A similar distinction may be found elsewhere. For example, an economic historian offers us explanations in terms of the relation of some events in an age to other events, whereas the historical novelist tries to express what it is to be an ancient Greek or a medieval man. A psychiatrist will relate symptoms to ills as far as he can, but he is likely to be more effective if he combines the scientific approach with some understanding of what it is to be anxious or depressed.

The suggestion, then, is that we may contrast a purely spectator account of things in their relations to each other with an account in which the speaker tries to convey what it is to be a person of a certain sort, acting in a certain way for reasons of his own. The former will be called a spectator or observational or "third-person" account, the latter a participant or agent or "first-person" account.

The physicist confines himself to the former, the historian makes much use of the latter. Biologists may not be sure, as witnessed by their hesitation about the use of the language of purpose. It is, however, when we come to philosophy that confusion about the two ways of talking reaches its height. Many philosophical problems may come from the assumption that the language of a spectator account is appropriate even though the topic can scarcely be discussed from this point of view. Are ideas in the mind as food is in the stomach? Can we step outside our ideas and compare them to things as we compare a photo to what it represents? Do we really "have" an idea or is an idea not better treated as a way of knowing, i.e., as belonging to a participant account? Are not the ideas I have in a game of chess my ways of being a chess player?

Deep problems are involved, and it is far from easy to say how a first-person account should go. But enough has been mentioned to summarize a hesitation about theories which reduce man, his acting and knowing, to a purely spectator account. This is appropriate and exhaustive in talking about computers. I can no more tell you what it is to be a computer than a physicist can tell us what it is to be a pendulum and to swing. But we do know what it is to know and to be human and act humanly. All these can of course be set in the third person and described from the outside as a physiologist does. If a behaviorist made no greater claim than to offer one account among many valid ones, there would be no difficulty. This arises when, as philosopher rather than physiologist, he tells us that no other account or viewpoint is valid; he reduces all to his own.

Our search, throughout this chapter, for some quality which would distinguish man from any possible computer may have been doomed to failure. For each quality was examined from a spectator's viewpoint. But man from this point of view is a machine, a complex of parts in relation to each other. However wonderful his mechanism, there seems no firm reason why artefacts may not eventually simulate it.

So the real question is not whether the pieces fit together within a spectator account but whether the account itself is exhaustive or requires that we go beyond it by adopting another point of view. It is perhaps this requirement that lies behind appeals to such terms as "consciousness," "originality," "revision and progress." Possibly consciousness is not a second world in which ideas are to be observed but rather a way of being "self-present," a knowing subject rather than an object to be known. Originality and progress may not be a rearrangement of the data that are already there but a new way of knowing that allows different data, a different "world," to appear.

All this can for the present be left in the vague form of suggestions. In particular, the question how one could *prove* that a purely spectator account is inadequate in philosophy has not been considered. Such a proof will appear in various forms throughout this book and will be briefly indicated at the end of this chapter.

The Independence of Facts

After this rather abstruse discussion we may turn to something more concrete. A philosophical theory is wrong if developed from presuppositions that are wrong. But the theories of the behaviorists and of John Locke, and indeed all theories which reduce human knowing to a mechanism, share a basic assumption about which we may express some hesitations. It is the assumption, apparently obvious and safe, that the world consists of a multitude of facts (things, events, processes, etc.) that are what they are independently of minds or human knowing.

Locke, we have mentioned, compared the mind to a mirror merely receiving what is already there apart from it. For the behaviorist, whatever sight, sound or touch is classified as a stimulus exists as a physical event in the world before it produces a response. The response may, on the principles of negative feedback, change the world and hence the stimuli that follow. But any event is what it is prior to the response for which it serves as a stimulus. The world is assumed by both theories to be "objective" in the sense that it does not depend in any way on knowledge by subjects. The mind is a sort of siphon or detector that comes across facts, then takes them in or responds to them.

This seems to be so, and any denial of it would appear to lead to a strange form of "subjectivism." We find facts and do not create them. There were three chairs in this room before I came into it, one behind the desk, one to the left of it and one to the right. These surely are facts which do not in any way depend on me.

Nevertheless, we may become less confident if, instead of asking how many chairs or books are in the room, we ask how many "things" or "facts" are there. The question is odd. How should we count them? Is each page in a folder a separate thing (because loose) and each page in a book part of one thing (because glued)? We can count things or facts only because we have classified them; and we do this in various possible ways, depending on our society and our personal needs and whims. I perceive the room as containing three chairs because I am used to sitting eighteen inches off the ground. Had I grown up in the habit of sitting on the ground or anywhere, I should either have counted more "chairs" or found no use for the notion. And it is difficult to know how one chair can be to the left of another except in relation to a situated knower who sees things to one "side" or the other.

Still it may be thought that ways of classifying and counting items of furniture or mountains or thunder rolls are subjective "additions" to a world of facts that are really there, in a certain number and with certain qualities, prior to any way we group them in knowing them. If so, there is nothing we could say about such things or facts. To ask what anything is means asking what it is for some human purposes. Water is that which I can use in washing or drinking or swimming or conducting a chemical analysis. Having specified what it is "for me," as an answer to the varied needs I have and questions I put, I find no sense in then asking what it is "in itself." Things are what they are for human knowers.

Perhaps these statements need to be qualified. There may after all remain some sense for questions about "things in themselves." But such questions would take us far into metaphysics, not a subject for which behaviorists have much use or on which computers have thrown much light. The facts we find in the world are always relevant facts, answers to some question with which we approach the world and in terms of which we see it as a world of objects of a certain sort. The radar analogy applied above to the gathering of information is misleading. Facts do not impress themselves on our minds like dots on a screen. If we were completely passive, we should know nothing. What things are revealed, and what they mean, is a function of the way we approach the world with questions and interests that are ours.

And if we think that the world "in itself" is the world of science, we should not forget that this world of mass and energy, of electrons and electromagnetic fields, is the result of highly sophisticated questions that developed late in human history. But as such topics are of so much importance today, and as science seems to go so far toward revealing an "objective" world independent of what we do about it, the present discussion can well be continued in the following chapter.

The Exclusion
of the Subject

To close this chapter, we may ask what sort of proof would show that the complete reduction of minds to machines is impossible. The proof is almost trite, and may seem an anticlimax, but it is weighty with consequences and will carry us far through the following chapters.

Briefly, the proof can be put this way. Any theory which explicitly reduces minds to machines, or the agency of knowing to the objects of a spectator account, is itself the product of theorizing, thinking, knowing. That is, what the theory explicitly states is denied implicitly by the performance of theorizing.

No such contradiction would be involved in any of the sciences or special disciplines because these do not pretend to account for everything. A physiologist can speak of man merely as a being that responds to stimuli, because no more is offered than a physiological account, one that does not pretend to take in all the physiologist himself is doing as a thinker and experimenter. The scientist abstracts from questions about his own questioning as a scientist.

But the behaviorist, or any theorist who claims to reduce man exhaustively to a mechanism, does not modestly offer us one limited way of seeing things. He denies the validity of any alternative account. However, only an alternative account which allows for the first-person agency of proposing and criticizing theories allows for the behaviorist to propose behaviorism and criticize alternatives.

This, as was said, is trite rather than subtle. But even trivial notions can lead to important results. What will come of this one must remain to be seen. A few suggestions to close.

1. The first-person agency of questioning, theorizing, criticizing, and affirming will be revealed and studied more fully in the following chapters under the heading of "subjectivity." In this chapter the approach has been largely negative. The aim has been to suggest the extent, yet finally the self-contradiction, of a purely observational account of man that ignores our grasp of what it is to be a subject.

2. Though the knowing, willing, questioning subject is not among the themes of the sciences, it cannot be ignored in philosophy. Indeed it may turn out to be the basis for such conclusions as can be reached in the metaphysical parts of philosophy.

3. Precisely because the knowing subject cannot be reduced to an object among objects, what can be learned of it does not come through direct questions (questions about objects) but through reflexive questions (questions about questioning).

4. However abstract this may seem, it is not irrelevant to the practical questions with which this chapter began, about how to identify our humanity and lead a full life in a technological age. Machines are here to stay. They may well take over all that we today classify as work, and the resulting problems are immense. But we cannot preserve our humanity by looking for some particular functions or services which we can keep from the machine. Our humanity is far more radical: it is that which questions the world in such a way as to reveal it in terms of particular functions or things or qualities. These mean only what they are for a questioning subject. A world full of computers, but without man, would be meaningless. To question and interpret, to give and renew meaning, belongs to man and to no machine. The very fact that we are worried about our powerlessness is our greatest power. No ape or machine is concerned about its "identity" or its failure or even its death. Our worry, concern, questioning, may prove positive and fruitful. At least this is a personal question we can keep before us throughout the remaining chapters.

3 | Can Science Tell Us All?

The previous chapter had a look at what thinking machines do and it asked whether this is really "thinking." Could they eventually take over all functions which we call "mental" and which we confidently suppose distinguish us from animals and artefacts?

The chapter offered no glib answer. What it suggested is that if I ask the above questions as an uninvolved spectator, the answer may be "yes": there seems to be no characteristic of human behavior which could not, at least in principle, be simulated by an extremely sophisticated machine. Yet I am not uninvolved in thinking, as I may be in the mechanical processes I study. I can give an adequate account of the swing of a pendulum without myself swinging. But I cannot give an adequate account of thinking without thinking: I am knowing what knowledge is, questioning what it is to be a questioner. Here, valid conclusions must belong to a participant account. And from this point of view a negative answer may be given to the original questions. For it is precisely this point of view which machines lack. An adding machine will solve my questions better than I can. But they remain *my* questions, for which I am responsible; they are not "appropriated" by the machine in a first-person agency.

The reply may seem unsatisfactory. A criticism might go like this. You have either supplied no proof or have offered a specious proof by retreating into a tautology (like "only U.S. citizens have U.S. citizenship"). How do you know that a machine will never ask its own questions, in the first person? Or if you identify this achievement with what we know from within as human thinking, then of course only humans can engage in human thinking: only you can comb your *own* hair.

Obviously much more needs to be said. But others can be left to say it. The topic of computers was chosen merely as a way of getting human minds working on philosophical questions. This book has been written for humans and its concern is with what we are. If machines do ever join us in the company of questioners by learning to say "I" and asking what it is to be a questioner, then we can unselfishly congratulate them. We wish them luck as they face the bitter personal problems that go with their success—including the problem of meeting the threat of technology from their own machines.

So let us turn now to a completely human society and ask if the sort of questions we raised in the previous chapter are also to be discovered here. This chapter will suggest that they are. It is not only machines that indicate we can dispense with the human subject; humans themselves have gone a long way toward doing just that. Indeed the proposal of this chapter is that the story of science represents a remarkably successful effort to lessen the part played by "subjectivity" in our knowledge and to dispense with a first-person viewpoint. The highly ambiguous terms "subjectivity" and "objectivity" need a great deal of clarification, and this will be one of the main tasks of the chapter.

Sensation:
the Purely Objective Datum

No machine ever makes a mistake. Its output is an exact effect of its input. If an electric clock tells the wrong time, it is because we set or regulated it incorrectly according to our purposes, or because the current changed or dirt, temperature variations, and metal fatigue added to the input.

Only a subject can make a mistake. In saying "The earth is flat," I say "I affirm it as true that the earth is flat." All my statements about what is so in the world involve some first-person element: I know, I think, I conclude. The more I am conscious of this ("self-conscious"), the more I realize that *what* I claim to be true may turn out to be false or at least inadequate.

Perhaps we grow more cautious in what we say as we get older. We become more "reflexive," less direct. The child shows little awareness of the personal factor, with all its risk. He is happily turned out to the world. In fact it is some time before he adds the pronoun "I" to his vocabulary. Tommy may say "Tommy wants that" before he says "I want that."

The history of philosophy seems in some respects to recapitulate the development of each one of us. Concern with subjectivity, with the problem of the "I," grew slowly, appearing at certain key stages. Socrates represents the first of these. For him, the most important questions we can ask are about man, about the values of human life, the "ought" each person faces. The philosophers before him, whom we lump together crudely as "pre-Socratics," seem to have been more concerned about the world. What their questions meant is far from easy for us to say, and it is probably wrong to see these people as primitive scientists. But they asked how the world was constituted, what was its underlying principle (*archē*). Thales (sixth century B.C.) replied it was water. Others spoke in terms of earth or air or fire.

In any event, they did not discuss the "I," or would have reduced it to some such principle. And before we look at the story of science as an impressive attempt to give an account of the world of atoms, animals, and men without reference to the knowing "I," we may consider that part of our ordinary knowledge which seems most effectively to exclude the knowing subject. This section will examine "sensation," its claim to priority in our knowledge and independence of what we are or do.

The Meaning of Sensation

Suppose we begin by saying, roughly and provisionally, that sensation is the type or part of knowledge which we get through the senses: sight, hearing, touch, taste, smell. At the moment, sensation tells me that the day is hot and humid, a police siren is sounding, and I have a toothache. Sensation would be opposed to any form of reason, in which I "think" beyond such immediate data to conclusions that are not simply given: thus I reason that a thunderstorm is likely, that there has been an accident or crime, and that I have an abscess.

To define sensation as that which comes from the senses is obviously circular. If I say that I know "through a sixth sense" that a friend some hundred miles away is ill, my right to refer to such a "sense" depends on whether my knowledge can be called "sensation," and we are back where we started. Also, there is a good deal more than immediate data in the original examples. Is the day hot or do I have a fever? Is it a police siren or the woman next door singing? Is it a toothache or earache or hypochondria?

Suppose we try to remove all thinking or interpretation and get at

the "purely objective datum," at what is given to me prior to any classification or understanding on my part. There are certain feelings, sights,
sounds, tastes, smells which I only subsequently (and perhaps errone-
ously) label and interpret.

This is what most philosophers mean by sensation, opposing it to
more complex forms of knowledge (such as perception, understanding,
reason). Sensation could be described in terms of two characteristics,
though they are basically the same. It is:

1. *immediate*: the raw material of knowledge, just "there," without any
processing by "middle-men." Classifying a sheer feeling as an ache rather
than a pleasure, locating it in a tooth, referring it to a cause such as an
abscess—these are all forms of "mediation."

2. *given*: the datum of knowledge which comes from the world. In sensation
we are passive and engage in none of the above activities by which a
knower goes beyond data and constructs some interpretation or theory.

To say this is what philosophers mean by sensation is not to say they
agree that there are no problems about the use of the term. The rest of
this section will indicate some of them.

Difficulties about
the Objectivity of Sensations

These problems are being discussed here in order to raise hesitations
about a common assumption that we know what we mean by "objectivity" and should look for it in that which is given to us as passive spectators of the "real world."

We are sometimes told that the scientist is objective because he "sits
humbly before the facts" and submits all his theories to the test of
further data. The following sections will try to make this claim slightly
more precise. But here we shall renew some of the doubts of the previous
chapter that facts are simply given to us rather than revealed in dependence on various ways of interpreting or questioning the world. In the
terms we have just used, are we wise to identify objectivity with the
immediacy of sensation, i.e., with freedom from any interpretation by
the knowing subject that goes beyond what is simply given? Or does
interpretation enter into our effort to get at what is "real"?

THE RELATIVITY
OF SENSATION

Marching proudly into any situation, ready-armed with our own
prejudices and theories, we are likely to distort our knowledge badly.

A politician convinced that the people support him, and full of his interpretations of current trends, may altogether miss the signs of a heavy loss at the polls. In some sense at least, objective knowledge does mean sitting humbly before the facts, or "letting the facts speak for themselves."

However, does this mean trying to abandon all theory and intellectual interpretation? Should we look to the pure data of sensation to present us with things as they really are?

If so, we should abandon hope. The immediate given is highly relative. The sensation of color which the wall of my room gives me varies with the weather and even with my mood. No one who has ever had a cold will fail to recognize the relativity in the taste of food. My feeling of warmth is much more immediate than that very theoretical instrument, the thermometer. But a pail of water will yield constant thermometer readings while one of my hands, transferred to it from hot water, feels cool and the other, coming from cold water, feels warm. To rely on the thermometer rather than the hand is to abandon pure sensation as an approach to reality and to call upon the intervention of theories and definitions we make.

If it were pure sensation that revealed the way things are, then the world would be thoroughly chaotic and "lawless." Sensations are relative to the situation of the subject, to his memory of other sensations he has had and even his anticipation of ones to come. The remarkably uniform findings of science do not come from sensation as such. Scientific objectivity involves theoretical constructs that take us far beyond immediate data.

THE ELUSIVENESS
OF SENSE DATA

An old adage in philosophy states that there is nothing in the intellect which was not first given in sensation. Perhaps all philosophers could find some way of accepting this. None, at least, claims to be doing no more than spin theories out of his mind. All allow for some reliance on what is given, not made.

However, some would take the adage more literally than others. The supposition would be that each of us first receives a series of items of sensation, or sense data, and then makes perceptual and intellectual constructions out of these. We are like children who are each given a box of colored blocks and then left to see what we build from them. "Objectivity" is to be found in the original gift. "Subjectivity" enters with the particular way each builds the atoms into molecules of his own.

So, it is suggested, the objective thinker is one who can analyze every statement he makes or word he uses into the atoms out of which it was formed. These are sense data and need no justification beyond the brute fact that they force acceptance as purely given.

This may seem plausible. Surely the simple comes before the complex? And much of the progress of science stems from its ability to break complex phenomena or statements down into simple ones.

However, is it so certain that we do start off with common, objective atoms of experience? Are there not alternative models for interpreting what goes on? Most games may have originated with a rough and ready way of playing, out of which rules were gradually crystallized until they could be expressed, in numbered series, as a rule book. Is not this the way most things go in life? If we want to be precise about business or politics or literature, we must be prepared to come up with simple statements in logical order. But there is nothing absolute or "given" about these. There are many different ways of analyzing experience, many different sorts of atoms we can propose.

No more is involved here than in the discussion of the supposed "independence of facts" in the previous chapter. The question "How many facts are there in this room?" helps us to see that facts are not already there in any "atomic," countable way. What facts we discover depends on the questions, purposes and interests with which we actively confront the world. So also with sense data. It may at times be useful to try to break down complex experiences or statements into very small items. But the items we find will depend on the way we conduct our analysis. We look in vain for any building blocks which are given to all of us as the raw material of our experience. And even if there were such "things," the secret would be well kept. No one could talk about them, as the concluding part of this section will suggest.

THE INESCAPABLE
SUBJECT OF SENSATION

An illustration may be overdue, and a vivid one is offered by the American philosopher, C. S. Peirce (1839–1914). He supposes someone in a balloon at night who hears a factory whistle breaking the silence. Peirce analyzes three elements or levels in this experience:

1. *Presentness* is the characteristic of experience in its immediacy. Here it is the sheer silence and sense of floating in a calm dark night. In another situation it might be the low hum of an electrical appliance. There is no change, no relation or comparison, no imagination of what else might be there. Just a presence, a sheer given.

2. *Reaction* is the characteristic by which one experience is set off in contrast to another. In the example, the screech of the whistle impinges as the opposite of silence, and the silence assumes a new quality in contrast to noise.

3. *Representation* is the characteristic by which we have experience of something as a thing of a certain sort. Here the screech is presented to the balloonist as the sign of a factory whistle in a city far below him. The relations lacking in mere presentness are now filled in, and his world becomes structured.

Without investigating Peirce's own conclusions, we may try to locate the "sensation" or "sense data," in the austere sense described in this section. The third stage, representation, obviously contains more than this. There is an active interpretation by a knowing subject of the screech as coming from a factory, like others he has known. And he could be mistaken: it might be a train.

The stage of reaction is far less complex but each term of an opposition is mediated by the other. In so simple an experience we may possibly like to say that the contrast is "given" rather than interpreted. But the knowing subject is clearly present as the one who holds together the two terms *as* contrasting.

Presentness may seem by definition to exclude all mediation. However, it is by no means certain that anything can be experienced except in potential contrast. Unless the balloonist knew noise and light as possibilities, could there be an experience of silence and darkness? If we follow Peirce's account literally and exclude all relations, even potential ones, could we recognize silence and darkness?

That is, there is no difficulty in holding that sensation is a part or aspect of experience, infused through and through with the categorizing and interpreting of a knowing subject (intellect, reason). There is passivity as well as activity in all our experience. But if we should like to identify any experience as a pure sensation, prior to interference by "subjectivity," then we cannot even point to it: pointing classifies as "this rather than that." We are reduced to a grunt. Brute facts are for the brutes. Human facts are mediated by interpretations that give meaning in a variety of ways. This sort of subjectivity cannot be excluded from whatever we are to mean by a claim to "objectivity."

Perhaps only in infancy are sheer sensations to be found. The baby stuck by a pin does not have pain, it is pain. Possibly this is a pure datum, but it is a strange model to take for the objectivity of our mature knowledge. And we are grossly mistaken if we think that science finds its objectivity in immediate data.

Science as the Study
of a Purely Objective World

The thesis of the remaining sections of this chapter can be put quite briefly. However some may interpret the dictum of "sitting humbly before the facts," the scientist is not trying to ape pure sensation. He is engaged on a highly intellectual interpretation of what we see and hear. Nevertheless, he has come surprisingly close to achieving what the last chapter viewed as the threat of computers, the elimination of the knowing subject. Obviously, scientists are needed if science is to be done. But *what* they do, the content of science, has reduced to a minimum all that belongs to the scientist's own particular situation.

Science offers no return to immediate data. Its project has been to "mediate" data by constructing a "third-person" world of objects where each is defined completely by its relation to the others, much as any number is defined entirely through its relation to other numbers. The "first-person" involvement of the knowing subject, or "I," seemed to become increasingly irrelevant. And it is only since the end of the last century that we have come to realize that the part played by the scientific observer and theorist cannot so easily be put in brackets as having no bearing on the content of science.

Now these summary remarks will be elaborated as a further investigation of the complexity of the terms "subjective" and "objective."

Francis Bacon:
the Elimination
of Subjective Idols

This is no place for an instant history of science. But some reference to two key figures in the origin of contemporary science may help us to understand its remarkable project.

The first of these is Francis Bacon (1561–1626), statesman, jurist, and schemer under James I of England. Some have tried to make him into the true author of Shakespeare's plays. His reputation, however, is secure enough as the author of the *New Organon*, a work which has been seen as playing a vital part in the rise of the sciences. That science made no spectacular progress until the sixteenth century is partially due to the influence of Aristotle's logic, or *Organon*. Though Aristotle himself was a surprisingly accurate biologist for his times, he left us a purely deductive logic. This gave the rules for deriving conclusions from premises, hence for clarifying what is logically implied in any truth we have already established. But it provided no method for finding new truths about the world.

However, science, as we understand it, consists in the discovery of truths by observation rather than by deduction. No deduction from metaphysical principles can tell us how many planets there are or what causes malaria. We need a logic of discovery, and it is this which Bacon supplied. What he has to say may strike us as rather elementary and obvious. Yet his treatment of subjectivity and objectivity shows the rise of the age, and spirit, of science.

For Bacon, the first step in valid discovery is the removal of all influences that bear on us in a way that will distort our work. These Bacon calls "idols," and we may refer to them as subjectivity in the sense of prejudice (pre-judgment). They involve prior commitments that come from our personal character and convictions or from the customs and language of the society in which we live. It is only recently, for instance, that a scientific investigation of human sexuality has become possible and some long standing misconceptions have been removed.

Nevertheless, the removal of such subjective contributions belongs to all respectable disciplines and does not indicate the peculiar success which science has had in leaving the knowing subject out of account. Bacon's analysis of the method of discovery goes some way toward this by focussing attention on the relations between things in the world. A student of Plato does more than report the frequency with which words occur, but Bacon tells us to concentrate on the things or events we observe, to list their characteristics, to notice the ways in which these come repeatedly together, and hence to discover the constant relations between objects in the world. The tracking down of malaria to the mosquito could serve as an example. But it is with Galileo that the scientific method takes its most important turn toward a radical objectivity.

Galileo:
the Objective Model
of Mathematics

Galileo Galilei (1564–1642) may be associated in popular repute with dropping unequal weights from the Tower of Pisa, or perhaps with early observations through a telescope. However, it has been said that his main contribution to science was the realization that nature is thoroughly mathematical—more exactly, it was his invitation to apply numbers to nature and accept only those results which can be expressed numerically.

This procedure involves an abstraction or transformation, the construction of "ideal cases" rather than the mere recording of what is actually observed. Thus, the ideal gas law expresses in mathematical form the theoretical movements of a molecule of gas, occupying no space, travelling in a perfect vacuum, and having collisions which are completely elastic. This has, of course, never been observed, but the scientist is happy to regard what he does see as an approximation to what "should" be because following the ideal relations of numbers.

This notion of Galileo has become so much a part of our common currency that we are no longer surprised. We tend to identify the "real" with what is numberable, however much of the detail of our experience may be lost in the process. The experiment described above of transferring our hands from hot and cold to lukewarm water leaves us in no doubt that the thermometer is "right." Yet a thermometer does not measure warmth. What it measures is distance, and we simply *define* that regular increases in warmth correspond to the expansion of mercury, because this latter is an "objective" phenomenon: i.e., we can easily apply numbers to it. In similar fashion, we convert color into wave lengths, intelligence into I.Q., and greed into the mathematical laws of economics.

The Point of View
of No One in Particular

Science has filled in the details since Galileo. But with the project of converting experience into mathematical form, we have gone as far as possible toward eliminating all reference to the knowing subject. We should, of course, remember that numbers are not data out there in the world: it takes a subject to "create" numbers by thinking and to apply them to experience. Yet in following out this daring proposal we reduce ourselves to mere spectators of third-person relations.

A number has no reality except its relation to other numbers. I cannot point out the number "seven" anywhere in the world or *be* the number "seven"; it is nothing but a series of relations to 6, 8, 14, etc. However, I can point out shades of red and blue. I can even, in a sense, "be" various colors, as when I say that I "see red" or "feel blue"; at least color preferences give scope for personality testing and jobs for interior decorators. But the reduction of color to numbers dismisses such first-person talk as irrelevant and leaves us with a thoroughly third-person account, a spectator's record of a world made up entirely of the relations of one thing or event to all other things or events. This is the impressive, though limited, ideal of "objectivity" for which science came to stand.

The "subjectivity" to which this is opposed need have nothing to do with prejudice. It includes any part played by a knower beyond the function of numbering. It is in this sense that the ideal of science has been said to be that of "giving an account of the world from the point of view of no one in particular." This is not to abolish the human point of view but to generalize it. Thus, once I know Newton's formulas for the laws of motion and the particular numerical values in the movement of the planets, I can work out exactly where a telescope should be pointed from any planet at any time to catch light from any other planet. Nothing in my present situation or particular way of seeing things makes any difference.

The final section of this chapter will look at some of the limitations in this project. But first a section in which we mention a few difficulties which scientists in the past hundred years have stumbled on in carrying out their own project.

Difficulties in Excluding the Observer

Much has been written on the problems and paradoxes of recent theoretical science. There is no lack of philosophical questions involved, but we need look only at the most evident way in which the question of the meaning of "objectivity" has been renewed. Perhaps little more is involved than confronted the philosophers who first worked under the influence of the new science.

Locke: Primary and Secondary Qualities

John Locke saw himself as the philosophical servant of Newtonian science. Just as the new scientists had detected and excluded the "anthropomorphism" by which the medievals had injected their own particular views into their account of the world (e.g., "nature abhors a vacuum"), so Locke detected and excluded subjective contributions from his account of what the world is in itself.

Locke allowed that some of our ideas do not correspond to the way things are in themselves. For example, color. The cover of the book before me appears blue. If I take it to the window it appears green. As dusk falls it appears gray. If I became tired or angry or take to drink, the color may change still further. Now Locke was bound to admit that, in any such example, the ideas of color change; but he was unwilling to accept that the qualities which comprise the book itself, really out there in the world, change. The world would be chaotic, unscientific. Nor did he want to claim that any one color is the "right" one for the book, e.g., that its green color in sunlight is what it is in itself or for God (suppose we were circling a different star, or our own sun grows older). So his solution was that color is not a quality of the world; the world itself is uncolored but contains qualities which have the "power" of producing various ideas of color in our minds. The same he applied to sound, warmth, touch, taste, and smell; these and many more he called "secondary qualities." To say an object is white, sweet, and cool "in itself" is meaningless; it has such properties only for a perceiving subject in some particular situation.

However, where do we draw the line? Locke refused to accept that all qualities are secondary. Admitting this would, he felt, be yielding to a complete skepticism or subjectivism. It would suggest that the knowing subject, rather than the world, is the "site" of reality and it would make nonsense of Locke's notion of the mind as a mirror passive to what is given. Also, as we shall see, it would be unfaithful service to Newtonian physics.

So Locke insisted that the world must have some qualties in itself, entirely independent of any perceiving subject. These he called "primary qualities." They are number, mass, motion, extension, shape (geometrical form) : in other words, the qualities that make up the austere Newtonian world, those which can be numbered without any conversion to thermometer or spectroscope readings.

The assumptions behind Locke's theory survived for a couple of centuries in science, but the philosophical life of the theory was short. His contemporary, Bishop Berkeley (1685–1753), was quick to put the obvious criticisms, which most subsequent philosophers have sustained. Do not the very arguments which make secondary qualities dependent on a knowing subject apply also to primary qualities? What would shape and motion be without a situated perceiver, and are they not just as relative to the situation from which he estimates and measures as are touch and smell? The question "How many facts?" has already suggested how relative the basic primary quality, number, is to the way we interrogate and interpret the world.

That is, if we may translate Locke's distinction as between secondary qualities which are "subjective" and primary qualities which are "objective," it would seem we are bound to say that all qualities are subjective: they depend on the situation and intentions of the knower. There may still be legitimate grounds for applying the term "objective" to the limited range of qualities with which science is concerned. But this is not to say that such qualities are "more real": they are simply those with which mathematical science can work, the ones to which numbers can be applied directly.

Relativity and Conventionalism

Newton had an admirable modesty about his theories. He admitted that they fell far short of establishing necessary principles. Nevertheless, like most of us he was deeply, if implicitly, involved in metaphysical assumptions. He did assume that he was exploring the world as it is in itself, unconditionally, for God. Space and time are absolute. A body either is or is not in motion, regardless of the situation of an observer who locates it. Two events either are or are not simultaneous, regardless of the situation of anyone who times them.

The success of Newton's physics was so great that as recently as 1880 few, if any, scientists doubted that his comprehensive system would cover all phenomena. Only a handful of minor ones proved uncooperative, like the behavior of electrons projected through a double-slit diffraction grating. But by the turn of the century, queries about a few exceptions had grown into major doubts about basic principles.

Details are not important here, and even the amateur knows something of them today. It proved impossible to pinpoint both the location and the velocity of an electron. And absolute space and time went out with the theory of relativity. What followed from the changes is that science abandoned any claim to "primary qualities" as telling us how the world is "in itself." The full personality of the observer was far from being restored. But at least it was admitted that the situation from which he observes enters constitutively into what the world "really is"—not only into its color but also into its motion and all other measurements.

Werner Heisenberg sums up, for his own field, this abandoning of the claim to tell what objects are apart from the observer:

> Particularly characteristic of the discussions to follow is the interaction between observer and object; in classical physical theories it has always been assumed either that this interaction is negligibly small, or else that its effect can be eliminated from the result by calculations based on "control" experiments. This assumption is not permissible in atomic physics; the interaction between observer and object causes uncontrollable and large changes in the system being observed. . . .[1]

These are the remarks of a scientist about the work on which he is engaged. He does not generalize about science as a whole. And his language may suggest he is discussing no more than a technical problem; talk of the "interaction between observer and object" could be taken as

---

[1] Werner Heisenberg, *The Physical Principles of the Quantum Theory* (Chicago: University of Chicago Press, 1930), p. 3.

implying that the object does have definite qualities in itself but that we are unfortunately prevented from discovering them.

However, the conclusions of this chapter would be less modest. No object could simply be "there," with determinate qualities "in itself," apart from what it would be for a knowing mind. There is no meaning to the ideal of objectivity according to which a thing would be an absolute datum for some fortunate mind gaining access to it, free of any interpretative activity. Such an ideal represents a strange mixture of sensation and science.

What we are to mean by objectivity remains a problem. But in approaching it, we must allow that whatever objects we find are not independent of the questions, interests, and conventions we bring to our discovery. Indeed, many scientists would admit today that their own discipline is highly conventional. The principles it sets up are to be judged according to the use we can make of them. They are accepted so far as they work. And success or failure in working is relative to the purposes of the worker.

Further, most scientists today would be less ambitious to supplant other disciplines than their predecessors, particularly in the last century. It is no discredit to the achievement of science, and no blindness to the manner science imbues our thinking today, to admit that scientific norms of "objectivity" leave much out of account. A few remarks on this topic will form the concluding section to the chapter.

What Science Cannot Tell Us

The following three chapters will suggest that some support for the metaphysical claims of philosophy can come from an analysis of "subjectivity." This chapter has prepared the ground by distinguishing some of the senses of this ambiguous term through a study of the way in which science has diminished and partially restored the role of the knowing subject.

As a summary, we may list (1) a sense in which science and all other disciplines renounce subjectivity, (2) a sense in which science and all other disciplines find subjectivity inescapable, and (3) a remaining sense in which science rightly claims an objectivity which distinguishes it from non-scientific disciplines.

1. All respectable studies renounce subjectivity in the sense of prejudice (Bacon's "idols"). Likewise they renounce it in the sense of that which is purely private or arbitrary, not open to appropriate discussion. This statement throws the problem on what form of discourse is "appropriate" in some fields, but an open mind on this makes art and religion no more private than science.

2. All knowledge is subjective in the sense that it requires a knowing, interpreting, classifying subject. A platitude, perhaps, but it needs to be stated. For it can be forgotten, especially in discussion of "things in themselves" or the independence of objects. Even to say that the world consists of things in the plural is to indicate that some human manner of grouping, counting, and manipulating is at work. An object is such only for a subject. The very success of science is an impressive illustration of this.

3. The remaining objectivity which makes a study "scientific" is the result of a method that limits itself to whatever can be numbered. The opposite is not easily referred to as subjective. However, the term could perhaps be retained in the sense that a numerical account is as thoroughly "third-person" as possible. So far as any account is not numerical, it keeps something of the "first-person" or "subjective." No value judgment is implied by this distinction. Some comments, however, may be added on the gain and loss involved in such a choice of viewpoint.

This remaining objectivity of science secures that preciseness and unanimity which mathematics allows and which has always been one of the strongest attractions of science. Failure to quantify, where this is possible, makes for a bad businessman, a poor president, and conceivably even a woolly writer.

Yet numbers are not all. To apply them is to transform with considerable loss. Our appreciation of a painting involves more than its market price, our estimate of a religion more than the census of its followers. A historian tells us little of an age if he does no more than construct a labyrinth of relations between statistics of population, industrial production, trade, armaments, and literacy. An archaeologist finding some skulls and implements may feel it his scientific duty to search for a numerical formula relating cranial capacity to the size of axes; but we hope he will also convey to us some sense of what it was to be a person who lived and expressed himself in that manner.

A final paradox. In many ways the extrovert attitude may be healthy which immerses itself in the object without worrying about the "I." But the dedication of science to the world of things and events in relation has led toward the disappearance of the object. Contemporary mathematical science offers little support for the imagination. The solid objects of the old science have gone. There are no minute billiard balls at the heart of matter, nothing that waves to support a light wave. For numbers are relations without any "thing" to be related. Once the appropriate equations have been obtained for an object of science, no individuality remains for the "it"—all that survives is the "I" who thought out and applied the mathematical symbolism.

By way of transition to the following chapters, one claim no scientist makes is to tell us that the world he investigates and symbolizes must be as he finds it. To go beyond what ''happens to be'' to what ''must be'' is to pass from physics to metaphysics. Whether there is any such passage is the next question.

4

Can I
Opt Out?

At the end of his formal schooling, Descartes chose to forget all he had been taught. Many of us go far toward this without any special effort. But Descartes' aim was positive. He wanted to see for himself. He was unhappy accepting anything because he had learned it from others, however wise and respected the source. Nor did he think it sufficient to depend on the authority of his own observations, which reveal merely that things happen to be the way they are. He wanted to *know*, and for him knowledge meant seeing "the reason why," not merely yielding to "the fact that." His hope was to discover some truth which proved itself indubitable. Then he would accept whatever he could understand as necessarily deriving from this basic truth.

We may sympathize with his ambition as much as we doubt of his success. In the following chapter we shall enter into such an experiment. We shall try to question all we have learned, go back toward a sheer beginning, and see what is disclosed in the attempt.

However, the proposal may be ridiculous. Can we set aside the accumulated learning of our own life and the whole tradition from which we come? Descartes was over-optimistic. In dismissing the subjects he had been taught at school, he put history in first place for rejection. But can we so easily step out of our history? For example, did not Descartes' philosophical project of "seeing for himself" come to him as an inheritance from a long tradition of Western thought? Were his questions not given to him? Could he have asked the ones he did without the ideals and language he had absorbed from his earliest days? In setting out to do philosophy, must we not first know what philosophy is, what passes for a philosophical question?

Perhaps the ambition of Descartes can be judged this way. He was wrong in thinking he could get along without questions that are given to him from history. But he was right to think that these are received *as* questions only so far as he makes them into *his* questions, appropriating them to "ask for himself."

In these pages we shall try to recognize the force of history while "doing philosophy," asking for ourselves. The title of this chapter may be strange, but it is intended to invite personal questioning. However, the chapter will not claim to start in a Cartesian void but will look for its problem far back in the history of philosophy. The questions of the Greek skeptics and the replies of Plato and Aristotle may have been badly put and may have misled us ever since. Yet we come out of that tradition. We receive their questions. Our task is, by questioning these questions, to make them our own.

Must Anything
Be as It Is?

The history of philosophy is well on its way before any "professional" or "academic" philosophers appear. In earlier ages it was much more obvious than today that philosophical questions grow out of personal and social problems which are felt acutely and resist all solutions.

The Greeks were evidently not the first to have such problems. But they were the first to formulate and generalize them in a way that we today recognize as clearly philosophical. Every society suffers some type of "alienation"; the assumptions and convictions from which it lives are questioned and there is a loss of orientation. We often speak of "skepticism," and the term comes from ancient Greece. So as we turn from contemporary doubts raised by technology and science to the origins of Western philosophy, we may first look briefly at the Greek skeptics and the dominating figure who tried to meet their questions.

The Skeptics and Plato

The early Greek skeptics were the product of a rapidly developing political life after the Persian wars. To engage in politics, a young man looked for instruction in the art of winning followers and influencing people. He turned to itinerant teachers who became known as ''sophists'' and later as ''skeptics.'' Both terms we associate with a cynical relativism, and it is not altogether surprising that this became the mark of such teachers. The techniques of debating apply equally on both sides of the motion, and conquest can become more important than truth, the role of the advocate more absorbing than that of the adherent. Also, the skeptics were widely travelled. They had seen the many differing customs and beliefs of people outside Greece and were in a position to challenge the assumptions others took for granted. They conveyed to their pupils that common beliefs are a product of ''convention'' rather than of ''nature.'' No absolute norm of truth or of goodness is imposed on us by the nature of man or of society. All is what we happen to make it to be: ''Man is the measure of all things.''

It is only with the later Greek skeptics that such general teaching and attitudes were clearly formulated as arguments for the conclusion that there is no final truth. Yet the Greeks had an extraordinary ability to generalize. From the variety of opinions on any subject, and from the shifting scene of the natural world, they became absorbed in the problem of change. All material things and human convictions, it seemed, are in a state of flux. But as no realities or values are permanent, does it not follow that we can have no certain knowledge, that all is mere opinion?

One can suspect the threat to society such questions could represent and the need for defensive measures. However, the reply which history has preserved for us came from no ''establishment'' figure. Socrates moved among the sophists and must have seemed to many people no more than a sophist himself. Indeed, Aristophanes mocked him as their representative. Socrates used their own method of questioning unexamined beliefs. He was more skeptical than the skeptics. But his purpose was positive and more philosophical. He invited the questioner to question himself, to reveal his own dogmatism and slogan thinking. Philosophy is not an uninvolved study of the state of the world but a personal inquiry each makes of what he is and ought to be. It is out of self-knowledge that abiding truths and values appear.

What we know of Socrates comes from Plato, and it is to him we turn for the reply Greek society was to offer to its own self-questioning. Plato started life as a politician and his interests may have remained to the end political and moral. However, he learned from Socrates that the problems of his time could not be met by patching up existing institutions. Lasting influence comes from those who are prepared to step back from the immediate flow of events in order to find our deepest purposes and the fundamental principles which guide us in our pursuit of them.

Plato called such a principle an *eidos,* which we translate as an

"Idea" or "Form." The word *eidos* is ambiguous. Yet it is important to notice that an Idea, for Plato, is nothing merely "in the mind." It was Descartes who introduced the latter notion, which has become our common understanding of the word. But an Idea, for Plato, was the most real of entities, with a more secure position than any of the things we can point out in our everyday experience.

Indeed, Plato's reply to the skeptics can be seen as the result of a radical questioning of common assumptions. Of course nothing around us, neither among the facts we find in the world nor among the customs by which any society lives, is absolute or necessary. All such details are questionable. They are "conventional," that is, hypothetical rather than imposed by the "nature" of things. It is right to be skeptical about them. But let us not be complacent about our skepticism. We should put our own questions in question, ask what is involved in the very shock we feel at the impermanency of things. If life were indeed no more than a mere flux of changing phenomena, we could know nothing about it. We can recognize change *as* change only if we know some standards or norms against which details can appear as inconstant and unsatisfactory. To recognize events and beliefs as shifting and particular, we must have some grasp of what is eternal and universal. To see things as merely "happening to be so," we must have some insight into what must be as it is.

Plato's thinking was much influenced by mathematics. He realized that we do not base mathematical conclusions on what we see and measure in the world before us. We do not hold that the diagonals of a square bisect each other at right angles because we have measured a large number of squares. In fact, the procedure goes the other way around. We know with certainty, the first time we think it out in geometry, that the diagonals must bisect each other at right angles. Then, if we find this is not quite so when we measure an apparently square table top, we conclude that the table is not really square. The material objects we perceive are grasped as more or less accurate "copies" or embodiments of geometrical forms, which we know by thinking out how they must be.

Hence, very briefly, Plato's "theory of Forms." Everything we find by observation of the material world, whether of nature or of society, is changing, particular, and contingent (it happens to be so). We do not have genuine knowledge (*epistēmē*) of it, only "opinion" (*doxa*) from accepting facts as they strike us. But we can be aware of the inadequacy of opinion only if this comes against some background knowledge of "Forms" or "Ideas" as eternal, universal, and necessary. The tables, men, and states we see are all deficient: they are more or less adequate copies of (or "participations" in) the Idea of a table, man, or state.

Again, these Ideas are not merely "in the mind." They are more real than any of their sensible copies.

Countless questions arise with this summary version of Plato's position, but two comments will be enough for the present:

1. The similarity to "ideal cases" in science is apparent (cf. pp. 49–50). So is the weakness of Plato's theory if based only on a generalization from mathematical forms: for these, we recognize today, are merely hypothetical and do not tell us how things must be. However, Plato himself showed grave hesitations about the validity of his theory in regard to the things of nature. It was in the realm of values that he thought it most applicable (cf. *Parmenides* 130: Forms are of rightness, beauty, and goodness rather than of hair, mud or dirt). Perhaps, then, an interpretation of Plato should start with human agency, with what I do and ought to do rather than with the way I appear to an observer.

2. Plato's theory obviously goes beyond a scientific account of what we happen to find. It introduces metaphysics as a claim to say what must be so in any experience, regardless of the detailed contents of that experience. And it seems to introduce the further claim of metaphysics to be "transcendent," to tell us about "spiritual" entities beyond the world of our everyday experience. Perhaps, however, this "further" claim does not take us from one world of material objects to any "second world" of necessary Forms. And as the notion of "a world of things or objects" belongs to a spectator account, so the problem of "two worlds of two sorts of things" may evaporate with an account of man as subject. These are problems we shall investigate later.

Science and Metaphysics

The present chapter is not so much concerned with the problematic nature of metaphysics as with the preliminary doubt whether we need even envisage such a discipline. Do we need to ask whether anything must be as it is? Can we not altogether avoid the question and remain content with our ordinary problems about the many particular details of our life which we find happen to be so?

The scientist, as such, asks no metaphysical questions. Indeed, scientists have been able to make such dramatic advances in their account of the world largely because metaphysical questions have been scrupulously excluded from science.

This seems to have been realized from the first by the philosophers who worked in an intellectual climate inspired by the remarkable progress of Newtonian physics. A distinction which John Locke made, between "real essences" and "nominal essences," may clarify this attitude. It corresponds in some ways to the distinction of the skeptics between "nature" and "convention." For Locke, we know the real essence of a triangle; we see into its properties in such a way that we understand the reason why they must come together to make up what a triangle really is. But a chair has no more than a nominal essence. What constitutes a chair depends simply on the way we happen to "name" things or classify them in terms of our purposes and conventions. Because of our postural customs, we supply the name "chair" to a manufactured object which supports us conveniently in a sitting position. If we ask whether a piano stool is a chair, the question is about the way we use language to group properties, not about the way properties must come together in a certain thing. It is not like asking whether a trapezium is a triangle.

Now Locke insisted that we know only the nominal essence of any existing thing, i.e., of any of the objects which the sciences study. He took gold as an example. Chemists have agreed that whenever they find something with a certain color, weight, malleability, resistance to acids, etc., they will name it "gold." They are not content simply to group these qualities together as we do those of a chair. They try to connect them numerically, e.g., relating weight and valency to atomic number. But such numerical connections are no more than a sophisticated account of the way we happen to find things together and to classify them. We could possibly have developed a very clumsy chemistry in which gold and sulphur are treated as the same substance because of having much the same color.

One of Locke's successors, David Hume (1711–76), distinguished similarly between "matters of fact" and "relations of ideas." All we find in the world or make an object of science is a matter of fact: we record the way facts happen to come regularly together. But wherever we understand why one property must follow from another, we are discovering no more than the relations between our ideas (in the sense of Descartes, not of Plato). Necessity of this sort is, for Hume, confined to mathematics and to the purely logical implications of our language. Thus, an eight-legged spider is of necessity not an insect, but merely because this is a logical conclusion from our definition that we will call only six-legged creatures "insects." Relations of ideas give us no information about what is to be found in the world. Once we have observed that a whale has mammary glands, we get no information in deciding thereby to classify it as a mammal.

What is the result? If Hume is right, the fifth task listed for philosophy in Chapter One, the metaphysical proposal, is impossible. There are no truths which tell us what must be so in the world. In a famous passage, Hume suggests we go through the books of our library, retaining all those which trace out relations of ideas (mathematics, logic) and those which are content to give us an account of matters of fact (science, philosophy as analysis of the methods, assumptions, and language we happen to have). But we should "commit to the flames" all books of metaphysics.

Many philosophers have, without the dramatic gesture, followed Hume's advice. However, one may wonder if the advice is not itself based on an approach tainted with metaphysics. The following two sections will ask whether questions about a "must" in life are quite so easily dismissed.

Practical Attempts
to Dismiss the Question

The phrase "dismissing a question" remains ambiguous. I may simply fail to ask a question because it never seriously comes to me. Or I may resolutely avoid facing up to it, although I know it is "there," even that it is important. Or I may find myself personally and explicitly confronted with the question and then dismiss it from my attention. This latter approach can, like the previous ones, represent a practical attitude with a minimum of theorizing; or the question may be dismissed through a theoretically developed argument which claims either to solve the question or to show that it is meaningless.

These possibilities overlap in various ways. For instance, my approach to the question of death involves various practical evasive attitudes and some theoretical ones. Here we shall try to consider some of the many strands in our possible attitudes to the question of metaphysics: Is there anything in life which must be as it is? In this section we shall look at some of the approaches listed above as "practical." The following section will resume the story of skepticism as an example of a theoretical attempt to dismiss the question of metaphysics by posing it and developing an explicitly negative answer.

No Question

It may seem the easiest thing in the world to live happily without ever asking abstruse philosophical questions. And so it is, if by "questions" we mean academically phrased ones. However, the story that Socrates used to philosophize in the market place suggests that such questions belong to our life without their technical form. Perhaps even those who passed Socrates by were taking a philosophical stand in their rejection of philosophy.

Sartre substituted a left-bank café for the market place, but he did try to bring philosophy down to earth through his novels, plays and discussion of current issues. And one of his main themes is that we cannot avoid involvement in vital questions. Refusing to take a stand is itself taking a stand. For instance, referring to the Algerian war of the 1950's, he writes in his principal work:

> If I am mobilized in a war, this war is *my* war; it is in my image and I deserve it. I deserve it first because I could always get out of it by suicide or by desertion; these ultimate possibles are those which must always be present for us when there is a question of envisaging a situation. For lack of getting out of it, I have *chosen* it. This can be due to inertia, to cowardice in the face of public opinion, or because I prefer certain other values to the value of the refusal to join in the war (the good opinion of my relatives, the honor of my family, etc.). Any way you look at it, it is a matter of choice.[1]

That is, we tend to think of a choice as a dramatic confronting of alternatives. But failure to make such an overt choice is itself a choice. Abstention from the polls, whether out of conviction or apathy, is itself a political decision. As Sartre put it, there is one thing in which we are not free and that is in our condemnation to freedom. Whatever we do, we must do something. However little we have thought out our choice and its implications, what we do constitutes a choice which is our answer to the inescapable (if implicit) question what we are to do. I may devote all my energies to some narrow purpose. I may drift from one short-term ambition to another. I may take up the easy life and shelve all problems as they arise. I may opt out of life by committing suicide. But I cannot opt out of the necessity of making some such choice. This is inescapable, in the strongest sense.

Hence it is not quite accurate to say that the question of metaphysics need never arise. A practical "must" runs through the most unreflective life.

Anything Goes

However, what has been said is minimal. The question whether any absolute necessity imposes itself is usually taken as involving more, as a question whether there is some overall meaning or purpose to life. It is here that the grave moralist steps in, telling us about the plan of life and the penalties set up inescapably if we do not heed him.

---

[1] *Being and Nothingness*, trans. H.E. Barnes (New York: Philosophical Library, Inc., 1956; also London: Methuen & Co. Ltd., 1957), p. 554.

He is not an attractive figure. Do we need even to ask his questions and enter into his game? Why should I not treat life as a joke where anything goes? I can submit to the necessity of choice by choosing something different each moment, without any limiting commitment. Why should I not taste experiences to the full, unhampered by fussy restrictions or stern purposes?

By all means. But it is possible that the inescapable questioning of life has a somewhat more precise structure than the sheer need to choose. Every choice expresses a question and an answer, and answers have a way of excluding each other. The choice to go through medical school and become a doctor may exclude the choices to become an atomic physicist and an Egyptologist. At least, my choice to be here at this time excludes my choice to be there at this time. The "must" we face is not only of choosing but of specializing. Even noncommitment is a specialization which excludes the experience of commitment. A great deal more may prove possible than the stern moralist allows, but it is not so that "anything goes." Even the happy dilettante finds himself inescapably asking about the limits of choice in a quite detailed manner.

Nothing Goes

We have seen, however, that there are various ways of dismissing a question. What the above comments have suggested is that anyone who gives himself spontaneously to living will reveal questions that are inextricably bound up with living. The more you do, the more you must choose and the more agonizing limits you must set to your choice. But suppose I lessen what I do, withdraw from the activities of life? "Apathy" may not sound attractive, but the word does mean "not suffering." Is it not a practical counsel, and even a respected religious teaching, that we find peace through liberation from all questioning and striving? And would this not mean opting out of the supposedly "metaphysical" elements of life which go with activity and choice?

Such withdrawal from life may belong more to the old than the young, more to societies in their decay than in their growth. But few can say they do not know what is meant. The stronger our desires, the more vulnerable we are to the shock of failure and rejection. Often it is those who have, by common standards, succeeded brilliantly who realize this most acutely. At the heart of success there can lie a terrible emptiness. The purposes, ideals, and ambitions that inspired us appear hollow. We learn to expect nothing in order to suffer nothing. Ask not, and you will not be let down.

Contemporary literature has much to say on this sense of life as a "waste land." But if we think such attitudes a prerogative of our own age, we may consult that grand old pessimist of the Bible, Ecclesiastes: "I the Preacher have been king over Israel in Jerusalem. And I applied my mind to seek and to search out by wisdom all that is done under heaven. . . . I have seen everything that is done under the sun; and behold, all is vanity and a striving after wind."[2]

However, it is in oriental religions that we find the most clear account of a withdrawal from activity, choice, and questioning. Gautama the Buddha practiced mortification for many years in search of salvation, his tongue cleaving to his palate while he was clutching and tormenting his thoughts. But all in vain. Then the great awakening came. He realized that all evil originates in striving, in the lust for life. Perfection is Nirvana, the escape from all activity to a state where there is no coming to birth, no going from life, no duration, no falling and no arising.

Such notions are not altogether foreign to Christianity. The ideals of mysticism have usually been expressed through images of utter passivity. The values of activity, of working in the world, and notably of philosophical inquiry, have often been held suspect.

These religious and secular ideals of withdrawal from activity have been presented here as practical rather than theoretical. Philosophical justification would be foreign to both the Buddhist and the disillusioned. However, both start with deeply personal questions, and it is definite replies to these which lead to a dismissal of questioning. Hence what appears as withdrawal or negation is in fact a positive affirmation. The very least which must be supposed in the Buddhist is a desire for perfection, the will to attain Nirvana. The Buddha is said to have called for an intense effort of the will, involving all one's powers. His final words are supposed to have been: "All accomplishment is transient, strive unremittingly." That is, if we are to escape from striving, we must strive to do so. Liberation from need is itself a need.

The conclusion of this brief examination of practical attitudes is that whether we try to drift without choosing, or hope to choose all without restriction, or aim to escape from all striving, we reveal inescapable necessities at the heart of our project. The question whether anything must be so is posed and answered affirmatively, however inexplicit and untheoretical our questioning may be.

Theoretical Attempts
to Dismiss the Question

The run of this chapter may by now be clear. Pascal wrote that "to scoff at philosophy is to engage in philosophy." So, to reject metaphysics is

---

[2] *Ecclesiastes* 1 vv., 12–14 (Revised Standard Version).

to do metaphysics. If Hume affirmed that metaphysics is meaningless, his affirmation was itself metaphysical: ''Reality is finally such that books of this sort must lack meaning.'' Some such practical self-contradiction is threatened in adopting each of the attitudes considered above. The conclusion is minimal. Metaphysics could remain trivial, and it might seem best to proceed at once to the following chapters, which ask whether further conclusions can be drawn from our inescapable striving and questioning. However, it will be wise to ask more precisely about the nature of this ''minimal'' conclusion and of the self-contradiction that leads to it. The rest of this chapter will do so through a look at skepticism as a more theoretical effort to dismiss the question of a ''must'' in life.

The Relativity
of All Particular Facts

The arguments of the Greek skeptics were drawn mainly from two sources, both already mentioned. The first was the variety of conflicting opinions, especially on the more ''profound'' questions of philosophy. How can we be sure that any opinion of our own is correct, and are not doubts cast on the whole discipline of philosophy by its inability to arrive at agreed conclusions? The second source was the relativity of our perceptions according to the disposition of the subject, the object, and its surroundings. I can never say what any thing is ''in itself'' but only how it happens to appear to me in all the particularity of my own situation.

Now the word ''skeptic'' originally meant only one who takes a good look before coming to conclusions. And we may pause to consider the value and undramatic nature of the above arguments. We should all take heed at the spectacle of conflicting opinions, and especially in philosophy where such impressive claims are made for them. As for the relativity of perceptions, this likewise imposes a healthy caution but need not impede the conduct of our everyday lives. We do learn to halt at red traffic lights and octagonal stop signs, even though colors, shapes, and distances are all relative. Nor need the sciences close down, for these claim only to tell us the ways in which the relativity of situations can be taken into account, so that we know how to observe and measure objects from various positions.

What such ''moderate skepticism'' does is to give us a valuable reminder that all perceptions we have, and objects we find, are relative to human aims. We can say of particular things only what they are for our purposes. But this is enough for our ordinary needs. Problems arise when we are confused about the intentions which define things, or when we lay claim to any particular facts as absolute, independently of such purposes.

It may be worth a further example to clarify this. Suppose I am buying a suit which appears to be gray under the electric light of the store. Remembering the warnings of the skeptics, I am careful first to take it out into the daylight or sunlight to see if it does not appear different, say blue, in those conditions. If it does, then I perhaps say that the suit "appears" gray but "is really" blue. All I mean is that it appears gray under "artificial" light but appears blue in sunlight—and that we generally agree to take sunlight as the "privileged" or "normal" or "standard" condition for judging colors. Hence, in such. an example, the phrase "really is" means only "appears from a privileged point of view." But privileges are conventional, set by society, and may be changed according to particular purposes. If I want the suit to wear only on formal occasions, in the evening under electric light, I may reasonably say that the cloth is really gray and only appears to be blue under the abnormal condition of sunlight.

So the skeptics need not be regarded as mixed-up people or as threats to society. They stand for a relaxed, undogmatic approach which takes the full circumstances of any statement into account before anyone jumps in with claims to truth or accusations of falsity.

The threat which they represent is not to our everyday life but to the discipline of metaphysics. Or rather, what they exclude is any metaphysics based on particular facts taken as absolute. For instance, Descartes illustrated in this way his search for an unquestionable fact on which to base his philosophy. He supposed he had a basket of apples, mostly rotten, and wanted to find a sound one. He would turn them all out of the basket and then examine them one by one until he discovered and replaced the good one. So he would turn all the accumulated facts out of his mind and examine each by trying to doubt it until he found one solid fact that proved indubitable.

The skeptics would question his project. There is no "one sound apple." All particular facts are relative, "of convention" rather than "of nature." What they are depends on how they appear to the investigator in line with his questions, interests, aims. A green apple may be sound for cooking, bad for eating, according to present tastes; and it is green only in "normal" light. This claim needs no further elaboration; we have examined it enough in regard to ordinary perceptions, science, and mathematics. Even if we are prepared to admit of something that "it is a fact," the question remains what is meant by the fact, and this involves an investigation of the purposes of those for whom it is a fact. Every particular fact is "for me"; none is "in itself," absolutely, ultimately, unconditionally, self-evidently, unquestionably, "for God."

Hence skepticism helps us to live our ordinary lives with appropriate caution and to avoid absolute statements about particular things. However, Plato made no absolute claims for particular things. And the minimal conclusions of the previous section about a "must" in life were not based on colors or measurements or any particular object of our experience. They arose from certain necessities in our very activity or striving and from the self-contradiction in trying to avoid acting. To see how such a basis for metaphysics differs from any claim to stand on one indubitable fact, we may examine the contradiction in which skepticism itself lands when it tries to become "total."

The Impossibility
of Total Skepticism

Even if all skeptics remained within the bounds of the "moderate" form described above, there would still be some value in considering what happens when we try to push such cautionary doctrines to the extreme of saying that "there is no truth," or "all is mere appearance," or "all is relative." The experiment is instructive.

Some of the classical arguments of skepticism do seem to have been taken as leading to such total negations. For example, there is the argument from error, which can easily be converted into an argument from dreaming. It starts with the observation that I have often been in error (or have often been dreaming), but that I was never aware of my error at the moment I committed it—else I could not have been mistaken. Two conclusions, a special one and a general one, are drawn. I cannot exclude the possibility that at this very moment, for all my certainty, I may be in error. And if I cannot exclude error at any particular moment, then I cannot exclude the possibility of error at all particular moments: that is, I may always be in error (or dreaming).

The general conclusion, that I could be completely mistaken about everything, certainly belongs to what may be called total skepticism. It is not a worry that besets most of us. But the pertinent question is whether the general conclusion follows from the special. If you add up all particular moments, you may indeed get "always." Yet adding up all particular possibilities of error could never yield total error because it would exclude any sure grasp of truth, without which error could not stand out as error. Likewise, I can dream only if I have waking moments with which dreaming can be contrasted.

What is important is not so much the skeptical argument as the reply. This may suggest a return to the Socratic method. The skeptic's doubts or questions are not met by pointing to any particular fact as indubitable: "Obviously you are not mistaken that the sun is shining, that's

simply a fact.'' Instead, the skeptic is invited to carry his inquiry further and put his own questions into question. Is error possible without
some grasp of a norm of truth? Again, we may notice Plato's derivation
of Ideas as norms by which we recognize the details of life as inconstant
and uncertain.

Or we may look at a way in which Aristotle replies to an extreme
denial of basic principles, such as the law of contradiction, which denial
may be taken as equivalent to total skepticism.[3] He rejects the possibility
of any reply founded on some particular fact or principle, for the skeptics would simply direct their questioning at any truth so proposed. Then
he remarks:

> **We can, however, adduce *negative* proof even of this law by refuting our
> opponent, *provided only that he will make some positive statement*. . . .
> In all such controversies we start by requiring, not that our opponent should
> affirm or deny any particular statement, but that he should say something
> which has some meaning both for himself and for others.**

That is, the skeptic is refuted, not by adducing any particular fact
against him (''positive proof''), but by inviting him to refute himself
(''negative proof''). His questions are legitimate and his limited conclusions are valid. But let him run those conclusions to the extreme and
try to formulate the doctrine of total skepticism, then he will reveal his
own refutation. To say explicitly ''there is no truth'' or ''all is error''
is to say implicitly ''it is true that there is no truth'' or ''I am not
mistaken that all is error.''

We have listed total skepticism as a theoretical attempt to escape from
any ''must'' or absolute necessity in life. That is, the skeptic does pose
the question of metaphysics and he reasons to a negative answer. Yet we
may see perhaps how the distinction disappears between theoretical and
practical attempts to escape from any ''must.'' For it is in the *practice*
of asking his questions and affirming his answers that the skeptic comes
up against the inescapable element that runs through all the conventions
of life. He is in much the same position as the man who chooses not to
choose or the Buddhist who strives not to strive. In the final section of
this chapter we shall ask what sort of contradiction this is and reintro-
duce the notion of ''subjectivity'' discussed in the previous chapters.

---

[3] Cf. his *Metaphysics* 1005b–1009a. The most readable edition and translation
of this difficult work, from which the following quotation comes (p. 125), is that
of John Warrington (Everyman's Library, 1956, published by J.M. Dent & Sons
Ltd. of London, and by E.P. Dutton & Co. Inc. of New York, and used here with
their permission).

Self-refutation
and Subjectivity

Nothing has been added to the minimal conclusions reached earlier. But it is worth remembering that these are metaphysical. The impossibility of total skepticism is no mere conditional impossibility, as is the dissolving of gold in hydrochloric acid or the meeting of parallel lines. It is not as though we have observed that up to now we have not been able to be complete skeptics, but that we may eventually succeed if we try long enough. We see that we could never be such. We have knowledge rather than opinion. We have found something that belongs to the nature of reality rather than to the conventions of society or of language. We have gone beyond nominal essences to a real essence, and this belongs to the world of existence rather than to the hypothetical world of mathematical and logical relations.

This brings up the question of what ''relations'' are involved in the truth we have discovered. Perhaps we should examine more closely the self-contradiction in which it appeared. We may list various versions of this:

(I affirm it as true that)	"there is no truth"
(I am not mistaken that)	"all is a mistake"
(I conclude it is really so that)	"nothing really is"
(I am meaningfully claiming that)	"all is totally meaningless"
(I am choosing)	not to choose
(I am striving)	not to strive

The contradiction is patent. But between what and what is it a contradiction? It is not a contradiction between two explicit statements, as though I were to say ''this figure is a square'' and ''the same figure is a circle.'' So if logic deals only with what is explicitly stated or symbolized, the contradiction is not ''logical'' or ''formal.''

The contradiction we are considering is between *what* I say or intend and my very act of saying or intending it. It is between what I explicitly say and my implicit claim to truth in saying it. It is between the content or ''theme'' of my thought and my performance of thinking it. It is between what I mean (meaning as a noun) and my agency of mean*ing* it (meaning as a verb). Since these various terms will be used in following chapters, we may summarize them in two columns that represent the opposition:

act, agency, performance	content, theme
implicit	explicit
meaning as verb	meaning as noun

Now to return to the topic of the previous chapter, science is concerned only with the right-hand column. All science says can be put in the third person, as a series of relations between things or events which are expressed by the content of our thinking. Science is "thematic" and abstracts from what is contained implicitly in our agency of "doing science." It leaves out all that comes in the first person and would belong to a participant account. In other words, science supposes but does not tell us about the left-hand column, the "self" or "I" or "subject" that asks questions, formulates theories, and affirms conclusions.

However, at least since Socrates a strong tradition has taught that the concern of philosophy is with self-knowledge. Even in his less problematic tasks, the philosopher turns his attention to the agency of the subject. The philosopher of science does not make higher generalizations from the objective world of the findings of science. He asks what the scientist is doing, what his implicit intentions are that reveal a symbolic world of a certain sort. And the suggestion of this chapter has been that the metaphysical task of philosophy involves a repeated "turn to the subject." It is not among the details and relations of an objective world of particular facts that we have found traces of an absolute necessity, but rather through the way in which a questioning subject expresses himself in the world and reveals structures that set inescapable limits to his agency. I can choose suicide or sanctity, but I cannot opt out of all choice. I can affirm that Ptolemy was right or Plato absurd, but I cannot opt out of all affirmation of truth or meaning.

It will be for following chapters to ask what is implicit in man's agency of questioning, affirming, and striving.[4] The task is not easy. We feel so much more at home in the world of objects, and our language is adapted for talking about this. Indeed, philosophers who try to give an account of subjectivity slip easily into pseudo-problems about relations between objects.

This may have been the fate of Plato's "Ideas." The proposal above

---

[4] And to question the "obvious sense" of even the minimal conclusions revealed in this chapter. For instance, Chapter Thirteen will ask whether subjectivity must involve a choice of one alternative and rejection of another. Some philosophers (e.g., Spinoza) hold that our ordinary experience of choosing between alternatives is merely an imperfect expression of our fundamental "self-determination" or "self-acceptance." This would mean a reinterpretation, but not a rejection, of the conclusion that choice is "inescapable." In mathematics we can master our definitions and questions in such a way that answers leave no room for correction. But in metaphysics, as the next chapter will stress, a surviving ignorance at the heart of our self-questioning leaves all conclusions open to renewed understanding. Here, necessity and revision do not exclude each other (e.g., I know with complete certainty that I exist, while the meaning of "I" and "exist" will always remain questionable).

was that they started their career in the realm of values. They were the implicit norms of acting well and judging rightly. The artist recognizes the inadequacy of his work to the Idea which it only partially brings to expression. But the relation here is not the same as that which a mere technician sees between his product and a blueprint, where each is before him explicitly as an object to be observed. The temptation, though, was to reduce Ideas from principles implicit in our agency to things we contemplate (literally, an *eidos* is an object seen). As these "supreme objects" could not be located among the material things of this world, a home had to be made for them in a "second world" of spiritual objects. From this we get a crudely transcendent interpretation of metaphysics and a host of problems about the relations between entities of one world and those of the other.

The story may have been put too bluntly. And it may be about Platonism rather than about Plato. But some such ambiguity in the notion of Ideas has reappeared in other philosophers' efforts to talk about subjectivity. At least this may serve as a cautionary tale as we come to our own attempt.

5 | Who Am I?

In these days of moon landings and radio telescopes, science fiction has become science fact. We are now prepared to find that what were once wild notions of discoveries outside our own earth are stated as cool "matters of fact" in the daily newspaper. With the number of earth-like planets scattered throughout the universe, is it not likely that signals will some day reach us from other intelligent beings? Might they be much more advanced than we are? How different could they be?

These are fascinating questions, and we wait for scientists to give the latest facts of our own home and far beyond. Here, it would seem, we are clearly limited to what observation tells us, as Bacon and Hume insisted. Not even the most intense "thinking" will help. Or will it? Are there any limits to what can be found, to what sort of beings can appear? Can these limits be disclosed through human thought without waiting for what telescopes and microscopes may reveal?

From Plato onwards, the claim has been made that thinking can somehow take us beyond the details of observation. Metaphysics represents the brave proposal to go ahead of "physics" and tell us in advance at least the most general lines, or structures, of what must belong to any fact we can discover or any being with whom we may eventually communicate, however superior to us in the scale of evolution.

In the opening chapter, six tasks were listed for philosophical questions. The first four, asking about methods, assumptions, concepts, and alternatives, can be set together and classified as clearly ''analytic'' or ''descriptive.'' Granted that such a thing as science does exist, how can we analyze and describe its methods, assumptions, and language? Here, science is taken as a datum: it could perhaps proceed differently, and most generations lived without any organized science. However, the fifth and sixth tasks of philosophy are more pretentious, asking what *must* be so in any experience we have or in any way man can live.

It is this bold, but problematic, claim of metaphysics which will form the topic of Chapters Five and Six. Chapters Two to Four have gone some way toward setting the scene. Their themes may have seemed disparate. They asked whether machines can in principle take over all human tasks, whether all knowledge can be reduced to the methods of science, and whether we can follow the skeptics in limiting our knowledge to the purely conventional. The answers proposed have, however, indicated a common notion. In each case it was suggested that a negative answer can be defended only if we turn from the details or content of knowledge to the agency or performance of knowing. That is, the proposal was for a shift of inquiry from the objects of knowledge to the knowing subject, the ''I'' who responsibly poses his own questions, decides to formulate experience mathematically or historically, acts according to purposes which determine what is normal or appropriate.

In other words, the suggestion with which this chapter starts is that an approach to the claim of metaphysics may be offered through the question ''Who am I?'' If we can find out what belongs to ''subjectivity,'' to the very agency of being a knowing, striving, and questioning subject, then we may disclose something of the shape our experience must take, whatever its changing content.

The proposal is far from clear. And warnings have been given of the danger of reducing the subject to the status of an object. So, to indicate more concretely what is to be avoided and achieved, this chapter will start with two historical sections. Descartes will illustrate what is not intended. Aristotle and Kant may suggest what is involved in an inquiry into the structures of subjectivity.

The Experiment of Descartes

Descartes has been allowed to speak for himself at some length in the first chapter. The quotation given there shows the philosopher's reflective temperament and desire for knowledge more comprehensive and more certain than any of the special disciplines can supply. It was not that Descartes feared what he had been taught at school to be untrue;

he did not take up a detailed study of history or astronomy to disprove the particular theories he had learned in such fields. His dissatisfaction was that the theories remained "particular." He felt he had been conducted through an encyclopedia, a maze of detailed information, without seeing the connections that make for an ordered whole of knowledge, for "wisdom" rather than erudition.

Hence he was more interested in what historians and scientists are doing than in the causes of a war or the number of the planets. He was concerned with the relations between different types of questions, and he set as his ideal the discovery of the "tree of knowledge," in which all particular disciplines could be seen as branching out from a fundamental study, which would be "metaphysics."[1]

It is in this context that we may understand his method of systematically doubting all he had learned. Descartes was no less willing than the skeptics to accept obvious facts as sufficient for ordinary purposes. He was as ready as any other man to believe his eyes or follow what thermometers and clocks told him. But he wanted more than this. He wanted to *know* what he was following. He was less interested in technical proficiency at using ruler and compass than in understanding why certain procedures *must* bisect an angle. The study he admired most was mathematics, because he thought it gave knowledge rather than mere techniques. What he ambitioned was the extension of such genuine knowledge to all fields. The task of philosophy, or metaphysics, was to help us see for ourselves why things must be as they are rather than merely to indicate what works or is sufficient for our limited purposes.

Few philosophers today are happy at the manner in which Descartes set up his philosophy and portrayed the tree of knowledge. But simply to dismiss his whole project is to lose the aim which has inspired most philosophers to their studies. It was with Descartes in mind that Husserl, founder of the contemporary school of phenomenology, wrote as follows of the philosopher's aim:

> Anyone who seriously intends to become a philosopher must "once in his life" withdraw into himself and attempt, within himself, to overthrow and build anew all the sciences that, up to then, he has been accepting. Philosophy—wisdom (*sagesse*)—is the philosopher's quite personal affair. It must arise as *his* wisdom, as his self-acquired knowledge tending toward universality, a knowledge for which he can answer from the beginning, and at each step, by virtue of his own absolute insights.[2]

[1] Cf. his prefatory letter to the *Principles of Philosophy* (Haldane and Ross edition, I, 211).

[2] Edmund Husserl, *Cartesian Meditations*, trans. Dorion Cairns (The Hague: Martinus Nijhoff, 1960), p. 2.

This is the ideal which has produced philosophers in all ages, the ambition to start afresh and see for oneself. The philosopher is never happy simply to take things as "given." He will do so for practical purposes in his everyday life, and he need have no lack of respect for experts in the special disciplines. But as a philosopher, it is not enough for him to recognize that authority or observation says so, or that a certain procedure works. He must try to think all out for himself. What others take for granted becomes questionable for the philosopher.

In this and the following chapter we shall enter into Descartes' experiment. We shall see what happens when we put into question all the details we normally take for granted, and when we turn to ourselves as questioners in this state of perplexity. That is, we shall ask if anything is inescapably revealed in our very self-questioning.

Nevertheless, an important respect has already been noticed in which Descartes' proposal differs from the one indicated in the previous three chapters. Descartes likened his method of systematic doubting to the search for a sound apple in a basket of fruit. The implication is that we can go through all the particular facts we have previously accepted and question them in turn, until we come across one such fact which simply proves unquestionable. However, agreement was expressed with the skeptics that every particular fact remains questionable. What each is depends on the conventions and purposes of the questioner. There can be no particular fact which is an absolute datum for any possible knower.

This section will not repeat the argument of the previous chapter but will ask what interpretation of "subjectivity" resulted for Descartes and how this differs from what is revealed in an analysis of the *structure* of questioning.[3]

Subjectivity
as Introspection

Descartes realized that he could find no unquestionable truth among the particular facts of the material world. Perhaps he was merely dreaming that the sun was shining or that he was sitting before the fire. However, he held it was indubitable that he *thought* he saw the sun and felt the fire: what proved certain was the *idea* of sun and fire that he found "in his mind."

It seems to be in this sense that he interpreted his proof of his own

---

[3] Descartes' famous "I am thinking therefore I exist" can, however, also be taken as a performative basis for metaphysics, though most of the texts turn against this. I have discussed these two interpretations of Descartes in *Perplexity and Knowledge* (The Hague: Martinus Nijhoff, 1972), Chapter 6.

existence as a conscious being (or "soul"), which merely happens to be united to a body set in a material world. The soul and its "contents of consciousness" are known immediately and with complete certainty. The existence of material things to which such ideas correspond is dubious and in need of proof. As a thinking being he could exist without a body and apart from the material world.

Hence Descartes stands for the distinction between a private mental world, to which I alone have access by introspection (an "inward look"), and a public world of material bodies, to which all people have access by perception (an "outward look"). The metaphysician who starts with such a notion of subjectivity invites each of us to go beyond the contingent facts of science and find indubitable truths by introspecting the "clear and distinct" ideas of his own mind.

The difficulties in such a basis for metaphysics stand out. How can I ever pass from introspection of my idea of sun or fire to any reality of which these are ideas? Any exit from a purely mental world comes to me as the idea of an exit, itself part of that mental world.

However, here we need only to ask if this view of subjectivity is indeed the one that rightly follows from Descartes' method of questioning all he had taken for granted. Two comments may be enough. The first is that while Descartes was able to doubt all the *details* of the material world (the sun, the fire, etc.), he did not show he was able to do so without himself existing materially (e.g., being situated somewhere, seeing the way things appear from a certain point of view, asking what he *can* do as a temporal being with a future and a past). On the contrary, the next chapter will argue that all *questioning* of the particular contents of material existence affirms the materiality and worldly situation of the questioner; what Descartes doubted explicitly he affirmed implicitly in his very agency of questioning.

The second comment is similar but refers to the "indubitable truth" Descartes found in his own consciousness or thinking. What he in fact revealed to be inescapable was his agency of thinking, or questioning. It was not any particular content or object of thought, however clearly presented. No idea I have of the sun is immune from legitimate questioning.

In other words, the philosopher's task of questioning to the limit leaves open to challenge all the particular objects or details of experience. But what is established is the reality of a thinking (acting, questioning) subject as the inescapable condition for any experience, whatever its content. That, at least, is the "turn to the subject" which will be investigated in this and the following chapter. Such a form of subjectivity is not reached by introspection. It is the subjectivity of a material agent, expressing and finding himself in the public world which admits of no division into compartments for thoughts and others for bodies. There are not two worlds, a mental and a material, but one human world in which subjects act in a variety of ways: knowing, willing, talking, playing, engaging in politics and business, technology and science, art and religion.

Subjectivity as Privacy

If Descartes' notion of subjectivity is based on introspection, then the resulting source of metaphysical truths will be private to each person who seeks certainty within his own mind. I alone know what idea of the sun I have at present.

Descartes has of course written down an account of what he found when he retired into himself. He invited others to see for themselves and was confident they would discover the same certainties. But his approach to a metaphysics of subjectivity leaves this term open to its common association with what is private, particular, "mine" rather than "yours."

That this is not the meaning of subjectivity derived so far in this book needs little further comment. What must belong to the agency of any questioning must belong to all questioners. Necessity involves universality. Though not all are bound to do Euclidean geometry or Newtonian physics, we are the subjects of whatever we do, and the structures of subjectivity belong to us inescapably. So understood, a metaphysics of subjectivity is public and communicable. Idiosyncrasies are no part of its topic. The method is one of demonstration and not of private conviction.

What form this demonstration will take remains to be seen. Clearly it is not the same as a scientific argument based upon particular facts that happen to be observed. Also, there is no place for that form of objectivity which comes from the application of numbers and gives the sciences their character. But the claim that a subject must, in the strongest sense, exhibit certain features calls for a form of proof that is open to the assessment of any questioner. Such self-questioning is no withdrawal into a world of one's own.

The Search for Structure

The warning of the previous section is that the question "Who am I?" cannot get an adequate answer through introspection. If I seek my "self" through an inward look, all that is revealed is a variety of contents of consciousness. The subject of thinking becomes an object of thought, a confusing assortment of ideas and images that happen to be present at the time.

Instead, the proposal of these pages is that we try to disclose what it is *to be* a subject. It is our agency of thinking, striving, questioning that we hope somehow to grasp and elucidate. Here words are not easy to come by, for most of them are adapted to talk about objects, things we observe in their many relations to each other. So this section will try to clarify a term which has already been introduced and will become central to the analyses which follow. It is the word "structure." What we shall be talking about is not the particular contents of thought but the structures of affirming or questioning any such contents.

The word "structure" or its equivalents (e.g., "form," "category") is of long standing in philosophy but has recently come into prominence in other fields. Today we speak of "structural linguistics," of "structural anthropology," even of "structural theology." There has been a shift of interest from the details of particular languages and cultures to the "framework" that is common to all languages or cultures and within which the varying details are expressed.

To suggest what part this term has played in philosophy, and to prepare for our inquiry into the structures of questioning, we shall refer to Aristotle and to Kant.

Aristotle and the Forms of Life

In the previous chapter Plato and Aristotle offered a reply to skepticism. Though the skeptic is right that all particular things we find are relative to our conventions and interests, we involve ourselves in a radical self-contradiction if we try to push such relativism to its limits. To deny all truth is to affirm one's denial as true. Some more than conventional norm is implied in our very recognition that this or the other thing is conventional.

OBJECTIONS TO PLATONISM

However, such argument for an unconditional element in experience leaves open the question where we are to find it and how we are to talk about it. The reply with which Platonism is traditionally associated is that absolute necessity is to be found in another world, beyond the one we perceive and the sciences study. The objects of our experience are particular, changing, contingent. But we do have some knowledge of what is universal, eternal, necessary. Hence the objects of such knowledge must be beyond experience, in a world we attain by reasoning.

It was suggested that this may not have been the view of Plato himself. But criticism of it began with Aristotle and has been repeated and developed by philosophers ever since. Plato says that the real bed is no object of our experience in this world but is a bed as it is "for God" (*Republic* 597). What this could mean is difficult to say. Whatever a bed is, it is presumably relative to human, not divine, postures.

That is, to ask what anything is "really," or "for God," or "in itself," becomes meaningless if we thereby reject any account of the way it can appear to human perceivers and users. This is not pure relativism. It is not to say I can mean whatever I choose. If I try to think this book is circular, experiments in rolling it will quickly show me I am wrong. But rolling (or any other test for circularity) remains a thoroughly human operation. Objects are such for human subjects and in terms of human tests. To displace objects into a second world is not to create absolute beings: it is only to raise insoluble problems of their relativity to this-worldly subjects.

THE ORDER
IN WHAT WE SEE

This is the gist of Aristotle's criticism. He was a biologist, an observational scientist of remarkable ability. The order, or "rationality," for which he looked was in no other world but at the heart of what he discovered in this one. Though agreeing with Plato that genuine knowledge is of the necessary and universal, he expected to find this embodied in the processes of this world rather than relegated to any realm of unchanging realities.

The collection of writings which has come to be known as Aristotle's *Metaphysics* opens with the statement that our urge to know is shown above all in the pleasure we take in our senses. That is, in order to know we do not turn from the sensible world to the rational but learn to grasp the rationality that is present in the world of sense. This was, for Aristotle, no abstract solution to a philosophical problem but a simple statement of what he did as a naturalist, as a precise observer of what makes a plant or animal to be an individual, maintaining a constant form as an oak tree or a frog, in spite of the varied influences bearing on it "from outside."

Darwin wrote that Linnaeus and Cuvier were "mere schoolboys to old Aristotle." In Aristotle's work we find a classification and description of around five hundred species of animals, and his acute attention to detail suggests first hand experience. But this detail is no chaotic list of facts. The expert is one who can grasp order in the flux of phenomena. And this order is to be identified with the structures which allow us to recognize species of persisting beings in what would otherwise be an unknowable disarray of details.

What Aristotle did was to bring Plato's "Forms" down to earth. What we know, the *eidos,* was no longer the inhabitant of an ideal realm but became convertible with the shape (*morphē*: cf. our word "morphology") or structural principle that gives order and intelligibility to the things that develop before our physical eyes.

THE ORDER
IN WHAT WE ARE

However, we miss much of Aristotle's thought if we identify structures with the "bare bones" of things as they appear to an observer. Even an anatomist may fail to answer our questions fully if he does no more than list the multitude of bones found in the human hand. We describe them, and their relations, most effectively if we see what they are *for.* Order is understood in the complex structure of bones once this is seen as for grasping and for gesturing.

Now numbers have no such "purpose," and scientists have generally tried to reject teleology (the study of purposes) from their account as a surviving anthropomorphism. Physicists simply relate the swing of a pendulum to gravity and to the rotation of the earth; they do not say that a pendulum is "for" swinging or keeping time. Hence Aristotle may not satisfy the contemporary biologist (though the latter still finds it difficult to eradicate such human notions as a "struggle for survival").

Nevertheless, other disciplines such as history involve a study of purposes. As discussed in the second chapter (pp. 35–36), such studies rely on a participant account: they try to convey what it is to *be* a person of a certain sort, acting in a certain way for reasons of his own. And it has been suggested that metaphysics is a study of subjectivity, of what it is to act as an "I," or to be oneself.

Hence, when Aristotle identified form or structure with activity (*energeia*) and purpose, he may have been outdated in his biology but could remain contemporary in his metaphysics. His writings which come under this name, and which he himself called "first philosophy," extend his investigation of biological forms to a study of the structures that must belong to any being. Thus, he held that every being must be open to analysis in terms of form and materiality, of activity and passivity.

More will be said of this in the following chapter, and of his consequent view of reality as a hierarchy of stages of life. But for the present we may take from Aristotle the invitation to ask what are the structures or most general forms, not of our behavior as it appears to observers, but of our agency in being subjects. Whether or not we think of an oak tree as being "self-identical" in all the stages from acorn to decay, we may at least find it worth inquiring what structure of self-possession or self-presence must belong to the most or least advanced being that could formulate any questions that may reach us from a situation far out in space. This we can ask now as metaphysicians and then wait for the astronomer to tell us how many legs the creature has.

Kant and the
Categories of Experience

The scientist, as such, is not concerned with subjectivity. As stressed in Chapter Three, he is of course a questioning subject and his own manner of questioning discloses the world as one of numerical relations. But it is objects and their relations, not subjects, which form the content of his study. For the scientist, that *is* (or exists, or is real) which appears as an object of appropriate observations. In slogan form: "To be is to appear for an observer."

Aristotle's slogan was different: "To be is to act." Whether he was right or not to apply it in biology, this formula is appropriate for a metaphysics of subjectivity. What I am as a subject is not how I appear to observers but how I am in myself, how I act humanly, questioning and affirming myself and my world.

The medieval philosophers continued in the tradition of Aristotle. But with the rise of science, the concern of philosophers for subjectivity was lessened. Descartes, for all his desire to "see for himself," interpreted seeing in the manner of Galileo. And empiricists, such as Locke and Hume, though regarding themselves as opponents of Descartes, followed him closely in the identification of "being" with "appearance as an object."

THE COPERNICAN REVOLUTION

The basis for a return to the subject was laid by Kant. His attitude toward metaphysics was subtle and will be discussed in the following chapter. But he set out to make a clear distinction between the way a scientist relates observed facts and the way a philosopher inquires into what must hold of any experience. Kant respected science highly; he himself anticipated the nebular hypothesis of Laplace and wrote treatises on the rotation of the earth, on earthquakes, fire, and winds. However, as a philosopher he felt it his task to investigate, not the detailed content of knowledge, but the inescapable structures of any human knowledge.

This project he referred to as a "Copernican Revolution" in philosophy. By this he meant that if we are to validate the claim of metaphysics to discover necessary truths, we must turn our attention from the particular objects we know to the "categories" of knowing them. We may translate this as a conversion from the content of our questions to that which belongs to the structure of any question we can ask. To use Kant's own illustration:

> **Reason must go out to nature in order to be taught by her. It must do so, however, not as a pupil who merely takes in whatever the teacher chooses to say, but as an appointed judge who compels witnesses to reply to questions he has himself formulated. (*Critique of Pure Reason*, B xiii)**

That is, so long as we remain passive pupils, taking in particular facts as sheer data, given to us by a nature that is already constituted apart from us, then we can expect nothing more than mere "matters of fact": here, Hume was quite right. There can be a place for necessary truths only when we realize that the facts we observe are not independent of the way we actively question the world and of any necessities that exist in our agency as questioning subjects. If, for example, it can be proven that a chaos of data is made intelligible only by questioning in terms of causal order, then a philosopher can tell astronomers that although they may have to break the principle of inertia if they are to admit quasars into their scheme of things, they can never find an event without a cause. If they speculate on galaxies not yet observed, or on societies with which we are not yet in communication, then causality must form part of the picture.

TRANSCENDENTAL PHILOSOPHY

Some terminology may be introduced here. Kant called the facts revealed by science *a posteriori*: they come "after" observation and depend for their truth on repeated observations. Such experience of particular data, which we can "point out" either directly or through instruments and calculations, we referred to in the first chapter as *empirical*. But there are some truths which we know must be so "before" we make any observations, or at least without our depending on repeated observations. Thus we do not have to wait for the broadcast or go to the stadium to know that the home team must either win, lose or tie a game that is played to a conclusion. Such truths Kant called *a priori*. The example rests on human conventions. But Kant held that an analysis of the structures of knowledge would reveal truths about the world which are *a priori* and yet independent of any conventions. The principle of causality is the example quoted. We hold it for certain and do not make its truth depend on repeated observations: if we do not yet know what is the cause of cancer, we look again, for we know there must be one.

Such knowledge of *a priori* truths about the world was also called by Kant *transcendental*. The term comes from medieval philosophers who took up Aristotle's proposal for discovering what must belong to any being at all. Such properties cannot be set in one class and opposed to other properties (as some things are red, others green) but they go across ("transcend") all possible classifications: e.g., whether red or green, the unity of a red or green "thing" must be present.

The term is unfortunate because it is similar in form, but strongly opposed in meaning, to the word *transcendent*. Kant regarded his work largely as a refutation of "transcendent metaphysics," which claims to take us by reasoning from what we experience to some second world of spiritual objects beyond empirical experience. He thought that such metaphysicians made the mistake of talking about a transcendent reality as though they were "acosmic" spectators and forgot their situation in space and time. An astronomer can legitimately speculate about the origin of the earth from the sun because he is giving an account of how an observer would have measured and recorded the event, long before us and from outside the solar system, yet from a perfectly possible situation in space and time. However, Kant would insist that if a metaphysician talks in all too similar terms of the origin of the entire universe, he forgets that there is no possible situation from which an observational account could have any meaning. Transcendent metaphysics is nonsensical because all valid statements must be made from within the limits of "situated knowledge." Without a *point* of view we have no "view" and can make no sense.

Briefly, then, Kant's project was to re-establish metaphysics by turning it from a transcendent inquiry to transcendental philosophy, an investigation of the inescapable structures of human knowledge and hence of all we can know. Such a study, he insisted, far from taking us beyond experience, is an attempt to make explicit what belongs most intimately to our experience. For instance, he commented caustically on a reviewer who ascribed to him a form of "transcendent" or "higher" metaphysics:

Not on your life *higher*. High towers, and metaphysically tall men like them, round both of which there is commonly a lot of wind, are not for me. My place is the fruitful *bathos* of experience . . . .[4]

[4] *Prolegomena*, trans. P.G. Lucas, p. 144.

It remains to be seen whether what such a method reveals of the depth of experience is fruitful or not. Yet the project of coming to grips with what we basically are as human subjects, rather than running from experience to experience, is one that has a long tradition, even outside the halls of philosophy.

To close this historical introduction, we may now be able to understand a famous quotation in which Kant indicates his plan for philosophy:

I call that knowledge transcendental which is concerned not so much with [particular] objects as with the form of our knowledge of any object, so far as such knowledge is to be possible *a priori*. A system of such concepts would be termed transcendental philosophy. (*Critique of Pure Reason*, B 25)

The Subject as Questioner

There are many ways of exploring our subjectivity to disclose the necessary structures it involves. We could, for instance, investigate Sartre's suggestion that some choice is inescapable in whatever we do, even if we try to shirk the responsibility of a definite choice. To examine subjectivity in this light would be to treat the self primarily as willing or striving: freedom would become the initial topic. Or we could follow out the argument of Aristotle that some commitment to truth is inescapable, even if we try to be completely skeptical. To inquire into subjectivity in this way would be to approach the self through the more "intellectualist" structures of knowing.

All roads converge. That which will be followed in this book starts with our subjectivity as questioners. We did, after all, begin the book with an account of the philosopher's task as a questioning of questioning. And it is safe to assume perplexity in any reader making his introduction to philosophy. That is all we need to get going. Our proposal, for the rest of this chapter, is to inquire into the situation of perplexity in which we find ourselves.

The Situation of the Radical Questioner

At the beginning we have no possessions. If we are to see for ourselves and develop a "self-acquired knowledge for which we can answer from the beginning," we can take nothing for granted. We have no indubitable facts on which we can build, no evident point of departure, no method for advancing. All we have is our very perplexity, our question where to begin, how to proceed, where to go. It is this situation of bewilderment we shall now describe and analyze.

The French essayist, Montaigne (1533–92), held that we are condemned to skepticism. He admitted that if we try to state our skepticism, then we contradict ourselves along the lines of Aristotle's "negative proof." But, he wrote, could we not find a "nonassertive language" in which to express our skepticism without self-contradiction? Clearly there is no such language; all we say is somehow "assertive." But still we may sympathize with Montaigne. Is there not something of a trick in glibly pouncing on contradictions in the position of those who deny any inescapable necessities in our life? Does the "position" of the skeptic need to be stated in any explicit form? Is it not something much less positive and less definite? Is it not rather a vague but profound malaise or hesitation at the heart of all we do?

Even if we do not profess skepticism, is not a nonassertive hesitation the best term to apply to the embarrassment in which any honest thinker finds himself? He does not rush to arms and assert one theory against another. He is not sure whether either is right, whether the difference is a real one, whether the whole dispute has any meaning. He is uncertain, puzzled, vacillating, confused.

There is no want of synonyms for "perplexity." And it is this situation, in any form from the least definite to the most articulate, that we may cover with the term "questioning." It is the distressing performance of realizing that we do not know. At the beginning (whatever that may mean), we have no more than our bewilderment. If any progress is to come (whatever progress may be), only our perplexity can reveal it.

The situation of the questioner may be far less definite than the systematic doubting to which Descartes invited us. But if we wish, we may repeat his experiment by questioning as radically as we can all we have previously taken for granted—not forgetting our very questions. It is not enough to join the many who doubt whether life has any meaning. We question whether it is even meaningful to ask whether life has any meaning.

The Content and Agency
of Questioning

At the beginning of the previous chapter it was suggested that Descartes neglected the influence of history in his attempt to find a beginning that was truly his own. No one ever "does philosophy" without some inherited ideas about what this is or in which direction one should go. Philosophy is what is taught and examined under that name in the country and at the university in which one happens to be. Or it is that which has been done by those customarily listed in books on the history of the subject. Or it is that which has been suggested in casual conversation or simply absorbed from the "atmosphere of the age."

Nevertheless, Descartes was right in thinking that no such inherited notions can be accepted as a simple datum. Of course we take our questions from tradition, as we do our language. But they can be taken *as* questions only if we make them into *our* questions by putting the received form of the question into question. And this, though difficult, is no more so than using language to criticize and amend language.

Hence no *content* of my questioning yields a starting-point from which I may proceed to find a way out of the perplexity of the radical questioner. If I ask how to begin philosophy, I cannot even assume that I know what philosophy is or what "beginning it" means. All notions I may have of this from various sources are themselves put in question and fail to justify themselves. Perhaps Plato and Aristotle and their successors were tangled in meaningless questions. The beginning philosopher comes from a long tradition, yet he stands alone.

Enough has been *said* about the perplexity of the self-questioner. The experiment is one each must perform for himself. The problem cannot be "given" by a book, nor can a solution. If any is to arise, it can only be from self-questioning which one *does*. The *agency* of questioning may prove more productive than the content.

Suppose, as is likely, that your present question is whether the above paragraphs are nonsense. Looking further at *what* is said and questioned only increases the perplexity. However, try turning from the content of such a question to your agency of being perplexed or indignant or in any way upset. The account must go in the first person. My explicit question is whether what I am thinking is nonsense. But in order for me to *be* in any way concerned about this, there must be some meaning to my concern, to my implicit activity of posing the explicit question about meaning or nonsense. The more concerned I am about the content of my particular questions, the more I affirm the meaningfulness of my agency of questioning in general. To put this in the form used at the end of the last chapter:

(I am questioning meaningfully)　　"Is my questioning meaningless?"

In other words, the suggestion is that once we clearly engage in self-questioning and turn from the content of our questions to the agency of questioning, we may find some way out of what seemed a futile situation of perplexity. Self-questioning is self-validating. Whereas any particular truth or meaning (any "theme" of questioning) is shaken when put in question, the reality and meaning of my own act of questioning is affirmed and renewed. From the most articulate skepticism to an undefined malaise, I implicitly affirm my reality as a self-questioning subject.

This may sound confusing. Or it may sound like a trick. But what is intended is something very simple, perhaps trivial and obvious. Suspicion should be reserved for any esoteric access to philosophy. The "access" indicated here is no special door, for we are already on the way. All this analysis of our perplexity suggests is that we live as questioners, that *our* questions at least implicitly turn on themselves, and that any manner we have of challenging this implicitly affirms it. The question "Who am I?" yields at least a minimal answer: "I am a questioner."

Perplexity and Progress

To close this section, two problems will be raised. Have I shown that I *must* be a questioner? And where do I go from there?

THE INEVITABILITY OF QUESTIONING

As to the first problem, it would follow that if we are necessarily questioners, then we are always questioners. Yet it seems that we are not always engaged in posing questions. The difficulty comes from a too precise, or too explicit, notion of what is meant here by "questioning." Four comments may help to clear up what is and is not claimed for the argument above.

a) What has been shown to be inescapable is the *implicit* agency of questioning. No such claim has been made for the content of any explicit questions. Nor has it been denied that we base our life on a host of practical certitudes. These are sufficient for our immediate purposes. We choose not to examine the ignorance which remains at the heart of our certainty and which prevents us from having "total" knowledge of anything. To say that man is essentially a questioner is to say that he is a "perplexed knower"; he can always question the knowledge he has (not excluding the above proof).

b) Even where we feel least aware of our questioning, our knowledge comes as an answer to questions we have posed, at least implicitly. This is no more than to repeat that no facts we disclose are independent of the way we question the world, "as judges rather than pupils." Though we may speak of "being struck by a fact," no one ever absorbs knowledge without being ready for it, inviting it by appropriate questions or at least by a questioning mentality. A mind as passive as Locke's mirror would know nothing. And different minds have a way of knowing very differently.

c) To say that man must be a questioner is to exclude the possibility that he could ever have a simply non-questioning experience. Might we not, however, receive something like a mystic intuition which altogether lifts us out of the questioning state? Questions of this sort could be profitable. It may well be that a study of mystical experience would lead a philosopher to modify his perhaps over-simple view of questioning. But questions of this type *are* questions. Any mystical experience that could challenge my present understanding of questioning would appear *as* a challenge, as a questioning of my present questioning state.

d) If anyone agrees that we are inescapably questioners but denies that this must involve *self*-questioning, it is again because he is reading in a degree of explicitness which is not claimed. It may be only in rare moments, and perhaps not always in healthy ones, that we ask explicitly about the status and meaning of our questions. But they are *our* questions, and the personal agency of questioning is at least implicitly self-critical. I can appreciate a question as *mine* only to the extent that I somehow reflect on it as the sort of question I am asking, adequately or confusedly, fruitfully or half-heartedly. Remove this completely and you remove the agency of questioning. It is because machines lack the self-criticism of an "I" that they need to be programmed by an agent who possesses it.

GROWTH THROUGH QUESTIONING

The other problem, where one goes from this bare beginning, can be answered only in the sequel. The rest of this book, or at least the more metaphysical chapters, will try to penetrate further into what it is to be a questioner. But three preliminary comments may help. The temptation of the philosopher is to be more concerned with method than results, so the remarks will be kept brief.

a) Whatever method follows, it can be described as *experimental*. A metaphysics of subjectivity does not rest on any particular thing we are supposed to "see" but develops with what we do. The sciences are experimental, yet within clearly defined limits. An experiment in physics presupposes that you have accepted a complex set of rules and principles. You can reject them but are then politely ushered out of the laboratory. However, in philosophy you are invited to experiment as far and as radically as you can. Try to become a total skeptic. Try to deny your freedom. Try to deny your materiality and worldly situation. Enter without restraint into the experiment and discover what you are forced to concede—not by the conventions of the game but by the very structure of your own questioning activity.

b) Such a method will in no way usurp the work of the scientist. We still turn to him for details of the content of experience. It is only the necessary structures with which we shall be concerned. If you want to know the time, look at a clock. But if you want to know what time is and whether some form of temporality belongs inescapably to all possible experience, then your questions are philosophical. Illustrations have so far been short of dramatic. Few of us are tempted to adopt the theoretical position or practical attitudes of total skepticism. But the method can be generalized as follows. Any position or attitude is shown to be impossible, in the strongest sense, if the experiment of stating it or living it is contradicted by our implicit agency of affirming it or willing it or asking the question it pretends to answer.

c) A method which encourages radical questioning may seem to sap our certainties and lead to ''agnosticism'' and apathy or despair. Descartes denied this, insisting on his constructive purposes. Once we have found a basic truth which is unshakable, we can build our life on it; the image is of an inverted pyramid, in which everything is made to balance on one thing. This image does, indeed, reflect a common attitude. Many people, in their search for certainty or security, do make their whole life depend on some conviction they take as unquestionable. And the posture tends to be defensive: the rock on which all is based must be protected against any questioning.

However, even the stoutest rocks can be shaken; no particular fact or principle is immune from legitimate questioning. But the ''starting-point'' we have been considering in these pages is very different. It is no particular point but is rather the inescapable structure of questioning. Hence, instead of protecting it, we are invited to experiment with all ways of questioning it. Whatever the method reveals, progress comes through renewed perplexity. The more you shake the foundations, the more you are able to disclose of what lies hidden in them. The method is positive and the attitude is relaxed, open rather than defensive.

The Structures
of Questioning

In the introductory chapter, a list was made of six tasks that philosophers claim to perform. The first four were classified as analytic, the last two as metaphysical. Whether the approach to metaphysics that is offered here allows for the sixth as well as the fifth heading is a problem to be raised in the following chapter. Yet this approach does not exclude the title of "analysis." What we are analyzing is not concepts or methods but the structures that give shape to anything we can do as subjects. To use one of Kant's terms, our project is now to disclose the *conditions of possibility* of questioning; we ask what must be so if we are in any way to ask.

Since questioning is itself an inescapable necessity, all the conditions required for it to be possible are of a like necessity. It is not metaphysically impossible for intelligent beings to exist somewhere without an atmosphere of oxygen. But it is excluded that they could be total skeptics. Some affirmation of truth belongs to the conditions of possibility for subjectivity.

Our inquiry may also be stated as a study of what must belong to a "transcendental subject." Historians and sociologists tell us what distinguishes one type of person or society from another. But the metaphysician is interested in what cuts across all possible divisions, even those which astronomers have not yet revealed. If any beings are at present questioning us with signals from far in space, such persons share in the community of subjects and in the conclusions of our analysis.

The results may remain highly general. Yet we do not have to look beyond our own earth for applications. A basis will be supplied for assessing some important views of man, whether theoretically expressed by philosophers or implied in a practical style of life.

The Need and Ability to Question

To close this chapter, we shall draw attention only to the two basic conditions of possibility for questioning and their relation. These are (1) that we should *need* to question, and (2) that we should be *able* to question.

1. Our need to question is our "not-knowing" or *ignorance*: unless we were in some way "separated" from knowing, we should not be perplexed, on the way to knowing, but we should be simply and utterly at home with all that is (whatever that would mean).

2. Our ability to question is some prior *knowledge*, without which we could not recognize our ignorance *as* ignorance: unless we were in some tentative possession of knowledge, we should have no norm by which to appreciate our inadequacy, no intention of asking to go further, not the vaguest anticipation of what this "further" could be.

To question whether these two conditions are inescapable is only to reaffirm them. In asking whether I am ignorant, I am implicitly affirming ignorance, else I should not be asking: I should have no perplexity about the reality and meaning of what I am. But likewise I am implicitly affirming some knowledge of what I am, else I should have no basis at all for putting myself in question.

Plato described our state of questioning as "midway between wisdom and ignorance." On the one hand:

> None of the gods philosophizes or craves to become wise, for those already in possession no longer seek. On the other hand, those who are purely ignorant do not philosophize or seek after wisdom. For the danger of ignorance is that a simple lack of beauty or goodness or intelligence would cancel our very dissatisfaction: one who did not even feel himself lacking would have no desire for what he lacks. (*Symposium* 203e–204a)

This may seem the height of abstraction. But there is no more personal question for each to ask than "Who am I?" Of course I know who I am. That is a topic on which I am the world's expert. Yet my most intimate self-knowledge is suffused with ignorance of the most painful and embarrassing sort. To my dying day, I remain a question to myself, "already" knowing and yet needing to know who I am.

The metaphor of "suffusion" is one we must now investigate. Each may readily admit that he is an odd "mixture" of ignorance and knowledge, and hence a questioner. But there is a danger of representing the relation in an over-simple way. We may think of ignorance only as a series of precise "gaps" in our knowledge, waiting to be filled once and for all time when the appropriate answer is found. And we may think of knowledge only as a series of definite facts which we have already learned and which, once known, are completely known. This is a picture we shall investigate and criticize.

The Relation of Ignorance and Knowledge

The appeal of the sciences lies largely in their ability to provide us with precise facts on which all of us can agree. At least at the elementary level, the scientist achieves this by making a clear distinction between what is known and what is not known.

Suppose we want to know what warmth water has before it begins to boil. We agree, as clearly as we can, on certain "knowns": what we shall accept as water, as boiling, as a temperature scale, and as the standard conditions under which we shall look for an answer. We leave only one "gap" in our knowledge, one region of simple ignorance. At which point on the temperature scale does water boil under those conditions?

As soon as experiments have satisfied the investigators (again, within agreed terms of what will count as satisfaction), the gap has been filled. Simple ignorance has been transformed into knowledge adequate to agreed purposes. The question has been solved, abolished as a question. We can now list the boiling point of water among the facts we know and proceed to some *new* question. Progress is linear. We set up a question, solve it, and advance to a new question and a new answer.

To represent this view of the relationship between ignorance and knowledge, we may speak spatially of the two as areas of darkness and of light. They are simply distinct. There is no light at the heart of darkness; ignorance is a simple lack of knowledge. And there is no darkness at the heart of light; what we know we know completely.

Such a scheme works only where we are able and willing to turn our attention away from the remaining questionableness of our knowledge and *define* certain facts as known sufficiently for our purposes. We define warmth as that which is shown by a thermometer. We thus formulate a ''direct'' question (What is the temperature?) and set aside all legitimate ''reflexive'' questions about our question (e.g., What is measurement, and why should changes in expansion correspond to changes in warmth?).

Scientists are no longer content with an analysis of their method in terms of a simple linear progress, an extension of pure light into areas of darkness. Historians of science now see it, not as steadily advancing from discovery to discovery (''development by accumulation''), but as passing through a series of revolutions in the way scientists have chosen to formulate the ''same'' facts symbolically. The Copernican Revolution in astronomy gave us no new facts about the heavens but rather a new way of looking at old facts. Much the same could be said for the major contributions of Newton, Lavoisier, and Einstein. They did not solve questions by filling gaps with items of knowledge. What each did was to put into question the very questions their predecessors had asked and the once accepted ''models'' or ''paradigms'' for answering these. In other words, they revealed the surviving ignorance at the heart of our knowledge and renewed the self-questioning that is involved in doing science as in all human agency.

If there were any ''area'' of pure knowledge in my life I should cease there to be a questioner. And if there were any area of utter ignorance I should not there be able to question. I do of course delimit ''items'' of knowledge and of ignorance in terms of my practical purposes. But such a model fails to capture the self-questioning implicit in all I do. Though we may talk of ignorance *and* knowledge, we are not speaking of a relation between one thing and another. As vague as the phrase may be, we must say that there is always ignorance at the heart of our knowledge and knowledge at the heart of our ignorance.

Since we are concerned with structures rather than with content, no example of what is meant by this relation can be given. Perhaps the notion of structure without content is best suggested by what we suppose to be the state of an infant. He possesses no items of knowledge, hence has no gaps of ignorance. Yet it would be wrong to say that he is totally ignorant. He is no complete "blank," for his ignorance is suffused with the structures of knowledge. From his earliest cry he reveals the need and ability to know, that eternal dissatisfaction of the questioner which produces scientists, revolutionaries, and philosophers.

6 | What Is Really So?

This is the question metaphysicians have traditionally asked. What they have meant is by no means easy to say. This chapter will try to indicate some of the problems involved and to go a few steps beyond the previous chapter. We shall look further into the most general conditions of possibility for the questioning from which we cannot escape. It is fair to warn the reader that the task is not easy.

Or is it? Should there be any profound problem about discovering ''what is really so''? Did not the fourth chapter show the meaning of this question as we normally ask it? For the skeptics (and for many contemporary philosophers), to ask what is really so is only to ask what appears under conventions defined as privileged. To say that ''the cloth appears gray but is really blue'' means that it appears blue in ''usual'' conditions of light. A question about what things really are, or what they are ''in themselves,'' is only a way of asking how they show themselves to a spectator who clarifies the rules of observation he chooses to adopt. The scientist, for instance, defines these in the way that best allows objects to be related mathematically.

Metaphysicians, however, in asking about the ''reality'' of (or beyond) appearances, have been looking for more than the above answer supplies. In the first place, they connect ''reality'' with ''necessity'' and "universality": what *must* be so *for all,* regardless of any conventions we choose as tailors or opticians or physicists? In the second place, even while respecting that we are limited to observing how objects appear to us, metaphysicians have sought some grounds for saying what is so "unconditionally," or what is so "in itself": in traditional, though confusing, language they have said they are studying *being,* or asking the question "What is it *to be* rather than merely *to appear?*"

This book has supported two claims about the metaphysical question: (1) a reply can come, not from any of the particular objects of experience, but rather from its *structure,* and (2) the structure we should investigate is that of *subjectivity,* i.e., of the first-person agency of questioning, knowing or striving. Putting the two claims together, we can say that the metaphysician asks what structures are inescapable if we are to be questioners, as indeed we must.

This chapter could go on at once to ask what more is contained in the predicament of knowing and not-knowing which makes us questioners. But there is a further problem which the chapter should face if it is not to gloss over the objection many feel toward metaphysics. They assume that this discipline proposes to take us "beyond physics" in the sense of giving conclusions that could never enter our experience. That is, affirmative answers are offered to certain "ultimate" or especially important questions, such as whether I have an immortal soul and whether there exists a Supreme Being who is the creator and ruler of the world.

So far, the project of metaphysics has been interpreted in terms of the fifth task of philosophy, as listed in the opening chapter; a necessity is sought beyond that of science but still within our ordinary experience of being questioners. Does this open the way for a reevaluation of the "ultimate" topics that propose a sixth task for philosophers? Can questions of God and the soul be drawn from an inquiry into the structure, and experience, of all questioning? Or does a metaphysics of subjectivity exclude such topics as a meaningless "beyond"? The question is complex and subtle. This chapter will do little more than pose it. And as contemporary discussion has been so greatly affected by the way Kant put the question, the opening section will again be historical.

The Problem of General and Special Metaphysics

The question of metaphysics was introduced in this book through the Greek skeptics and the replies of Plato and Aristotle. An ambiguity in those replies has already been mentioned, and its consequences will now be examined.

The Ambiguity
in Metaphysics

The skeptics asked whether all is not relative, utterly dependent on human conventions and in no way coming from the "nature of reality." Plato replied, not by offering any particular fact as unquestionable, but by inviting the skeptics to recognize the universal norms of truth which they must somehow know as a condition of their own questioning. Unless they had knowledge of universal, necessary, and eternal Ideas, how could they even wonder at the variability of particular things and beliefs?

However, if we grant that Plato leads us to something necessary, the problem arises what this is. And the tendency, at least among his followers, was to treat this as "some *thing*." The *eidos* became an object of intellectual contemplation. As the objects of experience are all particular and changing, the universal and necessary Forms must be beyond such experience, in a world of spiritual beings.

Whether or not Plato himself held this theory, Aristotle ascribed it to him and criticized it. However, it was over-simple to say, as we did in the last chapter, that Aristotle set the Forms solidly within experience, as the abiding structural principles which give order and intelligibility. The writings which he called "first philosophy," and which came to be termed "metaphysics," seem to indicate two projects. One was to generalize his biological studies and analyze those structures which must belong, not to this or that species of being, but to any being that is; metaphysics became the study of "being precisely as being." But the other task was to investigate what he called "separate substance," being or beings beyond the world of sense; and the most notable of these was the "unmoved mover" (uncaused cause) which many identify with God.

There are various interpretations of Aristotle. Some emphasize the difference between these two tasks of metaphysics; frequently the second is looked upon as an unfortunate survival of Platonism, which should be treated as meaningless, and valid metaphysics should be identified with the first task. Another interpretation is that Aristotle saw the second project of metaphysics as intimately involved in the first; to investigate what must belong to any being is to disclose its ultimate cause which is itself uncaused.

For instance, in his commentary on Aristotle's *Metaphysics* (Section 1170), the most influential of the medieval philosophers, Thomas Aquinas (1225–74), writes: "The study of first being (unmoved substance) is the same as the study of being as common (precisely as being)." As was suggested in the fifth chapter (p. 83), the medievals did not confine themselves to a spectator account in philosophy. Living before the rise of science, they did not regard it as evident that "to be is to appear as an object.'' Hence, talk of ''being'' was taken as belonging, not to a study of what is common to the objects of observation, but rather to an inquiry into what it is ''to be'' as a subject. Such views may have hindered the rise of science by treating nature anthropomorphically. Yet they enabled Aquinas to say that metaphysics has to do, not with generalities about objects, but with ''that which is most intimate to each person and underlies all he does.'' (*Summa Theologica*, I-8-1) He also held that ''all knowing beings know God implicitly in every act of knowledge.'' (*On Truth*, 22-2 *ad* 1) Hence Aquinas was able to unite Aristotle's two seemingly disparate projects into one investigation of that which ''underlies what we do in every act.''

However, it became increasingly difficult to appreciate and develop such views as science rose to prominence by a progressive exclusion of the role of subjectivity. And once it was generally accepted that ''to be is to appear as an object,'' the two tasks of metaphysics were sharply separated. This is shown most clearly in the division of philosophy made by Christian Wolff (1679–1754). On the one hand there is the study of being as being, the investigation of what must belong to anything that is: this Wolff called ''general metaphysics'' or ''ontology.'' On the other hand there is the inquiry which he called ''special metaphysics'' and which studies three main types of beings: material beings (cosmology), the soul (psychology), and God (natural theology). A crude analogy would be a division into general and special biology, with the latter subdivided into botany, zoology, and anthropology. Rather than asking what is implicit in the agency of being a subject, we treat beings as objects and classify them for better study, some within experience and some beyond it. This may not be altogether fair to Wolff, but it is much the view which Kant inherited and found so problematic.

Kant's First *Critique*

Kant's way of formulating the problem set the theme for subsequent discussion of the question whether metaphysics is a valid inquiry and, if so, in what form and with what limitations. We have already seen the main lines of the approach to philosophy which he followed in the *Critique of Pure Reason*. Here, we shall try to explain how this work claims to reestablish general metaphysics as ''transcendental philosophy'' and reject special metaphysics as ''transcendent metaphysics.''

KANT'S VERSION
OF GENERAL METAPHYSICS

Hume held that we can find in the world only ''matters of fact'' (cf. p. 62). We can associate them in various ways, as science does. But we can come across no absolute ''must,'' no necessary connections such as causality. Kant suspected that Hume had not gone far enough in his questioning. If I can know two events "atomically," as sheer matters of fact, then I cannot afterwards discover any absolutely necessary connections between them. Yet is it so certain that I can know any event just by itself without "already" (*a priori*) knowing much that belongs to it of necessity? If I hear a sudden loud noise, I may depend on later observations to find what caused it. But is it possible to hear it at all without knowing it *as* caused?

We have seen that Kant's basic proposal was that human knowledge does involve certain *a priori* structures. Hence if we can determine these we can say in advance what must hold for anything experience reveals, whether it comes through a microscope or as a conclusion from what is recorded by radio telescopes.

It would go far beyond our purposes here to explain what structures Kant found or how he claimed to do so. But it can be seen how his project of transcendental philosophy would satisfy the notion of general metaphysics. If we can discover the structures that are required for any experience to be possible, we shall have found what must belong to any object experience can reveal, i.e., what belongs to any being that is (appears to us as an object).

Thus, in the first part of his *Critique* Kant analyzes "sense" (*Sinnlichkeit*) and discloses space and time as inescapable structures of all our knowledge. We must take into account that whatever we claim to know, however abstract or "spiritual," involves some limitation to a spatial and temporal situation or point of view: try, for instance, to remove all spatial and temporal reference from talk of a "superior" Being existing "before" creation. In the second part of his book Kant analyzes "understanding" (*Verstand*) and claims to have found a dozen "categories" without which the world could not be known in any ordered or intelligible way: for instance, remove all causality from your view of a rainy day or a surprise event and unknowable chaos would result.

With this analysis of the structures of sense and understanding, Kant holds he has found the basic structures that must belong to anything of which we can have valid knowledge. However, he goes on to a third part of his *Critique* in which he studies "reason" (*Vernunft*). The distinction between this and "understanding" is important and leads to his rejection of any claim we may make to know the existence and properties of God and the soul.

KANT'S CRITICISM
OF SPECIAL METAPHYSICS

We can interpret Kant as asking how far we may push our questions without losing ourselves in a meaningless inquiry. If we can discover the inescapable structures of the questions we put and answers we receive, we may conclude that any "answer" we suggest which claims not to incorporate those structures is meaningless. Now the forms of sense, namely space and time, limit us to the knowledge of whatever can appear to us as situated knowers. If I look through a telescope at the planet Uranus, my knowledge of an object moving across the sky in no way violates the structures of sense and understanding. Nor is there any such violation if I postulate the existence of Neptune as the cause of deviations in the orbit of Uranus, even though I have "reasoned" to the existence of Neptune rather than perceived it: Neptune remains in principle perceivable, an object of appropriate observations. The more sophisticated conclusions of science (e.g., about electrons) would require a more complex account of how we reason from appearances to "appearances," but electrons can still be treated as objects of situated knowledge.

However, there is a different story when I ask, not what caused the deviations in Uranus, but what caused the world as a whole. Here the category of causality is being used to pass, not from one appearance in the world to another, but to an "answer" which could never appear because it would be outside the structures of situated knowledge.

We may ask what caused a loud noise or a stellar explosion. But to argue about the nature and activity of God or the soul, as of a thing with properties that causes events, is like trying to swim in a pool that has been emptied. Kant's warning is that we should recognize the limits of our thought and stay on the ground: to dive into transcendent metaphysics is to risk a broken head in a foolhardy venture. No wonder metaphysicians have come to such contradictory answers on questions of this sort.

It is this use of "reason" that Kant examines in the third part of his *Critique*. With more than a casual reference to Plato, he says that whereas understanding has categories, reason has "ideas": namely God, the soul, and the world as a totality (to simplify what follows we may ignore the last of these, as traditional cosmology will not concern us). Again, much in the tradition of Plato, Kant says that the categories organize *phenomena* (appearances "for us," in the world of sense), whereas the ideas of reason are *noumena* (things "in themselves," in an intelligible world).[1]

Kant's doctrine is that *noumena* are unknowable. This we may interpret as saying that we can know objects only as they appear from particular points of view and not what they are "finally" or "uncondi-

---

[1] The terms have become classical. Both are from the Greek. *Phenomena* means "things that appear," i.e., the objects of science and observation. *Noumena* means "things that are known," i.e., the realities metaphysics claims to disclose through reasoning rather than observing.

tionally." We can ask about the many ways in which a table appears "for us," but it is meaningless then to ask what the table is "in itself." Having asked about the many ways a person appears for us, the roles he plays and functions he serves, we enter the dubious realm of metaphysics if we then ask, as a further question, what the person really is in himself.

However, Kant adds that the ideas of reason are not useless. Though they are not "constitutive" of valid knowledge (as the categories are), they are "regulative." We have a "natural disposition" to ask metaphysical questions, to which there can be no answer. What does Kant mean?

Suppose I ask whether a certain person is a socialist. I set myself a task of inquiring into what he holds and what socialists hold. I may break off my questioning at any stage and give an answer adequate up to a point. But the ideal of finding what he *really* is (finally or absolutely, in himself, "in his soul") makes me realize that any answer remains provisional, and the questioning goes further. The idea of a "soul" is regulative of my questioning. However, if I ever claim to have reached his soul and to have proved that it has socialist properties, then I am making an idea constitutive, treating it as though it were a category. My conclusion is meaningless and, worse still, it puts a halt to the continued process of questioning. I make a similar mistake if I ask what caused the thunder or the war and reply "God." Talk of God and the soul never gives us knowledge but drives us ever onward in our search for results that are valid for situated knowers, i.e., in our search for provisional answers in terms of the *phenomena* of this world.

In summary, then, Kant's first *Critique* represents a reinterpretation of general metaphysics as transcendental philosophy, an inquiry into the structures of sense and understanding, the forms which must belong to all *phenomena*. The *Critique* claims further to show that the aim of special metaphysics, the proposal to give us knowledge of God and the soul as *noumena,* violates the limits of meaningful discussion. Yet Kant recognizes that the natural disposition to find "what is really so" belongs regulatively to our questioning.

THE PROBLEM
FOR THIS CHAPTER

In the light of this complex but important historical account, we shall now return to our own analysis of what is really so, as revealed in the structures of knowing by questioning. At the close of the previous chapter we identified the two most basic of these. There is our *need* to question in order to know (our ignorance) ; this will be examined in the following section. And there is our *ability* to question (our "prior" knowledge) ; this will form the topic of the final section. Insistence on the way ignorance and knowledge permeate each other in self-questioning warns us that the distinction between these two sections is made only for the purposes of exposition : each is complemented by the other.

The analysis of ignorance will support Kant's conclusion that all our knowledge is *situated*. We can have no grasp of what is really so *apart from* the many ways it appears to us through the limitations of a point of view. In traditional terms, all our knowledge is based on sensation, and this involves materiality and "embodiment." Comments on the precise "forms of sense" (space and time) will be left to later chapters. Here we shall ask only what it means in general to be a situated knower to whom reality must "appear." This may not take us far but will, as Kant intended, raise healthy questions about talk of man as a spiritual being with an immortal destiny "outside" the world and "beyond" time.

The analysis of knowledge, in the final section, will have more to say on the structures that are required if experience is to be ordered or intelligible. At least, we are invited to respect the sort of investigation into the categories of understanding which Kant made as his version of general metaphysics. But the question will arise whether his rejection of the topics of special metaphysics follows. Are the "ideas of reason" merely regulative of our questioning? Or are they also in some way constitutive? Is the notion of a "soul" only an ideal that leads ever onward to further questions about the appearances of myself as an object (*phenomenon*) ? Or is some presence to myself as a subject, some grasp of what I really am "in myself" (as a *noumenon*), among the conditions required for my very embarrassment at seeming only to play roles and serve functions in the manner of an object appearing "for another"? That at least is the question through which we shall return to the ambiguity in the project of metaphysics. Discussion of the topic of God will be left to the final chapter.

**The Structures
of Ignorance
in Questioning**

If I claim that there is an extra planet circling the sun, we all know *what* I mean ; the question is whether I am right or not. Metaphysics, however, is different. It is not concerned with matters of fact which simply are so or not. The assertion that God exists, or that the soul is immortal, or that the world is infinite, raises inseparably the question what is meant and the question whether it is true.

This is important to remember in examining a metaphysical method which claims only to disclose the structures of experience. If it can be proved that temporality must belong to any experience we can have, this proof will help us to understand what is the "basic" meaning of temporality which lies under our dealings with clocks, our indefinite anxiety, and our sense of responsibility. What we take for granted is questioned through our search for structures that are inescapable on any possible hypothesis.

This comment applies to the discussion that follows. It is unlikely that any reader is upset with grave doubts whether he has a body and exists in a material world. But questioning whether this can be proved to be necessarily so involves a search for the basic meaning of such terms as "body," "matter," and "world." The notions seem obvious enough. Material existence means having the sort of body we weigh, bathe, clothe, feed, medicate, and maneuver through crowds. Yet are all such properties necessary for any conceivable existence as a questioner? This could well be possible without need of soap or clothes or medicine. Perhaps there could even be questioners somewhere in the universe that do not feed or breathe. But the metaphysician asks whether there is some fundamental notion of embodiment without which questioning can be shown to be inconceivable—and not merely unlikely. In proving that materiality is inescapable, he asks what the notion means.

The Need
to Find Oneself

The relevance of this inquiry to the problem of "immortality" will be indicated in a later chapter. But some bearings for the present discussion can come from the account that has been given of Descartes' position—though his full views seem to have been considerably more nuanced.

In summary, Descartes held that he was immediately present to himself as a purely thinking being. He claimed he could "be himself" this way while questioning or denying the existence of his body and of the whole material world. Hence "this self, that is to say, the soul, by which I am what I am, is entirely distinct from the body, and is even more easily known; and even if the body were not there at all, the soul would be just what it is." Though he recognized that he happened to have a body and exist in a material world, he maintained that this was not necessary for a questioner—which his philosophical method of doubting revealed him to be.

Is Descartes right? Am I first immediately and indubitably present to myself apart from the material world? Do I only subsequently go out of this spiritual self to find a world of objects, including my body? Or does my very questioning reveal, as one of its inescapable structures, a basic meaning of embodiment and of situation in a material world? Is self-presence achieved only through self-expression, by going out of myself and finding myself in a world of objects?

The problem will be investigated in stages. A description of what is meant by "expressing and finding oneself" will be followed by an argument for its necessity, drawn from the ignorance in questioning. In the light of this, there will then be a brief examination of the properties of "situated knowledge," which Kant opposed so strongly to the claims of Descartes. And the section will close with a look at the way some contemporary philosophers describe "embodiment."

SELF-EXPRESSION

Descartes wrote in the early days of science, and almost all that the sciences of man have taught us since has raised serious questions about his view of our independence from the world. It is a commonplace today that what each of us is depends intimately on his body, his society, and his history. The biologist explains the influence of our heredity, the sociologist relates us to our environment, the historian shows how our normal way of thinking is conditioned by our own times. Above all, perhaps, the psychologist has convinced us how closely tied our mental and emotional life is to the peculiarities of our body and of our hidden past.

But we do not need to look to the sciences, for our commonest experiences throw grave doubt on any claim to the self-presence of a knowing subject apart from the material world. We do not "see into another person's soul" but learn gradually to recognize his ideas, feelings, and desires in the way he expresses them bodily—in his gestures, his smile, the inflection of his voice, in what he does in various situations and under various provocations. Similarly, if we want to know about any society, we study the wide range of its expressions in literature, in institutions, science and technology, art and religion. However, is there any basic difference in the way I come to answer the question "Who am I?" I do not learn whether I am cowardly or courageous, an athlete or an artist, by taking a look into my soul. I discover what I do in testing circumstances. I experiment to see how high I can jump. I see whether my intention to paint a masterpiece can be achieved on canvas and the result is accepted by critics.

The command to "know yourself" or to "be yourself" is not easily followed. I am not an open book to myself. I play roles, hide from myself, am often mistaken about my real motives; indeed, other people may see these more clearly than I do. I am dissipated, a stranger to myself rather than a sheer self-presence. I know myself, not by withdrawing into a private mental world, but by going out of myself into the public world and finding myself in my self-expressions or "objectifications."

Nothing of what was said in previous chapters about the inescapable presence of subjectivity is here being denied. I am present to myself as a subject, and this will be the theme of the final section of this chapter. What is denied by the comments above is that this self-presence is apart from, or prior to, any self-discovery through the many ways in which I make myself an object. I am "I" through becoming a "me."

IGNORANCE AND MATERIALITY

The above account has consisted of a series of assertions, each open to a simple rejection. Can they be drawn together in an argument?

I am necessarily a self-questioner. A condition for my needing to question in order to know is that there must be ignorance at the heart of whatever I know. Were there any "area" or "item" of sheer knowledge, I should there simply know rather than question. Self-knowledge can be no exception to this, or I should not be a self-questioner. Hence the ignorance which necessarily separates me from sheer knowledge must be at the heart of my self-presence. It is this absence of immediate self-presence which was described above as "dissipation" or "estrangement," the need to express and discover myself.

The questioner's experience of needing to find himself is basic and cannot be related to anything more fundamental. It is from this experience that we can come to a philosophical understanding of the root sense of existing materially or bodily. Having a body that I feed and clothe and medicate is one way of "coming to myself." These particular forms of bodily existence may not be necessary. But the immediate and indubitable self-presence of a purely thinking being is excluded by the conditions of possibility for questioning. The limitation or self-opposition which excludes it is our basic meaning of materiality. The details of my bodily existence are discovered gradually. My existing bodily is disclosed in my very agency of knowing myself by questioning.

If materiality is so understood, Descartes was involved in the same sort of self-contradiction as the total skeptic. The answer he gave to his question about the reality of his body and of matter was implicitly denied through his very agency of doubting or questioning:

(I am questioning materially)   "Am I material?"

Situated Knowledge

This notion of materiality as the need for self-expression and self-discovery lacks the rich details of "body" and "matter" for which detectives and sculptors look. It is not at once obvious how a first-person account of embodiment would be developed or how this makes possible the much more sophisticated (though to us more ''evident'') third-person account fashioned by physicists and anatomists.

Indications will be given later, notably in the discussion of time and space. But we can readily see how being an embodied questioner restricts us to knowledge from a ''situation,'' or limits us to a view of the world from a place in the world. Some of the more basic properties of situated knowledge may suggest what is involved.

The ignorance which makes us question is that limitation, or inadequacy, or lack of integrity, which separates us from the full achievement of knowing. To claim to have overcome this limitation is to claim exemption from the state of a questioner. We are excluded by this state from any ''intellectual intuition'' of the way reality finally is (whatever that might mean). Instead, our knowledge is imbued by ''sense.'' We do not grasp what ''is'' apart from the many partial ways it is given to us or ''appears.'' Questioning is a way of knowing that passes from appearance to reality, where reality is a further appearance that demands repeated questioning.

To know through appearances, or by sensation, is passive in that reality comes to me through many guises. It is given. I am a ''datum'' to myself. But the passivity of sensation is only an element of knowledge. The need to question means finding what *is* given. I have to make my way through appearances, sifting the genuine from the superficial. I discover what I can do with things. I find the fence is higher than I thought by trying to jump it. I find I am weak-willed by trying to keep my resolutions. I experiment, I experience things, I express myself. Questioning means repeatedly going *out* of myself, as the etymology of such words suggests.

To know experimentally through appearances is to know from a variety of particular points of view. Every appearance is partial and calls for a further view. The shape of the table comes to me differently as I walk around it. The meaning of water varies as I adopt the point of view of the engineer or the chemist or the artist or the man in need of a drink, a wash, or a swim. In questioning I pass from one way of taking things to another, building up a variety of partial views into some ordered whole.

This may be enough to convey what is meant by saying that as questioners we are situated knowers. The connection with embodiment is clear; it is my body which situates me ''here,'' gives me a point of view, and restricts me to appearances. The connection with time and space will be discussed later, but the outlines are suggested; we endure the process of discovery, passing from now to then and from here to there.

We shall shortly examine the other condition of questioning, the prior knowledge through which we are able to recognize our situation as a limit to be overcome. But whatever grasp of ''reality'' this may involve, it will not remove us from our situation or from our journey through the world of appearances. There is no intellectual knowledge which simply escapes from the limits of what is ''given through sense.'' It is meaningless for a questioner to aspire to knowledge from no situation at all, outside space and beyond time.

Embodiment

This rather abstract section may close with a brief indication of the way a first-person account of embodiment could be developed—as it has been notably by phenomenologist and existentialist philosophers. The following chapter will have more on this theme.

A spectator account is of objects. in their relation to each other. Physics describes the movement of bodies; it does not tell us what it is to be a body. We can of course regard our own body in the same way. And perhaps we usually do so when the topic arises; we speak of its size, weight, shape, and condition much as we should of any object of science. But we do not simply ''have'' a body as we have a table. I exist bodily in the world. My body is not only that which limits me to a particular situation and certain appearances. It is that through which I express and discover all I can possibly know. And for this primitive grasp of what it is to *be* bodily, we must turn to a first-person account.

Sartre distinguishes between the body as it is for others and as ''being-for-itself.'' When I commonly talk of my body, it is not strictly ''my'' body but rather a body for others. I join them and observe my body much as a doctor would.

When a doctor takes my wounded leg and looks at it while I, half raised up on my bed, watch him do it, there is no essential difference between the visual perception which I have of the doctor's body and that which I have of my own leg.[2]

However, my leg is not merely an object to be observed in relation to other objects. More primitively, it is a way of my being in the world: ''It is the possibility which I am of walking, running, or of playing football.'' That is, my body reveals the world to me as possibility and as obstacle. It is the possibility which I am of talking, writing, counting, measuring, painting, engaging in business, politics or space-travel. It is

---

[2] *Being and Nothingness*, p. 304.

also that which limits and frustrates my possibilities, revealing me as a coward, an invalid or a failure. And through its obstacles, the body discloses further possibilities:

> [A hiker] gives himself up to his fatigue as to a bath; it appears to him in some way as the privileged instrument for discovering the world which surrounds him, for adapting himself to the rocky roughness of the paths, for discovering the "mountainous" quality of the slopes.[3]

Such quotations may be enough to suggest what would be involved in a first-person account of the body and what sort of embodiment has been proved in this chapter as inescapable for a questioner. If signals come to us from outer space, we may let imaginations run wild about the bodies we may eventually observe, their size, shape, and features. But we know in advance what it is in general for such beings to exist bodily. Whether or not there are mountains to be climbed or even legs to walk, such creatures disclose their world as a set of possibilities through which they learn to express and find themselves. Whether or not they share our sickness and social problems, they at least face the basic problem of experimenting with different points of view, receiving all too particular data and correcting appearances. Whether such questioners choose to enjoy fatigue or not, the obstacle of ignorance remains at the heart of all they do, and "being oneself" is a command rather than an achievement.

The Structures of Self-knowledge in Questioning

This section will present the "other face" of the previous section. The slogan has been offered that there is always ignorance at the heart of knowledge and always knowledge at the heart of ignorance. Our inescapable ignorance has so far been studied as that which condemns us always to know through sense, or from some situation. Now we shall turn to the "prior knowledge" without which we could not recognize our ignorance or limited situation *as such*.

The Condition of Perplexity

Kant's *Critique of Pure Reason* is a brilliant defense of the thesis that we cannot step out of our material situation and know what is so "un-

---

[3] *Ibid.*, p. 455.

conditionally" or "in itself," apart from the way objects are organized in terms of our perception and manipulation. If I remove from my experience of an explosion all reference to the ways in which I can situate it spatially and temporally, interpret it as an event with a cause or a thing with properties, apply the categories of unity and plurality, then I do not escape from "my" view of it to get at "the thing in itself." I am left with nothing, or perhaps with what C.S. Peirce called "presentness" and Kant called the sheer "manifold" (indescribable immediacy) of sensation. The world "is" as it appears "for us."

Kant's analysis of the "categories of understanding," the most general structures which are required if any object is to appear to us in an intelligible rather than a chaotic way, is much too complex for us to examine here. In turning now to the structures of knowledge without which we should be unable to question, we shall not be concerned with the detailed categories which are required but rather with the subject who questions. For Kant, the categories are the ways in which experience is organized to appear for a "unity of consciousness"; putting it simply, there is no such thing as *an* experience but only *my* experience.

Here we run directly into the problem with which this chapter opened, Kant's acceptance of general metaphysics (transcendental philosophy) and his rejection of special (transcendent) metaphysics. The former discloses the structures of objects as they appear to us. The latter claims to tell us about certain realities (notably God and the soul or self) as they are "in themselves." Now, in the *Critique of Pure Reason,* Kant extended his conclusions ruthlessly to the subject of experience. I know myself as an object that appears (as a *phenomenon*), not as I am in myself (as a *noumenon*). The soul, like God, is an "idea of reason"; the search for my true self merely regulates my questioning, drives me on from one appearance or role or function to another. But I in no way grasp what I "finally" am.

Kant's clear distinction between categories (as constitutive of knowledge) and ideas of reason (as merely regulative) is important and attractive. Common talk of the soul and of God carries a sound of "absoluteness" that does not ring true to our shifting problems. We feel that the subtleties of our situation are lost when we are told what's what because "that is our nature" or "reality is finally that way." Surely the absolutes or totalities represented by soul-talk and God-talk are distant ideals that may direct our voyage but can never be attained (cf. p. 19).

However, is it possible for an ideal of *knowledge* to be regulative without being constitutive? The distinction may be valid for a voyage or for any other endeavor. The carrot dangled before the donkey can regulate his progress without ever constituting his meal. But if the carrot were in no way part of the donkey's "knowledge," the trick would not work. Must I not already taste the goal of knowledge if I am to pursue it?

Before this question is faced, two comments need to be made. The first is that even if some valid knowledge of the "ideas of reason" does belong to the structures of subjectivity, the force of Kant's distinction between such ideas and the categories of appearance will remain. Whatever can be said of the soul and of God, the language of a spectator account would be thoroughly misleading. For we should not be talking of objects that can appear to us but rather of conditions for the knowledge of any object. Hence, if we ask about the relation between the soul and the body, as between one object and another, or if we ask whether the soul is immortal in the way we ask whether gold is insoluble, we are making a grave mistake. We are applying the categories of objects to a subject. If special metaphysics is a valid discipline, then the search for appropriate language is serious and central. Kant's warnings need always to be remembered.

The second comment is that the account given of Kant in this chapter is one-sided. All that has been presented is his analysis in the *Critique of Pure Reason*, where he considers only "theoretical reason," our knowledge of the world of objects in relation and our pseudo-knowledge of God and the soul as objects with properties. Effectively, this is what has been called in this book a spectator account. But Kant followed this with a *Critique of Practical Reason*, in which he did try to renew the questions of special metaphysics through an approach that seems close to what has here been called an agent account; the self is grasped as a *noumenon* through our experience of being free moral agents. Kant's intentions are open to understanding in various ways. But it may be that what follows is more an interpretation than a criticism of Kant, if his full project is accepted.[4]

---

[4] According to Kant, order or rationality is brought to the world by both theoretical and practical reason. The former does so by organizing objects given to an observer through sense. The latter, however, is not based on a "receptive faculty." Kant refers to Plato and insists that ideas of what ought reasonably to be are not drawn from experience. There may never have been a just state in existence but we still have a norm of justice which it is our duty to realize as far as possible in the political world: we do not observe what *appears* to us but know what it is *to be* reasonable, free, and moral.

When Kant wrote repeatedly, in the first *Critique*, that God and the soul cannot be "known," he was referring to the conclusions of theoretical reason, if extended beyond experience to "absolute objects." But he maintained (notably in the preface to his second edition) that these negative results clear the way for an approach to

The Ability
to Find Oneself

This brings us back to our analysis of the conditions of possibility of being a questioner. So far we have examined only those which deny us any knowledge apart from appearances. Through our inescapable ignorance we are embodied, set in a material world, limited to a point of view. Yet such limitations are possible only if *known* as such. A machine is situated but recognizes no embarrassment at this, no desire to overcome its restrictions. The machine is not able to question its own operations, its success and failure, because it is not present to itself as a questioning subject.

Ignorance, alienation, and discontent can be recognized as such only if they are experienced as limitations in a knowledge that is already ours. The condition of perplexity is one of self-opposition: I am not simply at home with myself but must go out of myself in order to find myself. However, there are two sides to the hyphen, and the full situation must take both into account. Self-*opposition* is possible only if there is *self*-opposition. I must in some manner be present to myself if I am to recognize the many ways in which I remain a stranger *to myself*.

Can this self-presence, this ability which underlies the need, be taken adequately as a purely regulative ideal? Here we easily get confused by images and by spatial language. The interpretation of self-knowledge as a merely regulative ideal seems to rely on the picture of knowledge and ignorance as "areas" of light and darkness, with a steady progress of the former into the latter. This was criticized in the last chapter. In self-questioning, knowledge permeates ignorance as its condition. The goal of self-knowledge is not a distant "beyond" but an intimate presence. It is only because I do somehow grasp myself as an "I" that I can recognize the painful inadequacy of each view of myself as a "me."

Any book which claims to prove that we can know nothing at all as it is "in itself" is involved in the sort of self-contradiction that marks the theories of knowledge considered in the second chapter. In writing the book, the author is affirming that man "in himself" can know nothing as it is in itself. His explicit conclusions are denied by his own

---

questions of God and the soul through practical reason, where we are no longer limiting our concern to what "is" as an object.

Kant seems to have been consistent in holding that theoretical reason, for all its importance in science and in our ordinary life, is hypothetical and subordinate to practical reason. I have discussed the problems of interpreting this doctrine of Kant's in Chapter 8 of *Perplexity and Knowledge*.

implicit self-presence as a subject who knows and affirms what is really so.

Again, it must be stressed that such arguments represent only the other face of all that was considered in the previous section. This is no return to the purely spiritual self-presence of Descartes and no denial of Kant's analysis of situated knowledge—provided the analyst does not altogether forget himself in his work.

Two questions will now be raised: (1) how does our self-presence as questioners offer any opening to the topics of special metaphysics, and (2) how does the "reality" of our self-presence overcome the sheer particularity of the situations to which we are limited by our ignorance? The second question will lead to a concluding remark on the metaphysical notion of "grades of reality."

As questioners, each of us is condemned to ask what he really is. But I can *be* a question to myself only if I already *know* myself as questionable. The particular details I ascribe to myself are variable; they depend on conventions and may be rejected as erroneous. Changes in my self-estimate are common and sometimes traumatic. Yet only if I know myself as a subject can I be shocked at my failures in rendering an account of myself as an object, as a certain type of person.

Hence I can apply the word "really" to myself in different ways:

a) I am really a socialist.

This is no more than a statement of how I appear as a *phenomenon* to a political observer (myself or another). A change in ways of classifying behavior, or a growth of experience, may alter my self-concept: I appear far to the right of center when my savings are threatened.

b) I am really the product of heredity and environment.

This could be taken, not merely as above, but as a statement belonging to general metaphysics. Every object of experience must be known as caused by other such objects. Viewed purely as a *phenomenon,* I am the resultant of other *phenomena.* Here the word "really" introduces necessity (though of course the identification of particular causes belongs to observation, rather than to metaphysics, and is always revisable).

c) I am really a self-knowing subject.

Here I pass from an account of the structures of *phenomena* to some grasp of what I am "in myself." Underlying any way in which I can appear to myself as an object is an inescapable presence to myself as the "I" that struggles to recover itself through such objectifications.

It is with this third sense of the word ''really'' that some access is offered to the traditional questions of soul-talk and of special metaphysics. All Kant's cautions are to be respected, and when the topic of immortality is raised the conclusions may be far from dramatic. But the chapters on freedom and morality will suggest that these at least are realms in which the search for what is really so leads us to a further analysis of what it is to ''be oneself'' as a self-present subject. Persons are ''ends in themselves'' and not merely things to be classified and used.

Two comments. The first is that this notion of special metaphysics does not take us beyond experience. There is indeed no experience that is closer to us than that of our own self-presence.

The second comment is that no basis is supplied for an ''idealism'' that reduces everything to ideas in the mind of a knowing subject. What we are asked to do is to make a distinction between two ways of using terms such as ''is'' and ''exists.'' To be as a subject is to be oneself, to be self-present as the condition without which nothing could appear as an object. To be as an object is to appear through appropriate observations, tests, and manipulations. The sticks and stones that surround us are not thereby reduced to ''contents of the mind.'' If I ask about stones, I do so as a geologist or chemist or engineer or simply as a man mowing his lawn. Of course stones exist. Yet what I mean by their existence depends on my questions and the way I encounter things through tests. Stones are objects I analyze or kick out of the path of my mower. Chemical analysis and kicking are not maneuvers in a mental world but are sound bodily operations, open to failure as well as success.

UNIVERSALITY

Locke remarked that the problem of knowledge starts with the fact that all things which exist are only particular. We may feel we agree with him. In this room is a particular table, several particular chairs, and a lot of very particular books. However, as soon as we recognize that any object is what it is for a knowing subject, we begin to disclose the many forms of universality that make sense of the data of experience. The room I see is well organized in terms of the ''universals'' of posture and culture.

The previous section showed that the questioner is limited to a variety of points of view through which he makes his way. But sheer particularity would be utter chaos. We make our way by dealing coherently with things, experimenting with various forms of order. This ordering is the universality which gives shape to our experience.

If we ask what we mean by anything, we are asking what we can do with it, what part it plays in an ordered life. Universals are not contents of the mind but are ways of acting consistently and repeatedly. "Sharp" means ability to cut, and we organize knives, axes, and teeth under this universal, later extending it to cover spices and characters.

The pronoun "we" has been used deliberately because the more I order my experience in such ways, the more I am taken out of the particularity of my own point of view. Knowledge always remains situated, but the more it is intellectualized the more a point of view can be shared. I overcome what merely happens to be so for me and I communicate what can be known in the same way by all. The highly ordered world of science is a striking example.

Such universals, whether tables or temperature, mountains or mass, can be called "empirical." They belong to some experiences but not to all. However, if universals are to be understood in terms of the way in which subjects "come to themselves," there must be some universals which reveal more than the conventions of science or politics or ordinary getting and spending. It was Kant's project to discover universals that are "transcendental," belonging to any world a subject can inhabit.

The task of proving that any world of objects must have certain features will not be attempted here. The undertaking is not only complex but precarious. Kant unwittingly left his successors with a warning. Much of what he claimed to prove as necessarily belonging to any possible · experience has turned out to belong only to certain types of experience, notably to that of Newtonian science. The ways in which subjects can express and find themselves are more varied than we may think. The universals of science are basic to our own culture, yet the child's world probably has more to do with aesthetics than with physics, and a knowing subject can be thoroughly temporal without having any clocks at his disposal. The following chapter will indicate something of the variety of ways we can organize experience by different types of questioning.

Grades of Reality

This chapter has tried to suggest that metaphysics does not, in any of its projects, take us beyond our experience. Even the topics of special metaphysics are to be justified and developed, if at all, by a closer analysis of what is involved in our very agency as self-questioners.

We may be disappointed by this conclusion. Surely metaphysicians have aspired to more than this? Have they not been driven to their questions by the ambition to find a "greater reality" than our everyday experience contains?

Though many may feel an attraction for such a quest, others have always regarded it as meaningless. It is in this way that we have interpreted the Greek skeptics. They would have said that the question chosen for the title of this chapter represents no search for greater "degrees" of reality. What "is really so" is at no higher level than what "appears to be so." We have two appearances at the same level. One is merely preferred for conventional reasons or as a correction of some claim arising from confusion. We bring no inspiring news in pointing out that the cloth is really blue and the stick in water is really straight.

Science would seem to support the skeptics. Things either are or are not, and appropriate observations or experiments will find which applies to the cancer virus and the abominable snowman. There are no "grades" of being; all is at the same level.

Nevertheless, the claim that there are grades of reality seems to have been central to most of the great metaphysicians. This is basically what the whole discussion of "analogy" in the Middle Ages was about. The question what may be meant will draw together this section and the previous one.

If the notion of "being" accepted by ancient skeptics and modern scientists is followed, then all is indeed on one level. There can be no grades of "is" where "to be" is "to appear to an observer." The possibility of a hierarchical view of reality arises only with a first-person account, when we take "being" as self-presence. For situated knowers this is always a self-presence achieved through self-expression, and it is here that grades are to be found.

The term "dissipation" was used in the previous section to describe the "estrangement from oneself" that is involved in self-expression. A dissipated person is one who has lost himself and achieved little of a unified character. He is at the mercy of whatever influences bear on him from outside. However, someone with a well unified personality has made something of his life. He has also gone out of himself; indeed his expressions are more numerous and more varied than those of others. But he has found himself in these expressions. He has "returned to himself." What he is comes from himself and is no mere result of alien forces acting on him.

The illustration might have been taken from Aristotle. It is what he found in his biology and made central to his metaphysics. All living beings "have in themselves, as *selves,* a principle of action." (*Metaphysics* 1015a) This is their "form" or "activity." We think of the tadpole as retaining its self-identity in becoming a frog. However, there is also in all living beings an opposing principle, that by which they are not *selves* but are open to external forces. This principle of "dissipation" or "self-loss" Aristotle referred to as "materiality" or "potentiality." The higher we go up the scale of life, the more form predominates; the lower we go the more we find materiality in control. Man does what he intends regardless of opposition or misfortune; indeed he assimilates these, converts them to his own ends. But a plant is highly dependent on whatever comes to it.

However, it would be misinterpreting Aristotle to see form and materiality as two things, with one or the other in greater proportion. Materiality is not only a principle of limitation or opposition: it is that in which form expresses and realizes itself. Potentiality is not driven out but is actualized. The relationship is perhaps best illustrated by thought and language. It is through expression in language that thought "comes to itself." We do not dispense with material sounds through the growth of thought; they are "intellectualized." What we call intimate thoughts are not free of language but represent the achievement of a fine sensitivity of linguistic expression.

Thus, from this point of view there are "grades of being" as stages of presence-in-opposition. Aristotle's notions were taken over by the medievals and, perhaps with more than a passing glance at feudal society, developed into a hierarchical interpretation of the whole of reality. A quotation from Aquinas may illustrate this.

All things exist by expressing themselves, and the higher they are the more intimate is their self-expression. In the inanimate realm this takes the lowest form, that of the action of one body on another. . . . At the next level, the plant does express its own inner life in a seed but this becomes altogether separated from it. . . . The level of sensation is higher because the expression is more interior. . . . But the highest degree of life is that of intellect, which reflects on itself and can understand itself. Yet in intellectual life different grades are to be found. Human understanding, even in its ability to know itself, draws its knowledge originally from outside because bound to sensible images. . . . The full perfection of life therefore belongs to God, for whom to know is to be.[5]

The value of any such account for interpreting nonhuman realities is dubious. There science may have taken over, and we explain by relations all on a level. However, to explain man exclusively on one level is to lose his subjectivity. A work of art is an expression in which a subject struggles to find more of his meaning. So is a gesture, a ritual, a political or religious creed. So is the very project of symbolizing nature mathematically. We create various worlds of meaning in which we can "be ourselves" in different ways. We develop the city, the market place, the theater, and the temple as habitats in which we can live politically,

---

[5] *Summa contra Gentes,* IV–11. A long passage has here been condensed in a somewhat free translation.

economically, artistically, and religiously. The "contents of mind" are not items stored in some ghostly presence but ways of questioning the world in order to act out our complex selves and become more fully what we "really are."

The following chapter will develop this theme as we turn from a study of questioning as such to some of the different sorts of questions we pose in our effort to express and find ourselves.

7

What Do
I Intend?

The last two chapters have not been easy, and impatience with them is understandable. The conclusions may seem unworthy of the effort. We all recognize that we are questioners, that we live in a strange twilight of knowledge and ignorance, that we are situated in a material world through our body, that we learn what is so—even who we are—only through a variety of partial appearances.

The desire to investigate the obvious, to understand "the reason why" rather than merely to accept "the fact that," leads to the part of philosophy which is called "metaphysics." We have illustrated this historically through the work of Aristotle, Descartes, and Kant. Our own study of the conditions of possibility of any question we can ask has been a reinterpretation of their basic project.

More will come in later chapters. We shall inquire in what sense a questioner is bound to time, limited by his past and facing the future with hope or anxiety. We shall see what light can be thrown on our all too obvious fate of suffering and death. We shall ask whether, and in what way, being a subject involves freedom and morality. All of these are metaphysical topics, and they may fill out the slender conclusions of the last two chapters.

Nevertheless, the opening chapter stressed that philosophers face other, more descriptive, tasks. To limit philosophy to metaphysics is both discouraging and dangerous. It is discouraging because philosophy, if restricted to the search for what *must* be so, comes off poorly in comparison with other disciplines. Our urge to know is shown through the delight we take in our senses. And the delight of our senses is in a wide variety of facts. Hegel remarked, as an excuse for not going to church on Sundays, that the true worship of God consists in reading the newspaper. It may be that going to church adds something to the experience of life not found in the most detailed reading of the Sunday newspaper. But even a profound religious experience is suspect if it does not somehow turn our attention to the wide variety of details that make up the life of a situated knower. We measure the true depth of mind by "its daring to expose and give itself in its expressions." (cf. p. 21).

Restricting philosophy to the questions of metaphysics is also dangerous. A philosopher who does no more than ask what structures must belong to any experience may fear that his books will not become best sellers. But he should fear much more that his very project could lead to a dogmatism that invites no criticism or self-questioning. If his conclusions must hold for any possible experience, then no new experience can modify them, so why should he look any further? Kant wrote, in the preface to his *Critique of Pure Reason*:

> In this inquiry I have set completeness as my main target. I make so bold as to say that not a single metaphysical problem remains which has not here been solved or for the solution of which at least the key has not been provided. (A xiii)

However, Kant's commentators are far from agreeing with him. They point out that the structure of space to which he condemned all human knowers is solidly Euclidean, and the categories of understanding turn out to give us the world of Newtonian physics. Kant would have been less dogmatic in his metaphysical conclusions if he had not viewed them as so free from possible revision through the empirical investigations in which he was also interested. Admittedly he lived before the days of non-Euclidean geometry and post-Newtonian physics. But he could have realized that the space of religious thinking is nongeometrical and that the causality in mythical explanations has little to do with physics. Perhaps if Kant had had children of his own, or had observed those of others, he would have recognized to what a small extent children inhabit the sophisticated world of science or feel confined by its categories.

All we have claimed to find so far are some of the structures of self-questioning. They are necessary, but precisely as structures of self-questioning. That is, every word we have uttered about them remains in question. I am a creature of sense, with no self-presence apart from the material world. But what I mean by going "out" of myself to discover myself is a theme for constant reinterpretation. To say that the conclusions of metaphysics are necessary is far from saying they are not in need of repeated questioning. A broad study of what "happens to be" helps us to reinterpret our account of what "must be." This chapter, for instance, will look at some of the many ways in which we can exist spatially and it may destroy any illusion that the previous chapter has said the last word in proving that we must be "situated."

So we shall turn now to some topics which can be put under the more descriptive tasks of philosophy. The philosopher of science or of law starts with the fact that we happen to do science and set up laws. He then asks what structures are involved in this. But he does not exclude the possibility of a human society which lives happily without needing any code of laws or choosing to follow Archimedes and Galileo into the fascination and risk of science.

That is, the overused word, "inescapable" may be dropped for a time. Instead of investigating the "one possible world," we shall ask about our many different "worlds of meaning," the different sorts of questions we ask and ways we have of expressing and finding our complex selves.

Ways of Expressing and Finding Oneself

One of the many temptations into which a philosopher falls is of giving a highly simplified account of his colleagues' theories in order to expound his own by contrast. It may be clear by now that two theories have been used in this way throughout the last five chapters. The rationalism of Descartes has served as a contrast to our account of the part ignorance plays in questioning. And the empiricism of Locke has been made to stand as a consequence of forgetting the prior knowledge in all we receive as an answer.

The needs of exposition may have over-simplified history. But an account of questioning has gradually been developed which may now be summarized as "living in a world which I make my world." I find and become what I am only by discovering what I can do in the "otherness" of the material world. An assurance of my probity is of little value unless my self-estimate and good intentions meet the test when I discover a wallet of money in the street: I have to wait and see how honest I am. A questioner is a being who comes to himself, gradually and variably, through what he does in the world.

Yet the need to "wait and see" is misunderstood if it be taken as a recommendation for sheer passivity. In a genuine sense, the world in which I discover myself is my world. Good intentions have to be tested, but each person's world is much a result of his questions. The very fact that finding a wallet comes to me as a moral situation, and keeping it as a temptation, depends on the way I formulate my experience.

That is, if the element of ignorance in questioning means that we learn through facts we find, the element of prior knowledge means that these facts are not already constituted in the world without reference to the way we question. The number and type of facts each of us discovers in the room depends on the interests and purposes he has, the social conventions he accepts, the historical "climate of opinion" in which he lives. My inventory of the room in terms of desks, chairs, books, pen and paper, comes from a dominant question "how to study": I formulate or structure the room as a place for study. A child, however, might no less reasonably see it as a place to play. A botanist, a primitive hunter, and a visitor from outer space might find themselves in the same jungle but they would be inhabiting different worlds.

The world in which I express and find myself is a world of possibilities. Things mean what I can do with them. Children, hunters, and scientists live in different worlds because their questions or intentions are different. If we feel shocked at the "relativism" of this notion and insist that it is "basically" the same world for all men, that there must be some features common to all, then we are back to metaphysics, which we have agreed to leave for a while. No book that proposes a metaphysics can be accused of relativism.

If we ask which of the many worlds is "best" or "most true" or "most adequate," then we plainly need to clarify our question. No child would feel happy that the world of scientific measurement is better than his world of games and fantasy. And the hunter's world is adequate to his purposes. Perhaps, though, we could put it this way. The scientist sees and can do a great deal that the others cannot; yet in his spare time he enjoys hunting, and he has not lost the child's capacity to play games and indulge in fantasy. That is, his range of possibilities is far greater. Hence, without ever claiming that any human world is the "real" or "true" one, we may say that some worlds are richer than others. Questioning extends our possibilities, and some questions open up a "new world" in a more dramatic way than Columbus did. A man who is confined to hut and jungle could be happier than many a city-dweller, but his life is more limited. "Meaning" may be an overused and ambiguous word, but if questioning expands the worlds of possible activity it increases meaning.

So the theme of this chapter is that the world in which I express and find myself is *my* world. I discover and do not create. But what I discover depends on the particular sort of world in which facts are formulated. And this is a function of what I "intend," the particular ways in which I pose my questions. One philosopher for whom this became a basic principle started his career as an archaeologist. It was there he realized that discovery is no mere product of facts that a spade happens to unearth. Success comes by and large to the person who asks the appropriate questions:

> Meaning, agreement and contradiction, truth and falsehood, none of these belonged to propositions in their own right, propositions by themselves; they belonged only to propositions as the answers to questions.[1]

This may seem very obvious. If so, apologies are offered for repetition of the theme. But if not, it may be that we should modify a common image of knowing. We perhaps take it for granted that the mind and the world start off in a state of separation. The former is a receptacle, the latter a collection of facts waiting for a mind to stumble on them. However, if we could return to infancy, it is unlikely that we should find ourselves empty vacuum cleaners waiting for facts to come rushing in from the world "out there." The infant seems absorbed in what could be called indiscriminately *his* experience and *the* world; rather than a separation of subject and object we have a simple immediacy in which we could at best say "there is warmth" or merely "warm." Subject and world emerge from confusion gradually and hesitantly. It is only with the dawn of infantile questioning that he "recovers" himself from such immediacy by opposing himself to the world, recognizing it *as* a world of a certain sort. Through questioning, whether with limbs or sounds, he "steps back" from physical absorption and opens up a world of answers, one of "meaning."

Perhaps we can ask no more difficult and no more "reflexive" question than what we mean by "meaning." It is a topic we had best approach through illustrations, and the following section will offer some.

Symbolic Worlds

One Kantian scholar, Ernst Cassirer (1874–1945), suggests that man should be defined, not as a "rational animal," but rather as a "symbol-making animal," and that we can give a more extensive and more flexible account than Kant of the structures of human experience if we

---

[1] R.G. Collingwood, *Autobiography* (Oxford University Press, 1939), p. 33.

regard these as "symbolic forms." This is a theme on which we shall draw, but we must be careful to avoid misconceptions in such a use of the word "symbol."[2]

Development in
Animals and Children

A simple analogy may help, for a start. If we examine the sensory system of an animal, we can imagine the sort of "world" in which it lives. Only that "exists" which it can in some way receive through its senses. For an animal without eyes, or perhaps with very rudimentary eyes, differences in color are not "real." And even where a wide range of senses is present, we may suppose a considerable variation in the prominence (or "reality") accorded to features: for a pig, the world may be almost entirely one of smell.

Now if we start with the protozoan and retrace the course of evolution, we can imagine the way in which the world disclosed to animals grows in complexity and richness. Much of what a higher animal perceives does not exist for a lower animal. The ant might think most of the life of the anteater devoted to illusion.

But how much more sophisticated is the world that man inhabits. The greater part of his life must seem to any animal to be a withdrawal from reality. What more real than the smell of the prey one stalks? How foolish to waste one's time talking about it, or playing with numbers for constructing traps, or decadently reflecting on whether one *should* kill at all. The animal's questioning is happily limited to the nose which asks "Which way?" But man's questioning opens up the possibilities and responsibilities disclosed by language, by mathematics, by morality.

Rather than looking at the world of animals, on which we can only speculate, we can examine the development of a child's experience, through which we have passed. His earliest experience may be scarcely different from that of the higher animals. For example, the grasping or clutching movement is instinctive, and apes can be taught to manipulate an instrument such as a spoon for feeding. Suppose, however, that the spoon, or any other desired object, is at a distance. In the child the automatic movement of grasping eventually "degenerates," through various intermediary stages, into the gesture of pointing. Efficiency in holding things decreases as the deployment of all fingers passes into the use of but one. This, for the ape, would be a withdrawal from reality; the pointing

---

[2] Cassirer's book, *An Essay on Man* (New Haven: Yale University Press, 1944), offers an easily readable guide to the discussion of what distinguishes some questions from others.

finger cannot clutch an object. But the child has entered a whole new world of possibilities or "meaning." By withdrawing from the chain of instinctive actions and desires, he formulates a world of objects which have reality for him even when not wanted for instinctive purposes. He can point them out in sheer wonder. We say that he now "grasps" the spoon with his mind and knows it as a spoon. He now belongs to a world in which his basic need is to get things into his mind rather than into his hand or mouth.

However, the process of disclosing new worlds has scarcely begun. The gesture of pointing limits the child to what he can see. The next step comes as a further "degeneration" of immediate or purely physical contact. It is the rise of vocal language. Pointing was at least a poor copy of grasping. But a word is no physical derivative of the clutching movement. Yet the range of possibility has been extended immeasurably. The world that is now open to the child goes far beyond what can be seen. He can discuss spoons to his heart's content, fill his life with them even if every spoon ever made were annihilated.

The illustration has run far enough for our purposes, but it could be continued in many ways. For example, we could consider how our concrete everyday language "degenerates" into the highly abstract symbols of mathematics and science. Here we are at a far remove from our immediate, physical experience as a child, but perhaps no stage of our development is more dramatic, or more weighty with consequences, than the discovery that things can be counted and related numerically.

The point of such illustrations is that, whatever may hold for the evolution of animals, human development involves a "reflexive" activity which puts into question the world we take for granted and opens up some new world of activities that would have been meaningless at the previous level. In solving the questions of climbing and smelling, the apes have advanced beyond us. Our development is not (at least directly) along the lines of physical adaptation. Rousseau commented that "the man who reflects is a depraved animal." Because our questioning is reflexive, we have withdrawn from the competition and have disclosed possibilities in which the ape is a simple nonstarter. The word "physical" is vague, but we need an adjective to oppose it and describe such worlds of human possibilities and meaning. The term we have chosen to qualify the worlds of gesture, language, counting, science, art, morality, religion, is "symbolic."

Symbol and Reality

Misunderstanding can easily arise because we frequently oppose "symbolic" to "real." In so doing, we imply that we are first in touch

with the way things are and *then* may choose to reproduce them symbolically, either as a practical shorthand or for mere embellishment. It is
easier to talk of H_2SO_4 than of sulphuric acid or of a clear viscous liquid
that burns. We may find it more attractive to represent a college by its
crest than by its name.

However, we should recognize that we are here substituting one symbol
for another, not for a nonsymbolic reality. The language in which names
and descriptions are expressed is itself a form of symbolism. So, as we
suggested above, is a basic bodily gesture such as pointing. A symbol, in
Cassirer's sense, is any embodiment of human meaning, any way of taking
things intelligently and manageably rather than chaotically.

There is much that is conventional in all symbols. A country need
not express its national unity in a flag of this sort or in any flag at all.
But man could not develop social unity without some forms of common
symbolic expression, dress, music, folklore, mythology. There is no naked
meaning to which we can then first add a symbol if we choose. The
symbol *is* the reality, the first expression, the "existence" of any meaning.

Nevertheless, it is important that we understand the tendency we have
to oppose "symbolic" and "real" and to regard symbolizing as a withdrawal from reality. Such notions are implicit in the view of symbolizing
as a "degeneration" of what is "natural," as indicated in the growth of
the child, discussed above. Pointing, talking, and counting are symbolic
activities that show a progressive degeneration of the clutching instinct.
Hence a symbol is opposed, not to what is "real," but to what is instinctive, immediate, physical.

All of these terms are vague, and animals may not be as devoid of
symbolic activity as suggested. But the instinctive level is one where
response follows stimulus without our being aware of them *as* response
and stimulus. Experience is immediate; we are totally absorbed in the
"here-and-now" without giving it any interpretation. Meaning enters
through some interruption of the chain of events, some degeneration of
the physical response, some stepping-back from the immediate experience
to a symbolic formulation of it.

A stone in the way is instinctively avoided by an animal "without
thinking." But man withdraws from this instinctive level and sees the
stone symbolically as the embodiment of some type of meaning: he interprets it *as* an obstacle or a weapon or hammer or geometrical form or
chemical compound or object of worship.

Hence, symbolizing is not a withdrawal from reality. It is the interruption of instinctive, unthinking experience to allow some new possibilities of activity and meaning to enter. If Newton was struck on the
head by an apple, he did more than react in pain; he saw through the
incident a complex and abstract way of taking the world as a whole. Far

from such abstraction being a retreat from reality, the symbols of science have exposed us to experiences that would have been impossible if we had remained at the level of prescientific symbolism or at that of pain and response.

We may, if we wish, say that man lives in the same world as the animals. But we must then ask if we mean by this the world of the physicist or the biologist or the hunter. Each is a human world. We cannot step out of all human worlds, and each of us inhabits a variety of them. Reality comes to us as a complex of many forms of symbolism or types of questioning. How can we find our way around? Is there a sheer multiplicity of worlds of meaning, or is there some "rhyme and reason" to them?

Ways of Classifying Our Worlds

Philosophers are quick on the draw when asked for a reason that makes sense of a mere multiplicity. Here we shall mention, as examples, only two ways in which they have tried to put order into our many worlds of meaning.

Auguste Comte (1798–1857) expressed philosophically the view that many today take for granted, that knowledge is valid so far as it approaches the ideal of the sciences. This he summed up in his "theory of the three stages." The first, and lowest, stage is the *theological* one. This covers all forms of questioning which look for answers in a blatantly first-person account. Nature is personified. Winds are personal agents, blowing where they will. Thunder and lightning are explained in terms of the gods' anger. The second stage is *philosophical*. Here men still ask questions which look for answers beyond the events they observe. These explanatory principles are no longer personal agencies but abstract "essences." Sleeping pills work because they have "dormitive powers." Bodies fall because their "natural" movement is downward. The poetry of divinities is translated into the prose of essences. Maturity comes only with the third, or *positive*, stage when we accept that there are no powers behind what we observe. We regard our questions as adequately answered by science, which simply relates the events we observe and works out the laws which describe the patterns of recurrence.[3]

There is much to be said for Comte's theory. It has itself some "positive" value in describing the course that many disciplines have followed. The physical sciences went that way. Perhaps biology retains

---

[3] It is such knowledge that Comte termed "positive," and it is to this that the philosophy of "positivism" limits us.

some traces of the "theological" stage. Psychology and the human sciences may still have far to go but have largely accepted the goal. Also, our own personal development from childhood to maturity shows much of this passage from a first- to a third-person world of questioning.

The main difficulty with Comte's theory is the one we found with the theory of behaviorism. If it claims to be no more than scientific, one way among many of seeing things, then there is no problem. But as soon as it aspires to be a philosophical account of what is finally so, then it contradicts itself. To reduce all valid knowledge to a third-person scientific report is to exclude the first-person agency of giving such an account. Comte cannot reflect on his own philosophizing without violating his philosophy.

This is a difficulty which is ruthlessly avoided by the other theory we are to consider. Perhaps no philosopher has offered such an ambitious scheme for organizing our many worlds of meaning as did Hegel (1770–1831). If we take the term "structure" or "category" in its widest sense, Hegel went far beyond Kant's twelve and produced close on two hundred and fifty of them. But all that interests us here is his general principle for ordering our symbolic worlds. To put it very simply, Hegel proposed much the reverse order to that of Comte: he advanced from the most "positive" to the most "reflective." That is, at any spontaneous level of life, reflexive questions are implicit and are eventually raised. Instead of continuing to ask how we do given tasks, we step back and ask what it is we are doing. The answer must take a more comprehensive form which "accounts" for the previous level. But this higher level does not account for itself. So we put it also in question, reflect on it, and the process is repeated.

Inevitably, philosophy stands at the summit of the Hegelian system, for it is the reflexive questioning which has been implicit at each stage of the process. The philosopher is the only one who does not start with assumptions but can reflect fully on what he is himself doing without thereby stepping outside his discipline. According to Hegel, the theologian becomes a philosopher of religion. Faith seeking understanding is looking for philosophy. There is a philosophy of religion but not a religion of philosophy; and some such asymmetrical relation is supposed to situate and order our many other symbolic worlds.

What will be attempted here is far more modest and less provocative. Any such scheme as Comte's or Hegel's is notably metaphysical. It tells what must be so, from the nature of things or of human knowing. Yet in considering different types of questioning, we have agreed, for a time, to put any metaphysical account in brackets and content ourselves with describing what is given in each symbolic world and the differences between them.

If more is to come, then it should be allowed to appear in the course of an honest analysis. The danger, before which both Comte and Hegel fell, is of imposing a ready-made scheme. Our growth in knowledge of another person should be patient. We want to organize the hints we get of him from the ways he expresses himself, make a system of them, and hastily classify him. But in the end we shall know him better if we accept each facet of his tangled character, without "deriving" one from the other; we hold our information loosely and are ready for surprises. It is perhaps in this manner that we may best understand the complex worlds in which man has come to express himself.

One principle, however, may serve as a starting-point. Symbolic worlds are forms of "meaning," and these are possibilities of acting, ways of expressing and finding ourselves. Now it is only through my body that I can "externalize" and "re-collect" myself. Indeed, to express myself is to exist materially or bodily. The illustration we gave of a child's development in meaning was an account of the symbolic transformation of instinctive bodily grasping into gesturing, speaking, counting. Even the most abstract forms of scientific or artistic or religious symbolism are extensions of the possibility of bodily activity. All mental "grasping" is a derivative of the first clutching movements by which the infant questions and tries to make sense of his world.

The questioner is an embodied being. This is our starting-point, and it is one with which we never lose contact as our meaning grows in abstraction.

Embodiment as
the Source of Symbolism

The previous chapter devoted a few pages to a brief suggestion of what it means to exist as "embodied." Here we shall develop this theme with special reference to spatiality as a basic form of situated knowing; a similar discussion of temporality will be left to Chapter Ten.

Spectator and Participant
Accounts of the Body

If the body is to be considered as an expression of meaning, we must try to give a participant or first-person account. It is in this way, for instance, that we understand a piece of sculpture as an expression of what the artist felt and thought. To treat it in the third person as the product of an arm of certain strength and a chisel of certain sharpness would be to set it in the world of physics. Though this is a symbolic world, it is one in which the individuality of objects becomes irrelevant, and the meaning of a statue or a human body as such is lost.

Nevertheless, even a purely spectator account of the human body could well take note of the presence of something which distinguishes it from animal bodies. The example was mentioned earlier of the hand (p. 82). This has a complexity far beyond that of an ape's hand yet is less well adapted to the world of trees. Even if the question is irrelevant to an anatomist, most people would find that the structure of the human hand can be explained only in terms of symbolic functions. It has its remarkable ''liberality'' of movement, its freedom from adaptation to narrowly biological tasks, because the hand is a way of gesturing and of expressing meaning.

This applies, though less strikingly, to the body as a whole. A person's body reveals much of his character, as well as his weight and strength and other features that fit into the world of physics. His walk and standing posture, the carriage of his head, neck, and shoulders, the set of eyes and jaw, may tell us something of what ''life means for him.'' Our ordinary language suggests the same. We say he can stand on his own feet and can shoulder burdens, that he delights to sink his teeth into a problem, or that he is spineless and two-faced.

However, such phrases indicate the primacy of a first-person sense of ''being bodily'' over the spectator's account of an ''other body.'' It is not so much that I observe another well balanced on his feet as that I understand what it is to *be* balanced, feeling the ground securely under my own feet. It is the experience of sinking teeth into food which I know as an expression of character, rather than the sight of another doing it. And once I come to idioms such as ''stomaching it,'' the difference is clear.

Yet it is far from easy to capture the first-person experience of being situated bodily. This experience is so close that we overlook it. Or rather, it has been lost under the spectator account we have learned so well of the body as an object among objects. We feel that all has been said when we observe that the hammer is three inches in front of the nail. We forget that the hammer, before it becomes a thing of certain dimensions and weight, is an extension of our own bodily performance of hitting. And we forget that ''three inches in front'' is a highly abstract translation for a task of stretching, grasping, and reaching further to strike. The world is a complex of instrumental paths I follow in carrying out my intentions bodily. ''Three inches'' is a measure of exertion before it has anything to do with a ruler.

Our original symbolic world is practical and in the first person. It is from this as a source that we gradually build up the world of meaning for a spectator. If we may limit our attention for the moment to spatiality, we shall now try to say more of how this is originally experienced and how it is then extended through stages to the third-person space of Euclid and Newton which we take for granted.

First-person Spatiality

Contact with people who have not had the ambiguous benefit of a mathematical and scientific culture shows us how far we have come. "Primitive" man (where the adjective is used in this sense) lives in a space of action, of practical problems and intentions. It is the space in which he builds his hut, steers his canoe, throws his spear. It is strongly visual, tactile, acoustic, and olfactory, expressing an acuity of perception far beyond ours. Yet so firm a grasp of spatial activities shows itself of little avail when a map is introduced or when the description of a habitual journey is required. For here we must be able to "step outside" our own activity and view our body or our journey in terms of purely objective relations. My goal is eight miles east of my body, and this measurement and compass relation is transferred to "four inches to the right" on a map.

The space of a map, or of the world observed as map-able, has lost its concrete features. It is a homogeneous receptacle, indifferent to all possible directions, distances and places, and to whatever objects may be located in it. "Up" and "down," "far" and "near," "here" and "there" are all reduced to a conventional system of measurable relations.

This is the space we learned at school, in our geometry and geography. It is only occasionally that we are reminded how much effort went into the learning. Those of us with the greatest natural ability for such forms of bodily "spatialization" as sports or dancing are not necessarily the best qualified to explain our movements by diagrams or in writing. Familiarity with the symbolic world of first-person space does not automatically bring with it the aptitude to construct an objective spatial representation for an observer.

Even where such aptitudes have been acquired, they can be lost. An illustration comes with a sickness called "aphasia." The term covers a variety of ailments, but common to them is a loss of ability to form an "objective view" of one's own body. Thus, if a fly crawls over the ear of such a patient, he will brush the animal away with his hand; there is no failure of motor activity. But tell him there is a fly on his left ear and he may be unable to "visualize" his body in such a way as to direct his hand to that ear.

Our original sense of space is in the first person: it is that of actively "spatializing" ourselves. I go out from a situation to perform a task or achieve an intention bodily. I formulate a world of activity, not as a series of lines to be observed, but as a "workshop" of reaching and lifting, climbing and falling, striking and pulling. Things are that with which I have dealings, not that which meets my theoretical gaze. Children's first drawings capture this well. We miss the point if we ask what they "represent." Teeth are shown as they feel rather than as they look. The space is one of the agency of running, spinning, rising, and falling; it is a space of movement and rhythm, experienced from within rather than observed from without.

Again, our ordinary language retains something of this. If a new task or interest arises, I "make space" for it in the system of my concerns. Something may still be "a stone's throw" away. Our words are saturated with the imagery of "up" and "down," of "superior" and "inferior," and this has more to do with our primitive hope of rising and fear of falling than with any distance from the center of the earth.

We may be inclined to dismiss such survivals of our original spatiality as "subjective." But this is a word we have tried to rehabilitate. And if we wish to return to metaphysical themes, then this is the only spatiality we can hope to prove as absolutely necessary for a questioner. Kant's conclusions went too far. We could have lived humanly without ever producing Euclid or anything like a map or diagram. If the question "Where is heaven?" bothers religious people, then they can speculate on a state of spatial existence without worrying about coordinates.

Extensions of
Spatial Symbolism

In the above account, attention has been drawn away from the abstract space of science to our original experience of existing spatially. Yet we have stressed the continuity of even our most abstract meaning with primitive bodily activity, of all mental grasping with manual clutching. It should be possible to trace the course by which instinctive bodily actions have gradually been transformed symbolically into ones that realize progressively greater possibilities. So we may now give some indication of the continuity between our primitive spatiality and the theoretical form in which the scientist "houses" his objects. How has the latter developed from the former?

No more than indications can be offered. But we can recognize various symbolic worlds today which probably served as a link. They are the product of questioning which looks for an account in terms of both agent and spectator. Two will be mentioned: spatiality as it occurs in art and in mythical thinking.

Art has already been introduced as an example of a first-person world. Yet children's drawings do develop into adult ones, and with the change there appears representation for a spectator. However, we do not evaluate the worth of art, its adequacy as a reply to the questions which produced it, simply in terms of observed accuracy, as we do a blueprint. A portrait must "capture" the model but it also expresses the painter.

This dual function of representation and expression can be found as early as the cave paintings. In them we look for the artist as much as for the animals. Such paintings show, not only what he observed, but also his own "feeling for life." So also with all forms of ornamentation. Space must be filled, and man filled it with his feeling for what is right and harmonious. He carved details on his implements, he covered his pottery, his clothes, and his own person with designs. The lines of these emanate and return, recede and fuse, balance each other in rhythms; they build up tensions and resolve them.

In this we may find our sense of expressing ourselves bodily in a way that at least prepares for the abstract relations of lines and surfaces that make up a geometry. But it is in man's mythical thinking that we discover a more obvious link between our first-person spatiality and that of science. Many creation myths describe how the world was formed from the body of a giant, each part of the body being identified with a certain region of the heavens or of the earth. Man's myths, for all their fantastic tales, seem to have been his first comprehensive effort to make sense of his world. It remained a world of bodily actions, but order was gradually introduced into it. Things were organized and classified in terms of what we can do with our body.

Only broad generalizations can be given in support of this. The mythical world is divided into zones which reflect our bodily situation: above (the heavens) and below (the ground), before and behind, left and right. Things are then classified, not in relation to each other, but by being assigned to one of these regions of the projected body: the seasons, the elements, the classes of society, the various occupations, instruments, animals, ritual activities, intellectual and moral qualities. Abstract relations between things are represented as relations between the spatial zones, from "front" to "back," or from man at the center to the heavens.

If this sounds strange, we may remember that we learned to count, not by relating numbers directly to each other, but by referring each number to a finger. However abstract our knowledge, it is an orientation we make of ourselves in the world. Astrology sprang from an authentic search for meaning.

A slight acquaintance with cultural anthropology or with archaeology will suggest stages on the path that led from such concrete orientations to the featureless space in which the scientist sets up his symbolic world of indifferent things in numerical relations. Burial rites are intimately connected with spatial positions. Houses, plots of land, military camps, and whole cities are laid out with more than utility in mind. The east is the origin of life and salvation; the west is the direction of death and the place of departed spirits. Man faces south, with the clear presence of noonday before him, dawn on his left and decay on his right, and behind him the dark region of obscure threats. For the path of the sun is perhaps the most important feature of mythical space. Creation stories give first place to the origin of light, as this is the condition of all human working. The following chapter will consider this basic way in which we draw meaning out of chaos.

8 | Why Work?

The previous chapter turned attention from the basic problem of meta-physics to a study of the different sorts of questions we ask and the various worlds of meaning they open to us. Any such variety invites ordering, and we looked briefly at two ways of arranging our "symbolic worlds," namely the schemes proposed by Comte and by Hegel. The former sees all as culminating in science, the latter in philosophy. The value judgments they imply are strong.

In contrast it was claimed that no such scheme would be imposed in these pages. The reader may be skeptical. He may also be confused. At times the chapter seemed to have been supporting Comte. Progress appeared to consist in the advance from a first-person experience to the abstract, theoretical world of mathematics and science. At other times the "primacy" of the first person seemed to suggest that the theoretical stage was achieved only with a loss of the rich detail of the levels from which it came. "Degeneration" was the word used for this.

Some clarifying remarks could remove much of this confusion, but a genuine problem would still remain. Does "abstraction" give us more or less? If symbolizing is the passage from a practical to a theoretical level, is this gain or loss? When I express myself symbolically, do I really achieve a "higher" self-possession? Do I find myself or lose myself?

This is a problem we could examine in regard to any of our worlds of meaning. What does the mathematician do in opening up the world of numbers? Is he expanding human possibilities or losing much of his humanity?

Unless we happen to be professional mathematicians, this question may not come very close (though it was involved in the discussion of "subjectivity" in Chapter Three). However, there is one type of activity in which we are all likely to be engaged for much of our life, and where the question is acute. In our society it is assumed that the normal state is to be a worker. Now we may talk piously of work being the basic manner in which we transform or humanize the world. But this is not the way it strikes most of us. We work because we have to, and in most jobs the effect appears far short of humanizing. Do we express and find ourselves in work, or is it "alienating"?

No general discussion can solve this problem for individuals, though it may suggest guidelines. But the question needs to be tackled, even if in distressingly remote terms. We may allow Karl Marx to set the problem, for he it is who made work a topic for philosophers—and indeed an embarrassment for them, since Marx stands for the primacy of action over theory: "The philosophers have only interpreted the world, it is for us to change it."

However, some preliminaries are called for. First we may ask what view of theory and practice has been suggested in this book so far. Then it will be necessary to try to remove some of the vagueness from our notion of work.

Theory and Practice

Few terms occur more commonly in our talk than these. Democracy, we say, may be all very well in theory for new nations but it is hopeless in practice. The professor of economics has only a theoretical knowledge of the poor, whereas the social worker has a practical knowledge. The dreamer and the academic are "idealists," living in the world of theory; the politician and the administrator are "pragmatists," men of action who know what "really works," what goes in practice.

This book may seem to have tried consistently to water down this common distinction. As early as the opening discussion of what philosophy is, it was remarked that "practical-minded" people are often wild theorists who confront each problem with a different theory but make little effort to fit their theories together. We cannot act without any theory; this would be the sheer instinct or impulse of the animal, and evolution imposed on man the burden of acting theoretically.

Throughout these chapters, stress has been put on the activity or agency of knowing. The view has been rejected that we first know, by a passive reception of facts, and only then engage in action as something subsequent to knowledge. Sheer passivity would be pure sensation, and this is to be found only in the "immediate" experience of infancy. But as soon as a child can be said to know anything, it is some form of activity we need to describe. He knows what a spoon is when he learns to take it in his mouth in the act of eating. That is, he "grasps" it as a possibility of acting. He incorporates it into the complex of concerns that make up his life; he knows what it is "in practice."

As we develop, our knowledge falls more readily under the heading of theory. I know the dimensions of the spoon, the alloy of which it is made, and its value on the market. But this means that, instead of simply lifting it to my mouth, I know how to measure it, analyze it in the laboratory, and engage in the practice of barter. Theory is no more than an extension of the varied possibilities of acting. At the moment I am "doing things with words." And as any writer realizes, the more effortless the product seems, the more exertion has gone into it. Even the most theoretical knowledge is "knowing how" to do something in practice; if you know the differential calculus, you know how to "do it." And conversely, even the most practical of tasks, repairing a car, making a table, sweeping a room, is informed with thought, i.e., with "theory."

How then does theory differ from practice? All well established distinctions have some basis, and a philosopher who glibly reduces everything to a unity is losing something in the process. Two suggestions will be made, one favoring practice and the other setting a value on theory.

The examples with which this section began referred largely to practice as a more intimate acquaintance than theory. "Practical knowledge" of the poor means knowing in great detail, and from first hand experience, how poor people live. "Theoretical knowledge" is lacking in detail and is drawn from books, statistics, and other secondary sources. If a democratic system of government for a new nation works "only in theory," it simply fails to work because not enough of the particularities of the people and situation were taken into account, i.e., into theory, by those who framed the constitution.

What can be said in favor of a theoretical approach or mentality? The previous chapter equated theory with a progressively more symbolic understanding. Passage from the world of pointing to that of ordinary language and then to the highly symbolic world of science (e.g., from "that" to "salt" to "NaCl") is not achieved without some loss. Even the most elaborate chemical theory will not give us the taste of salt. However, the immense possibilities a scientific culture has supplied would never have been opened to us if we had remained in the world of concrete tastes, touches, and smells. "Abstraction" is a disclosure of new worlds rather than a filtering process which lets some items through and keeps many back. The man of a theoretical bent will not be happy following established procedures; he will step back from what he is doing, reflect on it, put it into question. And this is the "liberal" attitude from which discovery and creativity arise. The "idealist" may tend to lack intimate acquaintance with complex problems, but radical changes start with the dreamer who stands outside the techniques of practice and inhabits the "ideal" world of theory.

What conclusion, or problem, comes from this? Any symbolic transformation of the world is both gain and loss. We gain a greater self-possession through new possibilities of expressing and finding ourselves. But the "return to self" is not complete. There is a degeneration; we lose some of the vitality of the animal or the efficiency of the technician, and we lose something of the concrete detail of stages from which we step back. Spontaneity goes as the "pale cast of thought" takes over.

This has been a lengthy introduction. But it has given a context to the problem of work. Work transforms the world, whether done with hands or minds. We express and find ourselves in what we produce. But the danger of "alienation" has been there since Adam. History shows the ways in which the worker has been "expropriated." The product of his work ceases to be "his own," that in which he discovers and achieves himself.

The Ambiguity of Work

The question whether work is blessing or curse goes back to the origins of the Judaeo-Christian tradition. At the beginning of the Book of Genesis, two accounts are given of man's creation and "worldly existence." The first stresses his freedom and creativity, his work as "dominion over nature," as self-realization through what he does. But in the third chapter work is seen as a curse and as the penalty for sin: man is condemned to earn his living "by the sweat of his brow."

Does man live to work or work to live? Does some form of working belong to the achievement of life, or could we ideally get along without working? Such questions have been removed from purely academic discussion by the growth of automation, and any answer we give has obvious consequences for our view of society and our ideal of education.

Work and
Other Activities

We cannot go far with any question unless we give a preliminary clarification of its terms. With ''work'' this is not easy, for the word is used in ways that make it coextensive with any human activity. Above we applied work to minds as well as hands, to pure mathematicians as well as carpenters. And we spoke of theories or constitutions ''working.''

How can we limit the term? By the effort involved? But many forms of recreation on a Sunday are more fatiguing than the work we do on a weekday. By payment? But what an amateur athlete or artist does can be exactly the same as what another does for money. What is contrasted with work? Contemplation? Leisure? Free time?

No investigation of what work means can be complete without some study of how different ages have regarded it and what they have opposed to it. We should be wary of relying on the assumptions of our own age. So a rapid historical survey will be given shortly.

However, a provisional comment is that no particular activity seems classifiable as work ''by its very nature.'' What matters is the working situation, some determination by society of common needs and the ways they are to be met. We have made a whole industry of cat food, whereas other societies today and our own in the past set up no such need; one can rely on scraps from the table or mice in the field, or one may even feel no need for domestic pets. This relation of work to the satisfaction of socially defined needs will be examined further in what follows.

Labor and Work

Some distinction between ''labor'' and ''work'' seems to belong to every European language, ancient and modern. The Greeks, for example, distinguished between *ponos,* as fatiguing bodily effort, and *ascholia,* as the less strikingly manual production of something more lasting. Permanence is perhaps more helpful than effort as the clue to what is intended. The world of labor is close to that of the animal. Primitive man toiled to satisfy the pressing needs of his biological life. He was almost a sheer creature of nature, struggling to produce what was consumed as soon as it appeared. But the world of work is more ''symbolic.'' Man constructs tools which lighten his toil and help him to produce more than meets his daily needs. Working produces ''works.'' He does not merely catch the dinner to be eaten but constructs barns to store surplus food. He is no longer content with shelter for his head but needs more worthy buildings in which to worship, to hold assemblies, to defend himself against other men who want his wealth. He does not merely repeat tales around the fire but makes paper and records works of literature.

Through work, life becomes less ephemeral. Man establishes the relatively permanent features of a world of his own. Independence is won from rain and drought, and culture grows out of nature. Or more precisely, nature is progressively humanized through man's work. There is a continuity with biological needs, but each work of man transforms those needs. Fires in huts give way to centrally heated homes and a vast range of domestic needs is defined. Canoes and signals turn into cars and telephones and the need for presence at a distance is taken for granted.

Marx insisted on man's continuity with nature. But instead of a harmonious advance, he saw a "dialectical" process, one of renewed contradictions which were to appear among men themselves and form the basis for a doctrine of revolution. We shall say more of this shortly. But we may already get some notion of it if we return to the view of work as meeting socially defined needs.

Why did man advance beyond labor to work? It is not quite enough to say that he happened to produce more than he needed at the moment. Why did he expend the extra effort, and why did he not throw away the surplus? Did the additional product come before his new needs, or did his invention of further needs require satisfaction through work? No simple answer can be given, and that of Marx remains ambiguous. However, it is here that we can apply his famous distinction between "economic substructure" and "cultural superstructure." The substructure refers to the situation in which our life is set, the materials at hand, the means for working them, and the "productive relations" or social structures within which the work is done. The superstructure refers to our many ways of interpreting this situation, the self-concept which society expresses through its political life, law, morality, art, religion, and philosophy.

Marx held that the substructure "conditions" the superstructure. This is often taken as meaning that the mode of production in a society determines its cultural elements, and revolution in the former leads necessarily to corresponding changes in the latter. Marx's view of the relationship seems to have been much more subtle. But whatever he thought, we can suppose that the relationship is a complex and "uneven" one. It is not as though primitive man suddenly found he had produced more than his biological needs required and hence formed an estimate of himself as a being of culture. The way in which man feels his needs is largely dependent on the concept of himself he gains through his culture. Advertisers know all about that. Hence the material substructure, the manner in which we work to satisfy needs, is as much a result of our culture as an influence on it.

The possibilities of disharmony are many. Changes in culture can lag behind changes in nature, or vice versa. That is, changes in the humanizing of the world at one level can be at variance with such changes at another level. A new manner of production can evolve without corresponding development in social relations or law and morality. Conversely, a change of thought can define new needs which the substructure is not equipped to meet. In either case, some form of alienation results. How Marx saw this will be discussed in a later section.

Some Historical Views on Work

Ours is a work-centered culture. Those who do not work are either regarded as anomalies or understood as unable to work. The young are preparing to work, the retired have become too old for it (and retirement is a severe psychological problem). The unemployed are left out through temporary economic difficulties or their own unfitness. Hobos and hippies are voluntary ''drop-outs,'' and the phrase indicates society's negative view. Housewives turn to ''work'' for self-respect. And members of professions which once merely accepted fees now measure their value through salaried work.

If we hold such views as self-evident, it will be difficult to take the title of this chapter seriously. A look at history may at least raise questions. Three periods will be considered.

Greece

The Greek word for work, *ascholia*, has already been mentioned. Of particular interest is the fact that it is the negation of *scholē*, which means leisure (similarly, the Latin for business, *negotium*, is the denial of *otium*, leisure). The suggestion is that leisure was held to be the positive concept and the ideal; work is what those do who are incapable of appreciating leisure.

The contrast with our own view is clear. For us, leisure is ''free time,'' time off from work, and is intelligible only in relation to it. Leisure tends to be seen as idleness, for those who do not work, or as recreation for those who do, time to restore the power to work. The Greeks, however, regarded leisure as freedom *for*, not *from*: it is freedom for ''liberal'' pursuits, those which are pursued for their own sake, as ends in themselves. If I write books or compose music or administer justice in order to gain money, prestige, and power, then I am engaging in work. If I do so ''disinterestedly,'' as my expression of what is true, beautiful, and good, then I am leading a life of leisure. Those who cannot do this become workers and support those who are capable of leisure. This is the answer to the question "Why work?" which we should expect in Plato's *Republic* and Aristotle's *Politics*.

The Middle Ages

The declaration of UNESCO on human rights, that "everyone has the right to work," would have been as unintelligible in the Middle Ages as in ancient Greece. Aquinas allowed four grounds which could assign a moral value to work: (1) it is necessary, for most, to maintain their life, (2) it is necessary, for many, to avoid idleness and sin, (3) it is a form of penance, and (4) it enables us to give alms.

Basically, the Greek notion of leisure was retained, though the ideal of disinterested activity was set in the contemplation of God. Work did not belong to the "essence" of human life but proved necessary for most men. Its place was in "free time," i.e., in those times which could not be given to the essential worship of God. Hence in addition to Sundays there were around 115 holidays during the year. Such "holy days" were not proposed as times of idleness, which was put under much the same heading as work. Both idleness and work came from an incapacity for leisure.

Industrial Society

Many factors were involved in the transition to a positive assessment of work and the loss of a positive approach to leisure. At the level of the "substructure," there was the increase in trade, the circulation of money and acceptance of lending at interest, the invention of machines and growth of the factory system. At the level of the "superstructure," a new morality developed. Whether or not this came from the other changes, as Marx would hold, those qualities which increase productivity were raised in the scale of virtues, such as thrift, diligence, and self-control. The material prosperity of the rising middle class was looked upon as a sign of divine election. Work became a duty, and then the supreme duty of man. Such changes in society and its values were reflected theoretically by the Protestant Reformers, notably John Calvin. God was not the Absolute Truth, to be contemplated at leisure, but rather the Supreme Architect of the universe, to be imitated through work. Also, new philosophical "world-views" helped to desacralize nature and remove any theoretical ban on tampering with it; the earth exists to be transformed, and this is the meaning of work.

Though we may no longer look to explicitly religious or philosophical statements of such views, they form the common assumptions of our own age, the "ideology" which we absorb from our earliest days. The question "Why work?" has a very different answer from that which the Greeks or medievals would have given. We are not quite sure how to put it, because the notion that work belongs essentially to man is so evident to us. Man is a worker, a producer. For what? Perhaps for more work, or better working conditions, or more wealth to enjoy time off from the drudgery of work. Ambiguity appears when the question is pressed. But of one thing we feel certain. Only children and the aged can simply "do nothing" and get away with it.

This is the climate of opinion in which Marx appeared. The philosophy, or ideology, which he brought to expression saw man as essentially a worker, engaged in transforming nature and thus realizing himself. But Marx threw an almost Greek or medieval emphasis on the curse of work as we find it. No attempt to restate the problem of work today can afford to ignore his account of alienation and his call for action rather than theory to overcome this.

Marx on Work

Augustine, writing on the religions of his day, distinguished between the personal faith of believers and the *machinamentum,* the machinery or scaffolding of doctrines as seen by an outsider. He recognized that little was to be expected from a logical assessment of the latter. The sincere critic should concern himself rather with the part a religion plays in the life of the faithful, the way it formulates their deepest hopes and needs.

One who writes today on Karl Marx finds himself in a similar situation. Marxism has been of almost unparalleled influence in this century. It represents one of the great visions of what life and history are about. Yet, considered strictly as a philosopher, Marx may rank as no more than one of the many left-wing interpreters of Hegel. The two leading library classifications of this country list his works under economic theory.

Consequently, this brief account of Marx's doctrine of work will be set under two headings. First we shall consider his more technical reinterpretation of Hegel's notion of alienation. Then we shall say something on the appeal Marxism has had as an ideology.

Theory of Alienation

Hegel also has a doctrine of work, though it is largely through Marx that this has been brought into prominence. The reason is that for Hegel there is nothing special about work. In changing the world through the work of our hands or machines, we are simply taking part in one stage of the process by which ''reality'' has come to be what it is. Everything is to be understood as an expression of thought, ranging from very primitive levels (as in colors and their perception) to highly advanced ones (as in art, religion, and philosophy itself). Reality is seen as a development of thought or ''spirit'' by which it repeatedly comes to itself through such expressions. Each stage can be called an ''alienation'' in which thought stands outside itself, objectified. Hence there is no curse to work. Alienation, in this or any other form, is highly positive, the driving force of the whole development. Man is alienated in his work but recovers himself from this for the process to be repeated at higher levels, until he reaches the fully self-critical and self-present thinking of philosophy.

Marx took over Hegel's basic notion of a dialectical development but tried to convert Hegel's ''idealism'' into a ''materialism.'' In a much quoted image, Marx found Hegel standing on his head and put him on his feet. There are two main senses in which this can be understood.

First, Hegel's explanation of every stage of the development is in terms of thought, of the ''ideal'' rather than the material. It is the intention of thought to possess itself more adequately that leads it through its many material expressions. I am at the moment working with typewriter and paper to find what I think. However, Marx felt strongly that Hegel did no justice to the reverse process. It is because I have the body and temperament I have, and belong to the society and class and region I do, that my thoughts take this shape rather than some other. Here we return to his insistence that the material substructure conditions the forms of social and cultural consciousness. We come from nature and remain in continuity with it and should not forget this.

Second, Marx held that Hegel's emphasis on thought had disastrous consequences. It led his followers, such as the left-wing students with whom Marx associated in his university days, to assume that it was enough to speculate about the way things are. If thought is in charge, then its evolution in historical, political, and social forms will take place all in good time. For Marx, however, ''materialism'' meant that development takes place through political and social action bringing about tangible changes in our material situation which thought may later contemplate but could never effect. Marx upturned Hegel by converting theory into practice, philosophy into revolutionary action.

It is in this context that we may set Marx's reinterpretation of Hegel's notion of alienation. To explain what is happening in the world, Hegel looked forward to a final stage in which thought has completely come to itself, a paradise in which all work would be sublimated in philosophizing—dare we say, in leisure? But Marx felt that what is happening in the world is a result of conflicts that take us back to man's original working with nature. We should not look to pure thought but engage in the struggles of material existence. Indeed man's very preoccupation with philosophizing, his construction of an ideal world of thought or religion, is a form of alienation. It comes from the fact that he does not feel at home in the world. There is inhumanity in his economic and social life. It is this which we need to remedy, through action. The paradise for which we should hope is one in which all philosophizing can be sublimated in truly human work.

For Marx, then, alienation is no mere self-expression of thought on its way to self-possession. Alienation is self-expression gone wrong. It is a material situation in which we cannot find ourselves unless we take revolutionary action.

The details of Marx's analysis are not important for the purposes of this chapter. And the general lines are well known. The means of productive work develop beyond the existing social and property relations, and revolution produces a new economic structure which is in turn reflected by changes in man's cultural consciousness. A whole interpretation of history is built on this scheme. And its main topic is the struggle between the privileged class of the outmoded social order and the class which represents the new order.

It is in his treatment of capitalism that Marx's view of work comes out most clearly. For here he sees alienation assuming its most inhuman form. The capitalist is a nonworker who owns the means of production and all that the worker produces. It is not merely that property is in the wrong hands. Even the act of working is expropriated from the worker. What does this mean?

The basic humanism of Marx's doctrine of work is sometimes lost through emphasis on the question of who owns property. What counts for Marx is not what man *has* but what he *is*. Work is not a means to an end; it is man's way of *being* by finding himself in his material product. Hence property has value only as the expression of *my own* working. But in the capitalist system work is degraded to the production of a *thing,* outside the worker, a mere means to the purposes of a nonworker. The worker becomes an instrument with no humanity to express or find. Having served another's purposes during the firm's time, he hopes to be himself in his private home and private interests. But there is no "self" to be truly at home in the world or in society, for there is no work in which he can find himself.

Alienation appears not merely in the result but in the *process of production,* within *productive activity* itself. . . . The product is indeed only a résumé of activity, of production . . . . The worker feels himself at home only during his leisure time, whereas at work he feels homeless. His work is not voluntary but imposed, *forced labour*. It is not the satisfaction of a need but only a *means* for satisfying other needs. . . . We arrive at the result that man (the worker) feels himself to be freely active only in his animal functions— eating, drinking and procreating, or at most also in his dwelling and in personal adornment—while in his human functions he is reduced to an animal.[1]

One final question on Marx's philosophical theory. Where did it come from? Engels stated that the dialectic is a law of nature discovered by scientific observation and giving the same basis for predicting the future as other scientific laws. This is unsatisfactory. Historians rightly put little trust in generalizations from what has been observed in human affairs. At least, any such laws are far short of the necessity philosophers claim and the faith a Marxist shows.

Marx would need to have possessed some insight, beyond scientific observation, into what it means to be human or inhuman. However, this would be dangerously like the self-questioning of philosophical thought. It is not so easy to suppress theory in the name of practice, or—as Aristotle pointed out—to reject philosophy without philosophizing. In this sense we are all "idealists," with Marxists well to the fore.

Marxism as Ideology

As suggested at the beginning of this section, it is rather irrelevant to concentrate attention on the details of Marxist theory. So much more is involved, and all beliefs of wide appeal and long life represent a series of compromises. The attraction which Marxism has had for most people preceded their study of Marxist theory. Hence, to close this section, a few remarks on Marxism as an ideology.

The term "ideology" is here used rather loosely for any system of beliefs about man and his world which have consequences for the way we live our life. Such beliefs are often religious. They may be political or social. Or they may be philosophical, in the wide sense discussed in the first section of the opening chapter. The formation of some such ideology is universal. Without some unifying schemes and images we could not develop a way of seeing and judging things. From childhood each of us

---

[1] *Economic and Philosophical Manuscripts of 1844*, from *Karl Marx: Early Writings*, trans, T.B. Bottomore (New York: McGraw-Hill Book Company, 1964), pp. 124–25. This selection, with the foreword by Eric Fromm, gives an excellent indication of Marx's humanism.

grew up with the aid of some picture of the world, conveyed to us by innumerable gestures, hints, and requirements, and by the subtle ways in which language cultivates our vision and forms our feelings.

Central to ideologies are key terms such as "equality" or "liberty" or "progress." They are not altogether empty but are sufficiently indefinite to carry a wide range of values and sentiments and to show a remarkable adaptability. It is this which gives ideologies their source of renewal and their resistance to criticism.

The suggestion to be made here is that "work" is one of the key terms which would figure in an analysis of Marxism as an ideology. It supplies an image of "productive man" which ranks in appeal with the domestic imagery of filial man in traditional Christianity. The ambiguity of work as blessing and curse allows for the adaptability which Marxism has shown. Where stress is wanted on necessity, we have the view of work as springing out of nature and following its laws. Where freedom is to be emphasized, we are able to see work as the self-realization by which we recover our true humanity from a hostile situation and opposing forces.

Above all, Marxism is not merely a doctrine about work but a call to work. In a society centered on work and allowing little place for ideals of leisure and contemplation, we are attracted by a summons to action, to do something about the ills in us and around us rather than theorizing about them. Engels seems far from the point in claiming a scientific basis which allows prediction of the future. The revolutionary does not predict the future, he makes it. There are many problems in reconciling freedom and determinism in Marx's philosophical theory. But his ideological appeal is to man as a worker who recognizes the inhumanity of his past and engages in the struggles of today to create his future.

The theme of creativity, and its relation to theory and practice, will be taken up in the final section.

The Reappropriation of Work

Considered as an ideology, Marxism could be called a religion of salvation. The world is under a curse, and we are led on by the hope of recovering our true selves from exile. There is no passage to another world, but rather the transformation of this one to a state in which work can once more be a blessing. Alienation is overcome only with the final formation of a classless society.

As with most religions, the picture of paradise remains less clear than the details of what we should do to reach it. So we may ask, in conclusion, what are some of the ways of reappropriating our work, making it more human. This attempt to draw together the various topics of the chapter will remain highly general but may be more helpful than an effort to conjure up a picture of a world of pure leisure or of work without sweat.

Alienation and
Self-expression

A first comment is that Marx is right to regard as over-optimistic Hegel's view that all our objectifications are stages on the way to a more adequate self-presence. We need to distinguish between alienation, in which we lose ourselves, and genuine *self*-expressions in which we do realize and find ourselves. Or as this was put in the first section, man's transformation of the world involves loss as well as gain. Work can be dehumanizing and will remain so unless we do more than contemplate an unhappy situation.

In fact, the second chapter has suggested that we can give a more radical account of alienation today than Marx could. Technological society threatens to dispossess us more thoroughly than any of the inequalities of industrial society. Marx's worker did not completely lose himself because someone else owned his lathe; he was still at home in his work so far as he knew what he was doing. But computers may one day reduce us to mere technicians, deprived even of our right to make up our own minds. Then we should truly be dispossessed of our activity of working humanly. The question what is inalienably human would come home to more than the metaphysician.

The reply indicated in the second chapter was that we should look, not to any particular job that might be secure from the machine, but to our agency of giving meaning to whatever goes on. We shall return to this at the end, under the theme of "creativity." But first we may take a further look at Marx's "materialism" as a call for action rather than theory.

Nature and Culture

The first sense in which we interpreted his materialism was that the economic substructure conditions our cultural consciousness. It is at the former level that the disharmonies of alienation occur, and it is here that we resolve them by acting rather than by joining in the fray of theories that belong ineffectively to the superstructure.

An over-simple account of this doctrine is open to obvious objections.

It is itself a "doctrine" and hence belongs to the superstructure of theory. As we have insisted so often in these pages, we do not first have sheer facts, out there in nature or matter, and only then form interpretations of them. Every fact we indicate, of nature or economy, already embodies some interpretation. The way we "have" a form of mining raw materials, of producing the sort of goods we want, and of distributing them as property, depends intimately on what we understand ourselves to be, on our ideals and purposes and questions—nor can these be separated from our moral, artistic, religious, and philosophical view of life.

As with behaviorism and Comte's theory, there is a self-contradiction in any supposedly exhaustive account of how we get our theories which excludes the theorist's own agency of giving the account. Any statement which derives culture from nature belongs itself to culture. Indeed, the very notion of "nature" is a theoretical construct, and one with a remarkable cultural history from the Greeks to the present.

Marx himself seems to have regretted that his legitimate desire for a thoroughly scientific study of social and economic change should have led his disciples to see in his philosophy a deterministic materialism and a merely scientific method. In fact, to regard the cultural superstructure as a simple resultant of the material substructure is, according to Marx, the very vice of capitalism. For there, he held, all interests are reduced to economic ones and all human pursuits are translated in terms of money.

If we abandon the notion of a simple causal relation of substructure to superstructure, how could we then interpret the disharmony which Marx sees at the heart of alienation? An illustration from language may help. The child starts at the biological level of "nature." But as a questioner he already feels the needs of "culture." The need to find what he is leads to the development of vocal expressions. And the more his body grows in power to talk, the more refined and exacting his need for the self-consciousness of thought becomes. We cannot say that bodily movement causes thought or that thought causes bodily expressions.

In such terms, Marx's objection to Hegel would be that he ignored the child's basic struggles for expression and gave him prematurely an abstract language quite divorced from the needs he felt most "real." In general, then, a self-expression becomes an alienation when it is so far from my most urgent needs that I see it as imposed on me rather than as coming from me. It is in this sense that social structures, moral systems, religious and philosophical doctrines become abstract when they are solidified and no longer renewed in those forms of life which are closer to nature. The alienated worker needs a language in which he can find a meaning for his life, but the language he hears in church and in the law courts no longer says anything to him. Marx's advice for the philosopher is not simply to retire but to renew his thinking at its source by a visit to the factory.

Interpretation and Change

The second sense in which we tried to understand Marx's materialism was in terms of a call to action rather than theory as the way in which alienation is to be overcome.

Again, an over-simple account of this falls foul of obvious difficulties. Any call to action expresses or embodies a theory. Marx did not rush impetuously to the barricades. He sat down and wrote an immense corpus of books which make abstruse reading. History reveals few better examples of how a theoretical interpretation of the world changes the world.

How do we change things? If I move the furniture in my room around, the change is a relatively minor one, a reshuffling of the same things. A change in which they cease to be the same things is a change of interpretation. I see the room mathematically or artistically rather than in sheer terms of utility. Instead of moving the same pieces around, I may then design new furniture or inspire another with my vision to do so.

It is this notion of "newness" which leads to the theme of creativity in work. Marx certainly saw a new world and inspired others with his vision. When he wrote that "the philosophers have only interpreted the world, it is for us to change it," he was not making an appeal for us to give up thinking and let the forces of social and economic change take over. The world we are to change is the one of our old vision, the one we take all too easily for granted. The "theory" Marx rejected is one which is regarded as a simple reflection of data, an account of the world as it already is. The "action" Marx offered was original thinking.

Marxism looks to the future. But there are various ways in which one can do so. The future can be treated as little more than a projection of the present and past. From these we draw a picture of a state in which we exclude undesirable features and add desirable ones by a sort of extrapolation. What we anticipate is the "same again," but with optimistic adjustments. We look forward to a classless society that comes to us from the nineteenth century.

Alternatively, we may try to confront the future in its originality, as that which has not yet existed and can therefore not be predicted in any determinate way. We do not canonize any one human possibility or picture of an ideal state of affairs drawn from institutions we already know. It is here, in opening up new possibilities rather than in predicting variants of old ones, that truly original thinking is called for and the creative dreamer leads the practical man of affairs.

Technique and Creation

The gist of this section has been the solidly Marxist theme that the value of my work is in my working, my *agency* in whatever I do. And this applies wherever my work is to be classified on the scale from economic substructure to cultural superstructure. Indeed, as we have just suggested, a certain primacy could be given to the thinker whose thought is truly *his,* rather than a copy of what is already there.

For Marx, alienation is overcome so far as I am able to reappropriate work as my own. It is not easy to say what this would involve in detail, or in particular forms of employment. But it is a topic that is no stranger to these pages. What no machine can take from us is our ability to find and renew the meaning of our situation. That which is fully ''mine,'' and can never be expropriated, is *my* questioning. It is in my self-critical agency that I am and remain a ''self.''

Work degenerates to technique where the self-critical element plays little part : I am left with a mere ''job'' in which I am alienated, however the property is distributed. But work becomes creative to the extent that I am able to put what I am doing repeatedly in question and find new meaning in it.

The problem with which we started is that such questioning never comes without some loss. The dreamer is less efficient at his routine task. However, the ''loss'' is measured from a lower level. Pointing is degeneration for the animal, not for man. When we learn to talk, we do not much care that our growling is less efficient.

Perhaps it is the originality or creativity of work that reconciles it with the Greek ideal of leisure. A genuinely new achievement must be an end in itself ; there is nothing in existence to which it could be subordinated. And possibly contemplation has something to do with this— provided it is no view of the past but an openness to the future. These are themes to which we shall return in the chapters on time and morality.

9 | What Am I Saying?

"In the beginning," according to creation stories, we find not only the light in which we can work but also the Word in which reality comes to expression. The Word may be "with" God, or even "On the Word all the gods depend, all beasts and men. . . ."

Children and primitives assume that words give them dominion over nature. To utter a name is to gain power. When Adam named the animals he was not compiling the first dictionary.

We learn much about people, simple or advanced, by examining their homes and government and the way they make their living. But our judgment could well be reserved until they open their mouth or put their words on paper. We know a man from the way he talks. A language gives us privileged access to the mentality of the people who produced it and who live and think in it. Before we live in a world of bricks and mortar, we live in a world of words. We find ourselves there and submit to words. Yet they are our own. We produce them and take responsibility for them. It is this intimate symbolic world of language we shall examine in this chapter.

Philosophy appeared in conversation. The vocation of Socrates was to talk. His work consisted largely in questioning the common words we use so easily and assume we understand. But here we must try to go a step further. It is no particular word that is in question, but words themselves. What possibility of acting is opened by language? What are we doing in ''saying''? What basic intention or form of questioning is met by the world of words?

The problem is as fundamental as in the last chapter, and we find a similar difficulty in making even a provisional limitation of the topic. Language can be taken as coextensive with all we do. Some philosophers, such as Croce, treat it this way, considering any self-expression such as painting or dancing as a form of language. The artist does have something to say, and ritual dancing has been called man's first effort at serious thinking. In such terms, we cannot think without language; no exploration of outer space could ever find a society of intelligent beings without some such form of expression.

However, in this chapter we are no longer studying what belongs to any question, so we shall take language as one type of expression in which we engage. We shall ask about our ordinary vocal and written language of words in syntax. This may grow out of gestures such as pointing, and out of a babbling and lalling that could best be put under the heading of aesthetic expression. It may also grow into more abstract forms such as number systems, graphs, and chemical equations. But here we shall take words, at least provisionally, in their dictionary sense. Our ''ordinary'' language can be broken down into words, each of which is capable of rough translation into other words.

Language, as understood here, discloses or presents our ''common sense'' or ''empirical'' world of particular things and events. This book has tried to extend our notion of experience beyond the empirical. But the very term ''extend'' accords some privilege to the empirical world of objects in relation, where we pass *from* one *to* another.

Also, the need to draw words beyond the uses we first learned indicates some privileged position for language over nonverbal forms of expression. Whatever escapes our language seems to demand it. We feel we do not really ''have'' an experience until we can put it somehow into words, and then we are pained at their inadequacy rather than taking it for granted. Though we may try to imagine a purely aesthetic society that remains nonverbal, we should remember the self-critical element in all experience and notice that art critics work with words.

The Origin of Language

As we watch a child growing, we estimate his progress largely through his language. Parental pride in his first word is understandable. From that time much of what the parents have to give him will be through words. The traditions, attitudes, and values of a society are passed on to him through the language he enters. In countless subtle ways this develops his vision of things. Nor need "vision" here be confined to evaluation and feeling. Even our ordinary perception grows as our language is refined and sharpened. The acuteness of our "seeing" depends much on the words at our disposal.

We shall have more to say on how children find themselves through language. A genetic account of this sort helps us to understand what words do to formulate the world we now take for obvious. We recognize what words achieve by trying to recapture our primitive experience in which they first appeared.

However, each of us grew up in a world that was already linguistic. Words were there in the possession of speaking beings. Things had names, and these were "given" to us. But there seems a more radical question to ask. How did man first acquire language in a world that had no words to give him? The account of the naming of the animals in Genesis seems to suppose that Adam found himself in a world of culture. But does not the question of the origin of human language ask about the first appearance of culture out of nature?

Whether this is a valid question or not, it is one which has always fascinated philosophers as well as linguists. If it is not so much discussed by serious students today, this may be because so little evidence has been found on which to base the competing theories. Nevertheless, the assumptions behind such theories do indicate various views of what language is and does. So we shall begin by looking at several of these genetic accounts in order to clarify our own question about the sort of world that language makes possible for us.

Theories Based
on Imitation and Emotion

For an early discussion of the question, revealing options which later theories would exploit, we may turn to the disputes in which the Greek sophists and skeptics were involved. Are things "of nature" or "of convention"? Language was an obvious candidate for discussion. The more impressed we are with the fundamental part language plays in our life, and with our dependence on it for finding what life is about, the more we shall be inclined to feel that there is some part of language which must belong to the nature of things. Yet the conventionality of language is obvious. There are many languages, and within each individuals use words somewhat differently. We make words our own, as we choose. Is not language completely arbitrary?

Perhaps we should ourselves be inclined to look for a "natural" element in the *structures* of language and leave the *content* open to convention. But early discussion was concerned mainly with the content or detail of language. Words would be natural if they imitate the sounds of nature. If I talk of the "rippling brook" I am copying its sound, conveying the way it "is." So we find the notion that language arose originally in man's effort to imitate natural sounds, the theory of "onomatopoeia."

This was defended by the Stoics and it provoked an extensive, though largely fanciful, inquiry into etymologies, which was lampooned by Plato in the dialogue *Cratylus*. The ideal remained, however, throughout the history of linguistic studies and led to much more serious research into the roots of words. Over wide areas of language, certain phonetic constants may indicate more than merely conventional origins. Thus, labials are often found for flowing movements (as in "rippling brook"). Explosive sounds convey movement away, long vowels imply distance, "k" sounds come in questions. Also, a pantomimic sign language has persisted among some primitives along with vocal language, suggesting the origin of the latter from the clearly imitative intent of the former.

As would be expected, the sophists reacted strongly against such views. Man is the measure of the language he uses. To look for the origins of language in nature, or in divinity, is useless. The sophists made a serious study of language, but in accord with their aim as teachers of rhetoric. Language was for them the instrument by which man achieves his social purposes. It does not copy nature but gets things done. Words convey what I want and they urge you to do it. Words express what I feel and they arouse similar feelings in you. Rhetoric teaches us the art of moulding language to our purposes. The basic assumption is that the instrument is conventional; it is what we choose to make of it.

However, the view that language expresses feelings could easily be adapted to an account in terms of natural origins. This, which we may call the "interjection theory," is found as early as Democritus. It was supported by Epicurus and forms part of Rousseau's famous account of the development of primitive man into society. For there does seem to be a continuity between animals and man in the realm of emotion. Animal cries are an instinctive way of sounding off feelings of fear or rage or pain. In man these become interjections ("Oh, Oh!"), and from these the various forms of speech develop.

This theory received a certain impetus from the studies made by Darwin. He investigated the expression of emotion in animals and tried to show how each such expression was once a survival response. When a cat fluffs its tail and hisses before a dog, it is making itself larger and more frightening. In line with the theory of evolution, could not the origins of human language be set in such instinctive frightening or attracting responses, which have now become vestigial?

Turning back to the child, we realize that he cries from hunger and pain and for attention long before he can talk. His first words seem more an instrument of physical power than a statement of how things are. He tries to compel with sounds. Language sounds off our emotions and forces others to satisfy our wants.

Language as Symbolic Expression

It is certainly not to be denied that the imitation of sounds and the expression of emotions belong to the many things we do with words and that the origins of language are likely to have involved such functions. However, the difference between human language and natural sounds or animal cries is far more striking than the continuity. Through my words I do not merely copy what I hear but affirm what I think to be so. I do not only give vent to what I feel but try to say what I mean. What is involved is no mere response to sounds and urges but an attempt to interpret the world and understand emotions. The world which language opens is no longer that of biological needs and their instinctive satisfaction. It is a symbolic world, one of meaning. The needs are those of culture. I want to know what things are.

It is this element of meaning which the above theories ignore, and even a far more striking continuity could not make up for failure to consider this difference. My interjection when I crack my shin is no more language than is the movement of my leg when the knee is tapped. And if the repetition of sounds is speech, then parrots may run for office.

The fact that the development of language has been away from natural sounds and cries would also lack explanation if accounts in those terms were adequate. The child first refers to a certain animal as a ''bow-wow.'' But his crude imitation, far from becoming more efficient, declines to ''dog.'' That is, an attempt to understand what language is must allow for the fact of ''degeneration,'' discussed in Chapter Seven. What is achieved by the symbolic activities of language, art, and myth is unintelligible from a purely biological level. It is a waste of time to paint on the wall; this does not capture a single animal. Rain rituals produce no more rain than nature would otherwise supply. Man is a degenerate animal. Language introduces him to an unreal world of imagination, fantasy, and philosophy. Mistakes are made possible, indeed inevitable, that an animal would never commit.

It is through the strange fact of language, however, that we can best illustrate the real symbolic worlds into which man is introduced by stepping back from absorption in the physical world of stimulus and response. And the most dramatic examples are offered by those instances where entry to the world of linguistic meaning has come suddenly, rather than by the imperceptible stages through which children normally pass.

The story of Helen Keller is well known. Blind and deaf, thè child lived in a world without language. Hers was presumably an animal-like life based largely on stimulus and response. The feel of water would lead to drinking and washing, but the patient efforts of her teacher in associating tactile words with such stimuli produced no sense of language. One day, however, when she was six, the cold water from the pump gushed over Helen's hand while the word was spelled out. Suddenly she seems to have realized that this *meant* water. She spelled the word herself, then asked for the name of the pump, the trellis, and her teacher. She had been introduced into the world where everything has a name. On the way back to the house she learned the name of each object she touched and within a few hours had a vocabulary of thirty words. The world of language to which she had been admitted is a world of meaning rather than of mere copying or responding. And her face grew more expressive each day.

It is worth noticing that the moment of transformation was not one of biological need. It was not thirst which drove her to language. A similar conclusion seems to come from the accounts we have of the attempts to teach language to "wild-children" raised by animals. Efforts to make them ask for what they physically need, to vocalize their feelings of hunger or thirst, have failed. When the meaning of words dawned on them, it was in a situation freed from the pressures of the moment.

We may be as relaxed about animals talking, now or eventually, as about machines thinking. Such candidates for humanity would be advised to read a good book of human history before they go very far. Yet if animals have not learned to talk, it is because they are too busy. They are too close to their world and its needs to step back and talk about it. Baby apes who have been brought up with children make no attempt to experiment with their mouths and form new utterances. But children engage in babbling and cooing from early days, a play with sounds that give them sheer delight. It is distance from basic needs that introduces symbolism.

Perhaps the original development of human language is to be found in vocal play rather than in cries of distress, in useless ritual rather than in copying nature. Such a transition would be from one form of meaning to another, not from a supposedly nonsymbolic nature to culture. The latter transition cannot be "explained." This is not because we happen to lack the evidence, but because the search for any form of explanation belongs to some appropriate world of culture. Outside this there is a sheer immediacy but nothing we can talk about. All talk of "nature" involves subjectivity and is a manner of speaking that is part of culture.

Nature is the symbolic world of the biologist or of the hunter or of the artist or of the child grasping for names in the play of sounds.

The Structure
of Linguistic Symbolism

To conclude that language is expressive of meaning still leaves open the question what sort of meaning we express linguistically. Some philosophers who deny that words are the mere resultant of happenings in the physical world, and who admit that words "mean," nevertheless treat this meaning as though it were some sort of "copy" of things in the world. There is a one-to-one relationship between the facts of the world and the words of our language. I first perceive a table and then learn a word for it. My word is "table," yours may be "Tisch." But the two words have the same meaning because they "refer to" the same thing.

This is an over-simplification of *referential* theories of linguistic symbolism. But there are two basic assumptions which such theories make and which will be questioned in this section. The first is that the meaning of language is to be understood in terms of "atoms." Simple units of language, usually single words, mean basic units of reality, i.e., things, events, facts, etc. That is, words come before sentences, both temporally and logically; and if we want to clarify a sentence or larger unit, we should break it down into words and ask what each one refers to. The second assumption is that our access to the object of reference is through a perception of it common to all observers and in no way affected by differences of symbolism.

Both assumptions may sound reasonable. However, there are serious difficulties in any such account of the relation between a world of things "already out there" and a symbolic world of labels that refer to them. To take "meaning" as a noun and make it the relation of a word (in a symbolic world) to a thing (in a nonsymbolic one) supposes some contemplation from outside both worlds. Yet, as the final paragraph of the previous section remarked, we cannot get outside any symbolic world of meaning. By "spoon" I mean "spooning." I am isolating some part of, or part played in, my self-conscious activity of eating. Language opens up a world of possible activities, a network of "the same" tasks I realize I can do repeatedly. The world of language is not one of ready-made meanings which mysteriously "refer," apart from my many ways of acting, to things already existing as such "outside."

Now two conclusions may be drawn. The first is that the smallest linguistic unit which can express a meaningful doing is the sentence: "I am spooning food into my mouth," not just "spoon." The second is that my use of language and my perception of the world are unlikely to be independent. They could be, if we hold that language is not coextensive with the ways in which we can express and find ourselves. The artist first paints and then tries, very inadequately, to say in words what he means in his painting. But over large areas of our life the intent which presides over our perceptions is the one that directed the formation of our language. I lack the acute perception of animals which a primitive hunter has, and my language for talking about them is correspondingly unrefined.

This has been a brief, and perhaps confusing, summary of the theme of this section. The two questions, about words and sentences and about perception and language, will now be examined more closely.

Words and Sentences

We may start with a look at some of the earlier philosophical accounts of language which could be called "atomistic." Then we shall mention a more contemporary approach which stresses the use of language and the act of speaking. Finally, we shall suggest how language may have assumed its form of words in sentences.

LINGUISTIC ATOMISM

The origins of atomistic theories of language are themselves closely tied up with a fact of language. Greek supplied one word, *logos,* for "thought," "word," and "name." Now what is namable is a particular thing. When I name my dog "Fido," I am isolating a bit of reality as unique. There are not two of him, even if someone else happens to have chosen this name for his dog. Hence it was easy to assume a one-to-one relationship between a particular thing and the thought or idea we have of it, likewise between a thing and the word that means it.

John Locke shows this very clearly. He held that each simple idea is of a particular "quality" in the world, and that we should ideally have a different word for each thing. In practice, however, we form "general ideas" which cover various qualities, and the needs of communication limit us to words that stand for many things.

This assumption that ideas are atomic is to be found also in Descartes. Just as we can analyze all numbers into prime numbers, so he held that we should be able to break down our common confused meaning into simple and ultimate ideas. The fact that we have not been able to do so he attributed to the inadequacy of our ordinary language. To express atomic ideas we should need atomic words. These would form a "universal language." Descartes himself remained very cautious about the possibility of constructing such a language. But some of his followers set to work with enthusiasm. One, for example, found seventeen species of idea and proposed a language in which the words should have a different initial letter for each species and subsequent letters according to each subspecies.

The ideal of constructing a language which would avoid all the ambiguities of our ordinary words has persisted among philosophers, especially those with strong mathematical interests (e.g., Leibniz, Russell, Carnap). We are not concerned with the enterprise here but with the assumption that inspires it, namely, that from such a language we can read off the basic facts about the world. What seems open to question is the notion that our linguistic meaning consists in the reference of a word to a thing, and that sentences are subsequently built up from words to represent aggregates of things.

THE ACT OF SPEAKING

That such a notion will find little support in these pages should be clear by now. The view of facts or things existing in the world, fully constituted, waiting for a mind to get ideas of them and for a mouth to utter words which correspond to them, has been subjected to frequent criticism. What facts and things there are in the world is not independent of the way I question the world. Our access to facts is not through a passive contemplation that bypasses our ''embodied'' activities but through our many ways of classifying, counting, measuring, manipulating, according to our interests and questions. Hence if we ask for the meaning of language, ''meaning'' is to be taken as a verb. We should ask what we are meaning or intending when we talk in this way or that. We should look to the act of speaking, shown in the sentence, rather than to individual words within a sentence.

Even the behaviorist account of language, which tries to get away from the notion of ideas in the mind and of knowledge as a passive ''look,'' shows a surprising lack of interest in what the speaker is doing. But there is a strong tradition among contemporary philosophers that when we ask about the meaning of language we are asking how it is used by a speaker. This emphasis upon ''use'' is associated with Ludwig Wittgenstein, but it may be of value to mention here an analysis made by J.L. Austin of the activity of speaking (cf. his *How to do things with Words*, Oxford University Press, 1962).

Austin holds that when I am speaking I am involved in three ways of acting or types of linguistic action :

1. *locutionary.* This consists in uttering language (making sounds as words: i.e., not growls or nonsense). Suppose I say, "Don't talk during lectures."

My utterance, or locutionary action, would have been different if I had spoken in German, or if I had said, "Be quiet in class."

2. *perlocutionary* (*"through* speaking"). This is the action of bringing about some result of the utterance. In the example it might be silence or uproar in the hall, surprise or scornful amusement in the audience. Or the result might be "no result."

3. *illocutionary* (*"in* speaking"). This is my performance of "meaning" my utterance (e.g., as a command or warning or protest). What is involved in such linguistic action can best be suggested through contrast with the other two. I could perform the same illocutionary act if I had the same intention of commanding silence in making the three different locutions mentioned under (1). Also, the illocutionary force of my utterance does not depend on the result it produces in the listeners; the same illocutionary act would be performed whichever of the results under (2) came about.

The analysis is subtle. But your very effort to understand Austin may well illustrate his point. Do not simply contemplate the above words or try to refer them to any fact simply out there in the world. Make various experiments of saying something and try to distinguish what you are *meaning* from what you are *uttering* and what you happen to be *effecting*. For example, are you meaning quite the same in uttering "Please be quiet" and "I want silence"? How does your intention and anticipation of a result enter into your meaning, whereas the actual result does not (consider the boy who cried "Wolf!"). It may prove difficult to solve some of these border-disputes, but the point is that you do so by turning to your act of speaking and by asking what precisely you are meaning, not by studying what in the world corresponds to such words as "quiet," "silence," "please," and "want."

To illustrate this primacy of an act of speaking, expressed in a sentence, over individual words, we may consider the probable continuity of speaking with gesturing. A gesture says more than a single word can capture. Several sentences may be needed to express vocally what I am meaning in shrugging my shoulders. A gesture is evidently an act of gesturing. It would be difficult to compose a dictionary of gestures, and if we succeeded, it would be clear that the recorded stock of gestures (like umpires' signals) had been isolated from the activity of gesturing.

Another illustration likens words in a dictionary to tools in a carpenter's shop. The hammer is a hammer only in hammering. If I use it for scratching my back it is a back-scratcher. We do of course normally say it is a hammer while it is hanging on the wall in the shop, but we are saying that it was isolated from a previous act of hammering and can be used again, as the "same" hammer, yet only in another act of hammering. Similarly, words can be isolated from acts of speaking and stored in a dictionary, but only for use in further acts of speech (or perhaps for some different use, no longer as words, e.g., for voice testing).

The referential theory of meaning is most at home when words are taken in the way we commonly do in our search for examples, i.e., as nouns. I can refer to a ''table'' by pointing one out. For verbs, I can refer to a man ''running,'' or perhaps even ''referring.'' But if I look at this sentence, I find greater difficulty in suggesting what the little words refer to, like ''if,'' ''at,'' ''in,'' and ''like.'' It is such words which remind us most clearly that things and events are always in a context, and that the context depends on the speaker, his intentions and questions.

CONTEXT AND METAPHOR

The claim made in this section does not deny that the first words man uttered may have been single words, as they are with the child. But in hearing single words from a child we are isolating them from what, even in so primitive a form, is still a complete act of speaking. In pointing, the child is saying ''I want that'' or ''I admire that.'' The boy who cried ''Wolf!'' was speaking one sentence when joking, another when serious.

The last example draws attention to the context, or speech situation, which enters into the act of speaking. Except with intended deceit, as in the example, it is assumed that the context is common to speaker and listener. If at the dinner table I say ''water,'' my one word is part of a full speech situation which I suppose you to share. If you do not, and assume my context is of washing rather than drinking, then communication has failed and I try to remedy the mistake by making my context vocally explicit.

Some such process may well have been involved in the way language developed its form of words in sentences, with all the complexities of syntax. A full speech act expressing delight through a single sound, if misunderstood as an expression of want or fear, would be repeated in some modified way as two sounds. Misunderstanding of these sounds in some other context might be corrected by the addition of a further sound. Speculation is free on such matters. But the complex structure of many of the sentences in this book came about through the writer's attempt, on reading the simpler originals, to turn part of his context into explicit language in order to avoid possible misunderstanding.

In any event, the suggestion is that sentences developed by some crystallization of vague utterances into definite ones, not by the construction of complex wholes from simple linguistic units which were there before. This view allows language the flexibility it so clearly shows. If a word is crystallized from an obscure context it is by no means limited to use in a precise one. The same word can be used to help make some other context explicit. And when this occurs the old word will then be an integral part of a new act of speech. If we want to say it is the same word in a new sentence, then we must say that it "has a new meaning," i.e., new meaning is being expressed through it. In relation to the old ("literal") meaning of the word, the new one is "metaphorical." I "see" visually or "grasp" manually, then I see and grasp intellectually. For reasons that have been suggested, the language of the body offers abundant examples of metaphorical extension. But according to this view, all words are basically metaphorical. Our common distinction between "metaphorical" and "literal" is no more than a reflection of which uses have become accepted as standard.

The Organization
of Perception

The realization which suddenly struck Helen Keller, that everything has a name, comes more slowly to children of normal development. Still, there is a time, around the end of the second year, when an insatiable appetite for names seems to transform the child's life. Later on, learning lists of words will be drudgery, for these are fitted into a world the child has already formed. But at this age he is building up his first perception of an objective world of stable things in constant relations. And it is through language that he formulates this symbolic whole, just as it was through numbers that Galileo and Newton transformed the mass of particular phenomena into the unity and stability of a scientific world.

Without the symbolism of language the child would have remained close to what was described in the third chapter as sheer sensation. The world is so present to the infant that its features lack definition and constancy. All has a strong immediacy. He is not sure of himself or of an objective world in which a thing can disappear and reappear as "the same" rather than as another compelling experience. Space is limited to what he can reach and see at the moment, and time extends only to a short "coming" and "gone."

Later on we forget the way in which our initial perception of a world of constant things and repeatable events was intimately connected with the learning of our language. We are then able to acquire "another language" and apply new words conventionally to things we already perceive without them. But if we try to learn a language very different from our original one, or if we try to *think* in a language even close to ours, the arduous experiment may shake our conviction that we first see things and then label them with words. Our "own" language is an intimate part of the situation through which we find ourselves in the world. We are "embodied" in words, given a point of view from which appearances are organized.

THE INTERESTS
OF LANGUAGE

We are commonly taught a foreign language through vocabularies of words, where each word in that language stands for one word in our own—though it may surprise us to find that the new language uses the same word for two quite different words in ours, or vice versa. Also, the meaning we most usually put into foreign tongues is of the everyday sort that allows little scope for the subtleties where differences stand out. We find our way to the station in a similar manner in most languages.

Nevertheless, even where we should expect no difficulties of translation, some languages reveal interests and views of the world quite different from our own. For example, some primitive languages make no sharp distinction between singular and plural. It is as though man's earliest objective perception did not allow for counting. Such experience would tend to be of various indeterminate wholes, such as "grass," in which only later interests would lead to the discrimination of a plurality of blades or "grasses." A survival of such indeterminacy is found in the Greek neuter plural taking a singular verb.

It might seem a basic datum of perception that things are different from actions. Yet there are primitive languages in which nouns and verbs are largely interchangeable. Nor is this so strange. If we stand on the seashore, we perceive the waves breaking. That is the tradition of our language. But with a slightly different language we could have perceived the sea "waving."

However, it is when we pass from the perception of ordinary things and common actions to more personal realms that the language barrier grows. Few travellers stop to discuss their deepest feelings or philosophical ideas with the customs officials; but if they do, no phrase book will suffice. It is here that variations in context become all important and prevent any word having quite the same meaning as its "equivalent" in the dictionary. We have to try and think ourselves into the spirit (*esprit?*, *Geist?*) of the language that presided over the crystallization of its words and formed the sensitivity of the people who live through those words. We try to get the "feel" of the language, to recover the intentions and attitudes that have formulated the experience of life in a certain way. To translate conscientiously is to live again and perceive afresh.

THE FORMING OF SPACE

Basic to any perception of an objective world of things in relation is some structure of space and time in which they can be situated, identified, and reidentified. We have already distinguished between the first-person space of bodily activity and the Euclidean or Newtonian space which we have learned to take for obvious. Modern languages allow for talk and thought of things as located in ways for which the position of the speaker is irrelevant. I am on the earth but can talk easily of the movement of the planets as though I were outside the solar system, watching a mechanical model.

However, if I had grown up speaking one of the primitive languages we know, I should not have been able to engage in these feats of imaginative thinking. Such languages have to make explicit the relation of each thing or event to the spatial situation the speaker occupies when talking or thinking. The nouns, pronouns, adjectives, and verbs of simple statements of fact specify in which direction a thing is from me, whether it is horizontal or upright, and how it is moving relative to me, even when such details would seem to us totally irrelevant and distracting. Particles and inflections show whether the object is in front of me or behind me, above or below, close or distant, moving toward me or away from me. And even these relations are not put in this abstract form but frequently are expressed through parts of the body: e.g., "eye" or "face" instead of "in front of." We get here a vivid sense of our situation and "line of address." But language would have to pass through a considerable development before such detail could drop from our words and our perception, allowing science to be thought out as an account of the world from a "generalized situation." This leads to the topic of the final section.

The Growth of Language

Languages grow in so many ways that summaries are of little help. However, we may distinguish two directions of growth, calling them "univocal" and "analogical." In the former, there is a development from words that express highly particular perceptions to words of less rich but more precise meaning that apply in the same way ("univocally") to a wide class of things or events. The other direction of growth is one in which words break out of a relatively precise meaning to a looser but richer one, so that they may be applied in a variety of suggestive ways ("analogously").

Univocal Development

This is the growth shown by words as they are incorporated in the project of science. The intent of the scientist is to reduce a large number of particular things and events to a manageable number of classes and laws. As suggested above, primitive languages were no apt medium for this. There, words tend to be restricted to a high particularity of experience. For example, verbs differ accordingly as the agent is large or small, young or old, apart from others or in a group; they vary with movement over land or over water, inside or outside the house, toward the fire or away from it. Possessive pronouns differ according to the "intimacy" of what is possessed: goods, artefacts, house, children, parts of the body. Numbers, too, sometimes vary with the type of thing they enumerate: men, animals, spirits, canoes, cocoanuts.

The discrimination of such languages over a limited range of interests may defy our understanding. We do not see all the particularities that these languages distinguish. People whose life is centered on the camel may have over five thousand words to describe the beast in all its conditions, postures, and moods. Some of the distinctions we find in such languages may strike us as important. Three men evidently come together in a radically different way from three cocoanuts. But the numerical example illustrates the severe limitation that these languages put on thought. How could mathematics ever have developed if language had not brought to expression numbers as such, valid for any things at all? It is of the very notion of mathematics that numbers are not bound to any particular class of things.

So it is that the questioning which led to science—the attempt to understand things and events, not in their particularity, but in their most common relations to each other—has demanded, and fashioned, languages of increasing generality that formulate a precisely defined world in which a wide variety of objects stand out in the same way. The ideal of such languages is the technical dictionary. Words represent some class of things that can be recognized repeatedly or of events that recur. Laughter, considered as a personal activity, would not belong. It is not a recurrent event, but is different each time, part of a history. Yet we may also treat it as an event and find one word for it. As scientists we need to.

Analogical Development

Along with the tendency to free words from their particular vision and define a vocabulary of precise, universal terms, we find the tendency of words to break out of their exact, constant meanings and reveal their analogical possibilities. Here language reflects the history of our attempts to express a meaning to which no defined words can ever be adequate.

This is the already mentioned sense in which all words may be said to be metaphorical. More is intended in the context of any act of speaking than the words which crystallize from it can make explicit. The word for the potter's activity became the word for turning and shaping, then for imitating and creating, and for purely intellectual "forming." Indeed, a study of the history of the word "form" would give a good introduction to the history of philosophy.

It may be objected that in practice we learn our words from others, "ready-made," and we do not extend their meanings simply as we choose. Meanings are fixed by social authority, and it is the dictionary that the parental hand enforces. This is of course true. We all learn to think in a language that is already there. Even in the language of my private thought, I take part in a social activity and submit to the rules of a group. However, somewhat as one form of football became another through the impulse of an individual who picked up the ball and ran, so language evolves through the efforts of individuals struggling to express and find "their" meaning in it. Submission and initiative go together. Each person comes to grips with his language by exploring the potential of words and trying them out in new roles.

The life of a language lies, not in any fancy for coining new words, but in its power to revive old words with new meaning. Philosophy shaped the Greek language, as well as growing out of it. And Christianity, in taking over Greek, infused into its words a new complex of sentiments and attitudes. The words remained "the same" but became the focus for new possibilities of experience. Language is the home in which we are born, but we bring our own life to it.

10 | What Is Time?

Previous chapters have referred more than casually to a question for which we may now "make time." Language is eminently historical. A serious writer is unlikely to be content with a concise dictionary which tells him what a word means today. The shades of meaning can be baffling, for each word we use carries a long history. Anyone who is sensitive to words will want to know how they have developed, what different interests and ways of life have formed the context for their journey through time. It takes time for man to express and find his meaning, and language bears the mark of such experiments, innovations, and refinements.

The discussion of "work" illustrated this. No simple answer could be given to the question whether work is necessary. We had to ask what work meant in various ages. What constitutes work depends on socially defined needs and these vary remarkably with the way a society sees itself and its purposes. To pose any such question involves retracing a good part of history.

Questions about the nature of "truth" will be left to the final chapter. But it no longer seems self-evident that truth must be timeless. This may be the case with mathematical truths and with the sort of facts which make up a chronology. That Plato lived in the fourth century B.C. and proposed a theory of Forms is not a matter for reexamination in each age. But what that theory "was" is a topic of repeated reinterpretation. Kant suggested that it is our duty in each age of philosophy to try to understand Plato better than he understood himself. What Forms are is a question to which no timelessly valid answer can be given. Time, or history, enters into our account of what is so.

The interpretation we have given of "sense" and of "matter" suggests that temporality belongs inescapably to our existence. If this can now be proved, then any talk of "timeless" experiences (e.g., aesthetic or rapturous) would merely mean that a different sort of time experience from our ordinary one is involved. If we believe in immortality and speak of it in the language of "eternity," this would still call for understanding in terms of some form of time. As we have seen, any investigation of whether some feature must belong to our experience is equally an investigation of the basic meaning of that feature (cf. pp. 103–104). Such an inquiry into the temporality of our experience as questioners will form the topic of this chapter.

Two Attitudes toward Time

It may be that one of the most notable achievements of the last century was the growth of a genuine sense of history. We inherit this. If we are studying a form of government in existence today, we feel we do not properly understand it unless we learn how it got to be that way. If we are deciding which candidate in an election to vote for, we ask for a biography of each, for an account of how he became what he is. When we speak of a person as "mature" or "immature," we imply that his present character either does or does not incorporate his passage through a complex series of stages of development we regard as "normal."

In the abstract language of the philosopher, we tend to look upon "being" as a product of "becoming." Nevertheless, people—and notably philosophers—have not always accepted this. So, to be faithful to our own sense of history, we may preface our study of the necessity and nature of time with an indication of some of the different ways various ages have regarded temporality.

The Rejection of Temporality

The word "history" comes from Herodotus (meaning simply an "inquiry"), and it is perhaps with the Greeks that we find the first serious attempt to separate history from myth and explain the present from past human events, rather than in terms of mythical acts of the gods. However, there are notable parallels between the Greek attitude toward time, as a limitation or impediment to "being," and the mythical subordination of human activity to divine models outside our experience of temporality.

"BEING AND BECOMING"
IN GREEK PHILOSOPHY

Some account has already been given of the search of Greek philosophers for absolutes, for something certain and normative amid all the changes of nature and human opinion (cf. pp. 59–60). However one may interpret Plato himself, a way developed of accounting for things in terms of highly abstract dualities: being and becoming, the one and the many, universal and particular. Instead of regarding such coupled terms as different "aspects" of the same reality, or as various ways of coming to grips with it, the tendency was to think of two different types of object and two "faculties" for attaining them: there is an intelligible world of things that fully are and a sensible world of things that only seem to be.

That these two realms were characterized respectively as "eternal" and as "temporal" may have had much to do with the esteem in which mathematics was held. The truths of mathematics impressed with their precision, their certainty, and the universal assent they commanded. Once discovered, they left no room for change. By comparison, the facts of history, the details about the unpredictable deeds of man, remained vague and uncertain, open to a variety of conflicting opinions, subject to continuing reassessment. There seemed no "law" or "reason" to what goes on in our ordinary experience. So it was assumed that genuine knowledge is of timeless truths; we can have no more than opinion of what changes.

Mathematics also suggested a model for the relationship between these two realms. We do not discover about circles by measuring wheels. We apply the former normatively to the latter: a wheel is "true" to the extent that it "copies" or "participates in" the geometrical figure of a circle. So also the reality of human qualities and institutions was measured in relation to eternal archetypes. Any act we perform, or the state we construct politically, is just or good to the extent it shares in the reality of a "model" act or state existing timelessly in an intelligible realm.

As we have said, what such doctrines mean is open to repeated interpretation. No contemporary Platonist would be happy with such a crude outline. But it is not surprising that the topic of history plays little part in Greek philosophy. Value could not easily be set on innovation. We are called upon to copy in time what is "already" so timelessly and perfectly. "Becoming" does not enter positively into "being." The reality of our achievements is their repetition of what is so outside time.

THE REPETITION
OF MYTHICAL MODELS

This devaluation of time and history is shown more dramatically in the mythical accounts we find in primitive religions and in some of those beyond the Western tradition today.[1] There is a similar subordination of all human activities to nonhuman archetypes. Here, the latter are not intelligible "Ideas" but the sacred deeds of gods or heroes. We may speak of these acts as taking place in a "mythical time." But since this is regarded as in no continuity with our own time (in a remote past or "at that time"), it may be more correct to reserve the term "time" for our own experience and to regard divine deeds as outside time.

According to such notions, human activities have value or reality only so far as they imitate the original acts of the gods. Man's life is the repetition of divine models. Whether he is hunting, tilling the ground, warring, marrying and begetting children, he is not acting on his own initiative but copying what has been done perfectly by the gods and transmitted through the myths. Of these the primary one is a creation story, an account of how the primeval chaos was transformed into an ordered cosmos. Uncultivated regions (seas, deserts, inaccessible mountains) lack a celestial model, and if man conquers and develops them he is not engaged on a human venture into the unknown but is repeating the divine creative act. Only this can give the new territory its form and stability. Similarly, the building of a temple or city, far from being an original enterprise in architecture, is the embodiment of a design received from the gods.

Profane activities, lacking a divine model, are deviations from such archetypes and hence sinful. All that has value or meaning is a ritual reenactment. Human marriage reproduces a marriage between gods or between heaven (man) and earth (woman), from which resulted the cosmos and its fertility. Even in a basically historical religion such as Christianity, the calendar repeats stages of the cosmogony: man returns to chaos (Mardi gras), abolishes the past time with its sins (purification rites, such as Lent), and participates again in creation (resurrection, Easter).

Details, of course, vary immensely but it can be seen that the underlying notion is anti-historical. Man does not regard the future as radi-

---

[1] For a fuller account of what follows, cf. Mircea Eliade, *Cosmos and History: The Myth of the Eternal Return* (Harper Torchbooks, 1959).

cally new, open to his own initiative and projects. His life in time is interpreted as the duplication of what has already been achieved perfectly. Indeed, this can be put more strongly. The repetition does not so much take place "in time" as form a unity with divine deeds that withdraws man from profane time. In this sense, it is man's task to overcome time, to annul it.

Or, if we wish to retain some sense of time, we may say that man interprets it as cyclic. There is no irreversible progress of events but rather an eternal return to origins. Man remains close to the cycles of nature and does not distinguish history as a linear development of events taking place "once and for all time."

The Acceptance
of Temporality

The first indications among philosophers of a break with the Greek view of time come with Augustine. He was a neo-Platonist and it may be wrong to attribute to him contemporary notions of the historicity of experience. But he represents the first serious effort to synthesize Greek philosophy with Judaeo-Christian religion, and the main doctrines of the latter involve an understanding of time as linear and an idea of achievement which we today tend to take as "evident."

LINEAR TIME

Augustine accepted the Greek ideal of knowledge as a contemplation of eternal truth. However, in a variety of ways he tried to reconcile this with the notion that truth is revealed to us through the events of history rather than through timeless speculation. The two works for which he is best known are an autobiography (*The Confessions*) and a history (*The City of God*). Whatever may hold for purely factual truths and for those of mathematics, the sort of truth we attain through philosophy and religion is highly personal and depends for its acceptance and expression on the "maturity" of the knower, that is, on the history of individuals and societies. For Augustine, the appearance and formulation of absolute truth was not independent of the spread of Greek culture or the rise and fall of Rome. The truth we have is pregnant with the history through which we passed. Truth is temporal; it takes time to unfold.

Rousseau asked why God should speak to him through Moses. As scandalous as the notion may seem, it is this for which the Jewish and Christian religions have stood. It is through historical persons and events that we discover what is finally so. Biblical religion rejects the cycles of nature as a source of truth and directs us instead to unique events in history. Creation is not a model simply "outside time" but is rather the foundation of history. And history is linear, moving from the vocation of a people, through their various fortunes and toward a culmination which is to depend on what has been done by personal responsibility and initiative. Each decision on the way is irreversible. Though past mistakes may be "redeemed," the course is a straight line on which each stage is new.

Much remains of the notions of repetition and participation (cf. the example above of Lent and Easter). Yet emphasis is placed, not on archetypes outside time or in a remote past, but rather on a future which is not predesigned so much as dependent on what we freely make of it. God stands at the end of history. The future is no mere duplication of the past but is unpredictable, open to originality and creativity.

THE IDEA
OF ACHIEVEMENT

The source of such views may be much more complex than indicated above. The Greeks certainly showed and allowed for creativity. And the Christian Middle Ages were notably unhistorical in their thinking. But whatever the sources, a highly positive evaluation of time did grow in the West, along with an individualism based on the notion that each man makes his destiny. Various forms of evolutionary thinking appeared (e.g., Hegel, Marx, Darwin). Science showed a remarkable linear advance of knowledge. History grew as a discipline. And "progress" was taken for granted by all.

At least, progress was held to be open to all. No longer was it assumed that a son would simply step into the position of his father. Independence was won from ancestral models, and it became normal to aim at advancement beyond the status at which one began. Life became a field for achievement.

This century has posed serious questions. Individualism has become suspect. Evolutionary doctrines are less naive. It is no longer assumed that the advance of scientific or historical knowledge is simply linear. And the optimistic belief in progress has been badly shaken. We are less confident of our freedom to shape our fate and of any standards by which maturity is measured, and the new can be evaluated as an advance.

Yet even these questions may serve to emphasize the attitude of accepting time rather than rejecting it in favor of nontemporal archetypes. It was perhaps some survival of transhistorical models which enabled our predecessors to feel so confident that they were progressing toward a well defined goal (e.g., classless society or culmination of knowledge). Now we recognize more acutely that all we can say or think is temporal. We can no longer find support in archetypes. The eternal return of nature is not to be found in history. We must make *our* future.

The Necessity
of Time

In the previous section the phrase ''outside time'' was used rather glibly. It is a strange term, an odd combination of the spatial and the temporal. Yet changing the spatial preposition into a temporal one merely increases perplexity, as in the poetic phrase ''born of the Father before time began.'' ''*Before* time'' involves temporality and hence denies ''before *time*.'' Attempts to deny temporality seem to reaffirm it. Our language is saturated with time, and the resolute denial of any temporal element in ''eternity'' seems to leave us with an empty concept rather than a highly positive one.

So the question of this section is whether time belongs inescapably to any possible human experience. As with spatiality, the reply we shall propose is affirmative. An argument will be drawn from an examination of the conditions of possibility of questioning. It will be claimed that time must belong to any questioning experience.

However, the most fruitful aspect of such a discussion is not the bare proof that experience must be temporal. The interesting question is *what* sort of time has thereby been proved, what is the minimal—or original— experience of temporality we must have as infants or adults, in this life or in any ''future'' life we may hope for. This question will call for a ''first-person'' account of time.

It is only in this century that such an account has been developed by philosophers. However, some indications are to be found as early as Augustine's *Confessions* (Book XI). There he starts his inquiry by posing the following conundrum:

> **But the two times, past and future, how can they *be*, since the past is no more and the future is not yet? On the other hand, if the present were always present and never flowed away into the past, it would not be time at all, but eternity. But if the present is only time because it flows away into the past, how can we say that it *is*? For it is, only because it will cease to be.[2]**

Augustine soon realizes that this problem arises from *objectifying* time (though he does not use the word). If time is treated as an object which one observes, then the future does not now exist, nor does the past,

[2] *Confessions of St. Augustine,* trans. F.J. Sheed (New York: Sheed & Ward Inc., 1943), p. 271.

and the present is so ephemeral as to disappear even in the designation of a "now." Time, he affirms, is not "the movement of the sun and moon and stars" or of anything in the world. No answer to these questions can come from looking at such "clocks." Clocks measure time but presuppose temporality. If we are to understand what time is, rather than how it is measured, we must turn to our human experience of *being* temporal.

As Augustine puts it: "Thus it seems to me that time is certainly extendedness—but I do not know what it is extendedness of: probably of the mind itself." Or in the terms we have used, time is only derivatively something to be measured "in the third person"; the original experience of temporality is to be captured in a first-person account.

> Nor is it right to say there are three times, past, present and future. Perhaps it would be more correct to say: there are three times, a present of things past, a present of things present, a present of things future. For these three exist in the mind, and I find them nowhere else: the present of things past is memory, the present of things present is sight, the present of things future is expectation.[3]

In other words, I do not stand outside time observing a series of events which bear dates in the future, present, or past. My first-person experience is only of the present. Better, it is a "self-presence." But I am present to myself only as a complex anticipation and recollection. It is through a description of these modes of presence and nonpresence that we can give an account of temporality. For example, Augustine points out that what we later objectify as "a long future" is originally experienced as "a long expectation"; we hope or fear in a way that is "remote." Only then can we employ the movement of the sun or other physical bodies as a measure of our anticipation.

It is not till this century that the possibilities Augustine opened for such an account of time were exploited. Kant made time the most "interior" form of experience but treated it all too much as the "clock time" of Newtonian physics. It was Bergson (1859–1941) who turned the attention of philosophers back to our original experience of temporality. He was a biologist and realized that to understand what an animal is at any stage of its development is to take into account its whole past and future. Hence he distinguished between "physical time" and "lived time" (*la durée*): the latter is no mere succession of moments but is an experience which sums up the past and is "pregnant with the future." It is, however, in the phenomenologist and existentialist schools (e.g., Husserl, Heidegger, Sartre) that we find the fullest account of time as

[3] *Ibid.*, p. 276.

"lived" or as a "self-temporalization." We shall return to this but first need to offer a proof that experience is inescapably temporal.

The Temporality of Questioning

That our life as questioners must be time-bound is not difficult to suggest. A questioner does not possess himself in an instant. He is a searcher who must struggle to find himself. However, all this has been said before. We must now try to focus attention on the distinctively temporal element in man's need to go out of himself and return to himself.

The self-validating situation with which we start is that perplexity in which I put my own questioning into question. I ask whether I can avoid asking. But in asking whether I *can* do something, I am asking about the *possibility* of acting. Questioning necessarily involves the notion, or experience, of possibility. Remove this and you would have either a vegetable or a person who already knows without asking. A questioner is present to himself as problematic, as a possibility to be achieved or explored. To ask "What am I?" is to ask "What can I do?" But presence-as-possible is temporal: it is our original experience of the future. To this we shall return shortly.

However, it is as much an inescapable condition of questioning that possibilities should be limited. There would be no need to *ask* what to do if all conceivable possibilities were present "together" without the defining note of one rather than another; they would simply cease to be possibilities and become one grand actuality. Presence-as-possibility implies some impossibility or exclusion, a brute limitation or facticity. But if possibility is experience as future, the limitation of possibility is experience as past. It is what I "have been" or "already am" that defines and limits what I "can do." Only a person who already has wealth or power can be faced with definite possibilities of how to use wealth or power. Remove the past, the fixed "whence" of determinate possibilities, and you make questioning impossible or unnecessary.

Hence, temporality belongs inescapably to the experience of a questioner. He asks what he can do on the ground of what he has been. Whatever "present" or self-presence he achieves, he wins it by returning to himself from future and past, from "expectation and memory." We may now try to describe this more concretely and ask about the structure or relation of these three dimensions of our basic temporal experience: future, past, and present.

The Dimensions
of Time

Before starting on a first-person account of time, a description of "lived time" rather than of the "clock time" in which scientists locate observed events, we may remark that this is in some ways easier than the corresponding account of space.

First, we all have a strong sense of being bound to the temporal situation we personally experience. Whereas our familiarity with maps and diagrams makes it relatively easy for us to imagine being out of our own spatial position and in some other equally "real" position (e.g., the astronauts' pictures of the earth fitted readily into views we had already formed), no familiarity with the dates and events of history quite destroys our sense that only the present is real.

Second, we are convinced that time is irreversible. In the third-person space of science, it is indifferent whether a body moves up or down, to left or right. But if scientists use equations in which time flows backwards, the layman finds himself (at least as yet) unable to say what this would "really mean."

THE FUTURE

In their practical concerns, people take into account a certain period of time. Though a man of forty may spontaneously plan in terms of several years or even decades, the basic unit of reckoning in the twenties is said to be the year. For an adolescent it is the month. At eight, the child counts in weeks, each of which seems interminable. The concept of "yesterday" and of "tomorrow" is not found before the age of five, nor the concept of "today" as a unit before the age of four. The three-year-old child realizes that there are regular hours of the day. But in infancy one falls into a simple identification with a short "present."

The above details may be challenged, but the suggestion is clear that development from infancy to maturity is the achievement of a progressive freedom from absorption in the here-and-now. The infant does not experience hope or anxiety. He may howl when time for feeding approaches. But he cries because he is hungry and is absorbed in his hunger—not because he has clear expectations about the future. Growth wrenches the child from the "now" and throws him out into the future. He learns to face the human responsibility of reckoning with life as something to be done, as a possibility to be achieved.

There is a close connection between freedom and this original sense of the future as a possibility to be realized. What we regard as an impairment of freedom comes with some restriction of our way of living "in prospect." In the twilight of mental disorder, everything tends to become part of the "now." All details are of equal importance. There are no realms of the ideal or hypothetical, no place for imagination or humor, since all these take us constructively out of the present.

We may speak of things merely happening to us. But they come to us in the way we are prepared to receive them. They arrive as the realization of possibilities we have anticipated through hope or dread, as answers to questions we have at least implicitly posed. The future is our present experience as a field of possible actions in the world. It is not a date on a time scale, a preformed event which simply occurs, with the label of "now," when the clock has advanced. It is already present to me as that toward which I must take a stand, even if this be of indifference or evasion. The future is myself as possible.

I do not first say "I am" and then say "I shall be." What I am is a function of the possibilities with which I reckon. The questioner is separated from himself by being ahead of himself.

THE PAST

Plato relates the myth of pre-existent souls choosing their life before coming into the world. But the Bible claims that it was into the dust of the ground that the breath of life was infused. Possibility is set in facticity. We never begin anything absolutely, completely "from scratch." We start from a situation in which we find ourselves. We are "already" of a certain sex, race, class, and nation, with a given temperament, health, and mentality, supporting a whole history which defines and limits possibilities.

We may be more precise about the past which is constitutive of our present experience.

1. It contains transcendental elements, those which all of us have inescapably as human beings and which the metaphysical parts of this book try to specify.

2. It involves a "pre-history," those particular conditions which form the physical situation and mental make-up of each individual, his own "given" at the start of life; the roots are deep, as psychiatry reveals.

3. It includes all we have freely made of ourselves, the particular possibilities we have already realized and which then serve as the past which limits our remaining possibilities; such narrowing of the field may contribute most to the anxiety of age.

The intimate relation of future and past in our experience can thus be presented as one of freedom and limitation or necessity. However it would be wrong to see the latter as a mere determinism, over and done with, fixed for all time, utterly beyond our control.

My past limits what I can do. But equally the way I formulate my life as possibility affects the way my past enters into my present, the way it is "for me" in my act of self-presence. The life of Sophocles is said to have been achieved as a resolved chord. Yet a chord is never resolved, nor is it ever defined as a dischord, so long as the possibility of interpretation remains—and it does so, for us, until death.

The date of my birth is fixed in the archives, but what my birth means to me is a possibility still to be achieved. In this sense, Sartre tells us we are responsible for our own birth. Our past—the choices already made, our prehistory, even the transcendental elements—remain themes for reinterpretation through the attitude we adopt to the future. The same tragedy of defects at birth may have afflicted two people. But for one they constitute his present as one of bitterness and self-pity, for the other they are the occasion of a courageous approach to obstacles.

The "present of things remembered" is a re-collection, a constructive process. History is no mere "datum" but a task of renewal. We go into the future only out of the past. But what the past is or means for us depends on the possibilities we draw out of it.

THE PRESENT

This act of defining our future from our past, and our past from our future, is the original sense of our present. It is an act of achieving self-presence from possibility and facticity, a way of making oneself present in a certain way.

In terms of clock time, of course, the present is a "now" we designate. But Augustine's difficulty remains. If I say it is ten-nineteen and eleven seconds, it has ceased to be such while I was saying it. Even in clock time, what counts as "the present" is determined by human interests. For the policeman making a report it may be ten-nineteen. For most of us it is ten-twenty or even a quarter past ten. For others it is this morning, or this day, or even this stage of history.

At least in terms of "lived time," the present is not so much given as made. It is a common observation that some people tend to live in the future, others in the past. And there are schools of psychotherapy which regard the manner an individual makes his present as a clue to all his ills. Again, religions have been classified according to the way belief is focussed on future or past; prophets are not mere soothsayers but preach a conversion of the past through a vision of the future.

Such an account of the present need not introduce any norms of how we "ought" to achieve our self-presence. Nevertheless, writers on this topic have usually been quick to distinguish between an "authentic" and an ''inauthentic'' present. Psychologists and religious teachers have followed them. Whether this is legitimate would take us beyond the topic of this chapter into that of morality. But one comment may be in order.

It is often said that no *ought* can be drawn from an *is*. This would be true if we were dealing with an account of man in the third person. There we should expect to find no *ought* lurking in a description of man's temporality. However, here we have been describing a more basic experience. According to this, man is not a being who first *is* something and subsequently *can* become otherwise. In our experience of being temporal, what we are is achieved from an anticipation of our possibilities. Hence if it could be shown that the sensitivity or perception with which we formulate our possibilities involves any moral element, then there would be an ''I ought'' at the heart of ''I can,'' and hence also in what ''I am.'' Failure in the *ought* would mean failure in the *is* of self-presence which I achieve. The command, ''Become what you are,'' is paradoxical but not meaningless.

A final comment is that such ideas could open the possibility of reinterpreting the mythical view of time. The sense of the future as one of personal decision and initiative may seem lacking. But the notion of an ''eternal return'' might be one way of expressing the achievement of the present as a recovery of identity from dispersion in time. A brief note on the religious notion of transcending time in ''eternity'' will be added at the end of the next section.

Forms of Temporal Experience

This chapter has been concerned with the question whether time is a necessary element of any possible human experience and, if so, what sort of temporality can be shown to be inescapable.

The affirmative answer given to the first question will affect our approach to many of the themes remaining in this book. If all human action must be temporal, then all we do or say or think is historically conditioned. In the most intimate way I am bound by the age in which I live. Should a consideration of freedom allow me to claim a genuine authorship of my actions, still there would remain a sense in which I am a product of ''my time.'' No man is a timeless individual; he suffers all the limitations history puts upon him. And if an examination of morality allows for more than purely relative norms of conduct, these will still be historically conditioned in a way that poses grave difficulties for the location of any specific rules binding ''all men at all times.'' Perhaps we should be less ready to identify the notion of ''absolute'' with that of ''timeless.''

However, it is important to remember what form of temporality has been proved to belong to any possible human experience. All that has been shown is that man's self-presence must involve some possibility and facticity, some future and past as indicated in a first-person account. The time measured by a physicist, or in any spectator account, has not been proved to belong inescapably to existence as a questioner. There are many ways in which we may happen to objectivize and measure temporality, and the chapter will close by referring to a few of these.

Language and Time

The language with which we are familiar is adapted to identifying and relating events in time. We assume that the indicative mood is the basic one and that this expresses occurrences which were so, are now so, or will be so. We feel completely at home with the narrative form of history, with our ordinary descriptions of what is the case, and with the predictions scientists give us of what will happen at a precise time in the future.

However, such evidence as we have of the development of languages suggests that man's view of life was not always so clearly set in the manner of a chronology of dates. The ''moods'' of language which we call subjunctive or optative may come closer to translating primitive verbal forms than our indicative does. The sharp sense of a sequence of definite incidents may have developed slowly. The world was a theater of human desires and feelings before it became a laboratory of events to be recorded and timed. At least, an infant has little use for a clock.

The ''tenses'' in which we now express our verbs were not always so clearly defined. Future and past seem first to have been conveyed as a mere absence from the present, often carried by spatial words, and lacking in degrees more precise than ''near'' and ''remote.'' When distinctively temporal inflections developed in verbs, they were mainly adapted to distinguish actions as completed or continuing, as momentary or prolonged, as intense or merely repetitious.

That is, primitive language seems to have been concerned more with the temporal quality of personal action than with any quantitative measure of events in sequence. As with spatial words (cf. p. 165), a spectator account of events in time became possible when linguistic forms appeared which enabled the observer largely to neglect his own temporal involvement and see things as ''acting by themselves.'' Here there is a close connection with the growth of causal categories in language. A present event is the effect of a cause located ''in'' the past and producing a further effect "in" the future, with little regard to the way such occurrences express the facticity and possibility of the observer. The threat of rain in the afternoon is the result of falling pressure rather than a present warning to finish my work quickly. As such forms of ordering and measurement are introduced, one event can be seen as coming after another and yet before the present of the speaker. We can express our facticity in imperfect, past, perfect or pluperfect tenses.

However, the argument of Chapter Three applies here, that no language can reduce the observer to a completely timeless noninvolvement. Even in reporting simple facts (e.g., the desk is rough, heavy, and six feet wide) I am expressing a temporal activity in which I engage (e.g., running my hand along a surface, measuring, anticipating, and remembering). And no chronology or clock would tell me anything if its language were not the thoroughly human one of possibility and limitation.

Clock Time

The time we take today for "obvious" is that which clocks give us. It is a completely homogeneous receptacle for events, which differ temporally only by their situation in this empty container. According to the clock, the difference between a medieval document and one from the Renaissance is simply three hundred years: any "sense of the times" is irrelevant.

The growth of such a purely spectator version of time is, however, far from obvious. Only suggestions can be given of the many stages through which man passed from his earliest experience of time to that which made modern science possible. Times were highly particular long before they became indifferent dates. A definite time was always a "time for" or a "time when": a time for hunting or ploughing or sacrificing, a time when the rains came or the battle was fought. The indifference of a time scale required a high degree of detachment and a commonly accepted physical event which could be defined as "regular." Since light is the condition for most human activity, it is not surprising that the sun became the first clock. Our highly particular "times" were converted into a homogeneous series of positions occupied by a natural body.

It is important to remember that the regularity and repetitive form of the sun's movement, or of any other such clock, is a matter of definition rather than of experience. For the poet and for the historian, each dawn is unique. However, we have learned to ignore the novelty and accept each as "the same again." Why? Not because we wanted to enter more fully into the experience of time but because we wanted to withdraw from it and formulate an account of what we observe in terms as close as possible to the ideal of timeless truth described at the beginning of this chapter.

Aristotle shows this clearly. He recognized that the process of history is linear and felt that this escaped law and intelligibility. The best analogue he could find for the necessity of eternal truth was the cyclical movement of the heavenly bodies. What can be defined as sheer repetition is the closest we can come to necessity in what is changing: ''If the coming-to-be of any things is cyclical, it is 'necessary' that each of them is coming-to-be and has come-to-be.''[4] There is law or rationality in experience so far as we can say ''the same again.''

Indeed, the Greeks developed a cyclic view of history itself, making of it the human counterpart of the rotation of the heavens and repetition of the seasons. Historical knowledge would be the discovery of laws of recurrence. Herodotus thought of history as regulated by ''nemesis,'' a law of compensation which continuously restores the balance of things and from which no man can escape. Thucydides held that the purpose of history is to teach men wisdom in future crises, which must repeat the pattern of previous occurrences.

Though the notion of an eternal return has been abandoned in history, it may—with some important qualifications—be said to be the very basis for the natural sciences and for the great success man has had through them in imposing his will on nature. Numbers can be applied to experience only so far as this can be interpreted in terms of the same event coming again and again. The clock is not so much an instrument of science as the symbol of the whole scientific enterprise. Yet it is suggestive to reflect that our common experience of clock time is very close to the mythical account of activity as a repetition of archetpyes achieved perfectly and timelessly.

Psychological Time

If ''objectivity'' is identified with numbering (cf. p. 55), then only clock time is objective. But enough has been said in this book to question whether dependence on subjective activity and interpretation need always be written off as prejudice and distortion. Though a largely first-person account is ''primitive,'' it may disclose much that is lost in the objectifications of a spectator account. In a genuine sense, a tedious journey may take ''longer'' than an interesting one, whatever my watch tells me.

---

[4] *On Generation and Corruption* 338a. This quotation from Aristotle and those in Chapter Twelve are taken from the translations in the edition of the Oxford University Press.

This sense of the personal value of time is often opposed to clock time as "psychological time." The term may suggest an inaccurate estimate, and it is perhaps most commonly in this way that we use it. We get a shock when we realize that a boring lecture is only half over according to the clock and we accept the latter as "right," our own sense of time as misleading.

However, our frequent use of the terms "good time" and "bad time" may indicate more promising lines for an investigation of psychological time. What matters most is not what the clock tells us but the way we have used "our" time or "made" time for something of value. Here we remain close to the original experience of making ourselves present through a free and responsible expression of our possibility and facticity.

A final suggestion is that if the religious notion of "eternity" is to be interpreted, it may be wiser to think along such lines than in terms of clock time. If eternity is taken as endless time, the same again without even the problem of incorporating apparent novelties, the prospect is as unattractive as the idea is false to what such religious talk seems to intend. It would perhaps be better to take as a point of departure some experience of time well spent, of an achievement or self-realization that we report as an "instant" because the dispersion into past and future has been overcome in a remarkable way. The language of creativity would seem more appropriate than that of repetition.

11

Why Suffer?

Few questions are more personal than this. Suffering visits us all. None has escaped pain, sickness, failure, frustration, grief, and depression. We have all suffered the loss of others in death. And no assurance is firmer than that this will eventually, perhaps suddenly and absurdly, be our own fate.

Is there a "reason" for suffering? Or does it remain an irrational, unaccountable part of human existence? Academic philosophers are seldom consulted for advice on how to face suffering. It is here, above all, that theories seem inept. Yet the theme that suffering is an inescapable part of our life belongs to the central topics of Western philosophy. This chapter will try to situate our personal plight within the general analysis of what it means to live as a questioner. However each person faces the mystery of suffering, he is at least implying some theory of what it is about.

Suffering comes to us "from outside"; we do not invite it. Though modern English has lost the connection, other languages tell us that to suffer is to be passive. The word "passion" covers our confrontation with all forces that tend to overwhelm us from external agencies and from our own nature so far as we lose control. We suffer death, adversity, and our own moods, those irrational powers that are in us but not of us.

Hence the philosopher's task is to relate such personal experiences to an account of what it means to be passive. Though the topics of this chapter are more dramatic, the theme will return to the inquiry of Chapters Five and Six. There, in a most abstract way, the attempt was made to prove that a questioner must be both active and passive. He is in command as a self-present subject. Yet he is so only by objectivizing himself, finding how he appears through a variety of data, received ''from outside.'' The idiom of ''expression and discovery'' was largely intellectual. Here the notions are basically the same, but the language is more that of ''striving.'' The questioner is one who becomes what he is only by struggling to master the obstacles of materiality, of self-opposition and self-loss.

To stress that what we confront is *self*-opposition is not to dismiss our conviction that suffering comes from outside. As we shall see, philosophers can be divided into those who emphasize the ''interiority'' (rationality) or the ''exteriority'' (absurdity) of suffering. But the anguish of my situation is missed if I forget that suffering, though uninvited, is *mine*. If it were a sheer ''other,'' it would simply elude me. Passivity is possible only at the heart of activity. However alien the tragedies of life may be to what I intend, I do at least retain the active voice in saying that ''I suffer'' them.

Hence this chapter will begin with a brief summary of the way in which the knowledge and ignorance of a questioner shows itself as a structure of activity-in-passivity. Then this will serve as a metaphysical basis for a more descriptive approach to irrationality, to adversity, and finally to the extreme form that suffering takes in death.

Activity and Passivity in Questioning

We speak of being passive to forces that affect us or frustrate our intentions. Yet it is important to realize that the notions of activity and passivity belong to a first-person account and are not at home in the report of a spectator.

The physical sciences, at least, seem now to have reached the point of eliminating such notions. I may, if I wish, say that gravity is acting on a falling object or that a tree was felled by the wind. But any interpretation of physical forces in terms of push and pull, exertion and submission, is anthropomorphic. Talk of such forces is no more than an observer's record of how one event follows another. The cause of an event is itself the effect of a further cause. It is arbitrary whether we look upon the wind as cause or effect, and we are reading ourselves into the picture if we translate as agent or patient. The ideal of a spectator's report is a purely mathematical account—and numbers neither act nor suffer.

The notions of activity and passivity find a place only in a first-person account of what it is to be a person of a certain sort, with purposes he makes his own rather than merely with behavior as observed by another. I am active in running for a train because it is my project to get to work on time. I am passive so far as my intention is impeded or frustrated by my fatigue, my miscalculation, or my sheer misfortune. There is room for a complex description of the ways I suffer and of the degrees of interiority that my passivity takes. But the description will tell of my struggle to be a subject, not of an object in a network of forces.

The account of temporality in the previous chapter could be translated into an analysis of the way both activity and passivity constitute what I am. The original sense of the future is of possibility, of my ability to act in various ways. This, however, is defined and limited by my past, by what I have already been made. In this sense, my past is what I "suffer." Whether victim or beneficiary, I am the recipient of the body, temperament, and social situation in which I was born. My possibilities as an athlete are conditioned by my lot as a six-footer or as an arthritic patient. Yet the precise form my passivity takes will depend on my activity of interpreting it. Poor health may become a stimulus to success or an excuse for withdrawal. Riches may lead to effort or to sloth. My past is not a sheer determination from outside. *What* I suffer depends on the way I "actively" suffer.

Proof of the necessity of both activity and passivity, and an account of their relation, will come from a renewed analysis of the place of knowledge and ignorance in questioning. The right to translate the self-presence of knowledge into the language of activity arises from the fact that what we have been examining in all previous chapters is the *agency* of questioning. The inescapable structure of knowledge is my ability to question, to confront the world actively with the intention of disclosing what is so. Self-presence is an achievement, not a datum.

In the same way, ignorance is no mere "void" but a highly personal frustration, a passivity that can cover the bitterest suffering and pain. The inescapable structure of ignorance is my *need* to question, to struggle for self-realization in order to become what I am. The obstacles are intimate. Even when I feel most at home with myself, I find that the "self" is a stranger, a series of roles I play and about which I can be mistaken. Self-knowledge is won through self-opposition, through enduring failure and trying again. I am bound by my limited point of view, by my changing moods, by my hidden past. I suffer myself in order to be myself.

So the relation of activity and passivity is that of knowledge and ignorance. There is submission to ''otherness'' in all I do: I come to myself only ''from outside.'' Yet without some achievement there could be no suffering: through the obstacles of spatial and temporal existence I do find myself and recognize these *as* obstacles. This, at least, is the abstract scheme with which we shall now approach some of the more evident forms of suffering and examine the accounts that philosophers have given of them.

Irrationality

The first topic is in some ways the most confusing. If we say that someone acted under the influence of ''passion,'' we mean that he was led by forces that were in him but not of his control. He acted ''irrationally,'' i.e., in a way that was not self-directed through reasons he clearly saw and chose. Passion limits a subject's ''own'' activity.

Yet it is here we see most poignantly that suffering is the way to true activity as much as its limit. Without passion we lose the sensitivity and intensity that belong to being human and acting truly. To describe someone as thoroughly rational is not always a compliment. Rationality and irrationality are not simple alternatives. If we are to clarify what is involved, a historical excursion may help.

The Principle of Sufficient Reason

The notion that what is ''fully real'' must be thoroughly rational has a long history in Western philosophy. For Plato, ''the perfectly real is perfectly knowable,'' and Aristotle's scale of life (cf. pp. 116–17) culminates in the ''self-thinking thought.'' That is, to *be* fully is to attain complete self-presence and self-realization, the highest level of ''truth'' and ''goodness''; in relation to this norm, all particular beings can be assigned some limited degree of being, intelligibility, and value.

The tradition goes back even further. One of the pre-Socratic philosophers, Parmenides, expressed it in his statement that ''knowing and being are the same.'' In other words, to the extent that I fail to be rational, I fail even to be. In modern philosophy, this sense of a fundamental harmony has been repeatedly affirmed, in particular by the philosophers we call ''rationalists.'' For Leibniz it became the ''principle of sufficient reason'': ''No fact can be real or existing and no proposition can be true unless there is a sufficient reason why it should be thus and not otherwise, even though these reasons most often cannot be known to us.'' (*Monadology,* § 32) Or, as Hegel put it: ''What is reasonable is actual, and what is actual is reasonable.''[1]

Two comments may make this abstract metaphysical principle seem less obscure and perhaps less outlandish. The first is that it translates our common assurance that for every genuine question we ask there must be an answer, even if we have not yet found it or even if no one ever will. The burden is here put on the word ''genuine.'' But would science or any intellectual pursuit be possible if we were sure that there is a final irrationality, an absolute ''no answer'' to our quest?

The second comment is that the principle of sufficient reason is found in religious dress as belief in ''Providence.'' The believer seems convinced that there is a good reason for all that happens. He says: However great your sorrow and problems, however little you understand them yourself, basically all is well and right. You are in God's hands. He is all-good, all-wise, and all-powerful. Though life may seem chaotic and unjust, in the final account reason and justice will prevail.

Nevertheless, many modern philosophers have reacted strongly against such forms of rationalism. Attacks have been levelled at Hegel in particular, starting in his own day. And it is not only the Marxists who have seen religious views as ''the opium of the people.'' Briefly, rationalism of this sort has been taken as foolish and as dangerous. Surely it is foolish to look at the world and say complacently that all is ''finally'' reasonable and right. Is it not mere escapism to make such statements in full sight of the absurdity and waste and tragedy that confront us, the earthquakes and famines and plagues, the freaks of nature and follies of man, the misfortune of the good and the success of the evil? Worse still, such teaching of an ultimate rationality is highly dangerous. For it offers an easy passage to the doctrine that whatever is so is as it should be, that might is right, and that injustice should be tolerated patiently. Hegel is often regarded as the philosopher of totalitarianism, and religion is criticized as turning our attention from the wrongs of this world to a complacent belief that they must be resolved in some future life.

What is the alternative? The empiricist would say that there is no point in introducing any metaphysical claim that life is finally either rational or irrational. Let us simply go on asking questions, both theoretical and personal, and gladly accept such answers as may come to us and such compromises as we can make. For most practical purposes, this attitude can serve. Yet it is not only metaphysicians who have looked for some more comprehensive statement. Our question about the place of passion in our life may receive more light if we examine the views of those

---

[1] In the preface to his *Philosophy of Law*; he also defends this as no remarkable doctrine but as a common principle of experience in his *Encyclopedia,* § 6.

who affirm some ultimate irrationality or absurdity. The existentialists (e.g., Camus) have much to say on this. But we shall look a century earlier at Friedrich Nietzsche (1844–1900). He was one of the most eloquent critics of a dispassionate rationalism, and his ideas became popular during the turmoils of the present century.

Nietzsche: Dionysian and Apollonian Attitudes

As a student, Nietzsche came across the writings of Schopenhauer (1788–1860), whose philosophy bears some similarity to the doctrines of Buddhism. Nietzsche was also impressed with the view of life as a tragic expression of will and passion. He refused, however, to find any solution in a withdrawal from striving. He sought instead to affirm life to its fullest, and he found a clue to this in his analysis of two basic attitudes which he traced back to the Greeks (cf. particularly *The Birth of Tragedy*).

According to Nietzsche, the Greeks recognized acutely the terror, mystery, and precariousness of life. Their achievement was to transform it through the medium of art. This, however, was accomplished in two ways, symbolized by the gods Dionysus and Apollo. In the Dionysian or Bacchic rites the votaries overcome all restraints and seek union with the primordial forces. All veils through which we normally see things are cast aside, impulse and passion are allowed to sweep all barriers away, and existence is triumphantly affirmed in its darkness and horror. Apollo, however, is the symbol of an attitude that treats life as rational, regular, and harmonious. A veil is drawn over the elemental forces and they are transmuted into an ideal world of form, order, propriety, and intelligibility. We step back from our primitive experience and contemplate the *logos* of things.

From this analysis Nietzsche became a critic of culture. And his criticism of most cultures, notably that of his own day, was that the Apollonian attitude has forced the Dionysian underground. The *logos* has dominated; instead of life we have biology, and psychology has made us soulless. Our politics of democracy and socialism has established a uniform mediocrity hostile to genius. Christianity has devalued the body, stifled impulse, instinct, and passion. The result of such repression is that we face the revenge of vital forces, the repeated threat of a new barbarism. The veil of order is drawn thinly over violence.

For Nietzsche, true culture must involve full recognition of each of these basic attitudes. The irrational is not, as we think, a mere lack of rationality. The Persian sage, Zarathustra, was far closer to the truth in speaking of an eternal conflict between ultimate principles of light and of darkness. It is from the irrational that genius appears. Ideas and values do not come from an accepted harmony : man creates them from the abundance of his own life of impulse and passion.

The Challenge
to Reason

This account of Nietzsche's position has been given simply as an example of the way some maintain that the irrational is a basic force that cannot be "put in its place" by any intellectualist account of the world. Illustrations could be multiplied from other sources, notably from such thinkers as Kierkegaard, Rudolf Otto, and Karl Barth, who feel that religion presents us with a genuine account of the mystery of life and is constantly threatened by the rationalizing of philosophers and theologians.

Such challenges to the "Apollonian strain" of Western thought have appeared at all times. They have served as a constant reminder that every intellectual account is inadequate to the originality and creativity of life and reflects the limitations of its author. Temperament plays a great part in all experience, even in the most abstract thinking. Aristotle, Aquinas, and Hegel were all conditioned by their own "past," and their systems suffer from this.

However, to agree that particular rational accounts are all limited by background and in need of challenge is far from admitting that this challenge can be seen on the model of some final irrationality. Our very concern to find a place for the elemental forces that upset and create will not allow any model that leads to self-destruction. There remains a sense in which the rational is absolute and the irrational is relative. Nietzsche did not simply immerse himself in the darkness of the primordial. He brought his most passionate feelings to the light of rational expression in language and so communicated them to us. Again, his ideal of a unity or synthesis of two attitudes is itself an aim at harmony or form and hence "Apollonian."

There are various ways in which this can be put as an argument to show that any attempt to set reason, truth or knowledge below anything else, or simply apart from it, is self-destructive. If I say that "life is finally absurd or irrational," then I am affirming it as meaningful or rational that life (including my assessment of it) is irrational. The activity of denying rationality or of setting any absolute limit to it implicitly contradicts what I am trying to say or to think.

Such an argument may appear as a trick. However, it is offered, not as a cheap rejection of the impulsive or passionate forces of life, but rather as an invitation to a deeper experience of them that may effectively challenge accepted norms of "reason." For such forces come into their own as a revision and extension of rationality rather than as an alternative to it. Critics like Nietzsche have helped us to recognize more fully the complexity and subtlety of reason, the many different ways in which we know, and the varieties of experience that are brought to light as intelligible and communicable. We are self-questioners, open to repeated challenge from the ignorance at the heart of our knowledge.

This does not prevent us from retaining some pejorative sense for the word "rationalism" and applying it to certain philosophers. There is both foolishness and danger in a fixed system of thought and in an optimistic disregard for the tragedy of life and the brutality of fate. But the more we recognize the obscurity around us and in us, the more we affirm "reason"; for it is only within the horizon of rationality that anything can stand out as absurd.

Much that we have learned in this century has appeared as a threat to our complacency in man as a "rational animal." The violence with which Freud's views were met is a phenomenon that Nietzsche could have quoted to his purpose. But the fact remains that Freud's achievement was supremely rational. He brought us self-knowledge where before we had been lost in ignorance and misunderstanding. Yet this achievement can be secured only through a firm realization of the primacy of reason. If knowledge is subordinate to libido and if all theories are no more than the outcome of purely sexual states, then so is Freudian theory. If all doctrines are said to be the mere resultant of economic or geographical or temperamental or any other "non-rational" factors, then so is this doctrine itself and nothing has been said. Put sex outside reason and you take all the fun out of Freud.

Perhaps Nietzsche is right in hoping to restore creativity by renewing our appreciation of the Dionysian elements of life. Our present situation fits all too well his vision of violence under the mask of order. But the dualism that sets up ultimate principles of form and the formless, though of long-standing appeal to the popular imagination, is of little use for an account of the *self*-opposition which is our most intimate experience as questioners.

Adversity

The above account of irrationality has been more concerned with finding an appropriate way of seeing its place in our life than with describing how passion can aid us to "enlarge" reason and become more sensitive to what is so. Indications of what such a description would involve will be left to the following chapter. There we shall ask how the symbolic world of art helps us to bring our life or feeling and passion to the light of expression.

Our temperament is "suffered," in the broad meaning we are allowing for this word. However the interiority of suffering, its status as *self*-opposition, becomes less easy to accept as we pass from our moods and irrational impulses to forces we think of as clearly external. Physical sickness, sudden tragedy, and the opposition of others are thrown at us from outside. In this section we shall put them under the term "adversity" and consider the tendency of philosophers to stress either the uses of adversity or its remaining mystery. The extreme case of an assault from outside, death, will be left to a final section.

From our account of the place of activity and passivity in questioning, we can conclude that some suffering must belong to all. And as we are passive to what is at least partially external, then we can say that suffering must *come* to all. But the precise form that adversity takes is a matter for description rather than metaphysics. There may be societies in which sickness and social problems do not feature. Medicine and technology may eventually master many of our ills. However, some struggle against adversity must be an intimate part of any Utopia we imagine. To remove all obstacles is to remove all questioning. Strife can be sublimated, but if it were to disappear, even the qualities we most desire would lose the very framework in which we understand them. As Graham Greene pointed out, centuries of war in Italy were the setting for the world's greatest art, while a corresponding period of peace in Switzerland gave us chocolate bars and the cuckoo clock.

Does this "explain" adversity? No philosopher has thought that reading his books will remove our pain or even set our minds at rest. Yet some have gone to great lengths to develop a system of thought in which the necessity of suffering is proposed as a key to the development of experience. Hegel has already been mentioned in this connection, and a further word may help to clarify the philosophical alternatives.

Hegel's system stands as one of the most comprehensive efforts to see a reason in adversity. Though the assault and "negativity" of suffering appears always as a curse, it is a blessing in disguise. For it is no accident but the very principle of life. Man's existence is a repeated "recovery of self" from the many ways in which he seems to lose himself and to be at the mercy of outside forces. Subjectivity is not a possession we simply have. It is achieved in many "grades" through objectifications which we suffer. Life offers no simple passage but is "a process of repeated self-opposition," involving all "the seriousness, the suffering, the patience, and the toil of negativity." We find our true strength, not by shrinking from death, but rather by enduring it in countless forms. The power of a subject is to ''look the negative in the face and transform it into being.'' (from the preface to the *Phenomenology of Mind*)

These quotations indicate Hegel's vast project. On a theoretical level, it is an effort to interpret all that comes to us ''from outside'' as really ''our own,'' as an aspect of man's search to express and find what he fully is. On a practical level, the invitation is for us to experience all adversity as constructive, to use it in such a way that we make sense of apparent ''facticity.'' Hegel tells us to take ''otherness'' seriously but to realize that it is no irreducible force: the deeper our experience of suffering, the more we can appropriate and humanize it. Life is tragic, but tragedy is human.

The criticism Hegel himself suffered at the hands of Marx has been considered in Chapter Eight (pp. 144–45). According to Marx, Hegel's ''idealism'' trivializes the sheer otherness we find in nature. We cannot explain the evils of life in terms of man's progressive self-realization. Mind and its interpretations are themselves the product of an ultimate other. No theory or attitude of mind will convert negativity. There are material and social situations in which we simply cannot express and find ourselves. Suffering is alienation, and this cannot be explained away as a necessary stage on the road to becoming fully human.

The claim that adversity represents an irreducible otherness is of long standing. Religious people, in particular, seem repeatedly to have been drawn to the view that suffering is a mystery which calls for faith rather than for explanation. The interpretation of Greek philosophers, that evil is a mere lack or ''privation'' of good, though officially adopted by orthodox Christianity, was never left undisputed. The young Augustine accepted this doctrine as a condition for his return to the Christian religion, but it has been questioned whether he ever really abandoned the Manichean faith in an eternal conflict between equal principles of good and evil. Suffering, like the scorpion presented to him in one of his disputes, is a stinging reality rather than a mere absence.

In modern times it is existentialist thinkers, from Kierkegaard to Sartre, who have presented the most radical alternative to Hegel. Whether theist or atheist, they have stressed our inability to account for the sheer tragedy of life. For Sartre, a Hegelian-type philosophy aims at a final reconciliation of all opposition; but this ideal of ''being one's other'' is, he claims, chimerical. Man ''is what he is not and is not what he is'': in his struggle to appropriate all in his own self-identity, he is condemned to perpetual failure (cf. *Being and Nothingness*, pp. lxv, 622–23).

In these different philosophical approaches to adversity there seem to be opposing temperaments at work. That which leaves it as a mystery rather than trying to incorporate it in an ''explanation'' is probably the

more popular. Faced with any personal tragedy, we feel that all attempts
at supplying a reason are hopelessly short of the mark; something is
there which has come upon us inexplicably and must persist outside any
account we can give. Nevertheless, to affirm that suffering is a mystery or
an irreducibly alien force is still to make a theoretical statement. And
the question remains whether this theory does more or less justice than
other theories to our situation as we confront adversity.

Again, we must ask what are the conditions of possibility for experi-
encing anything *as* a mysterious or absurd incursion into our life. The
absurdity of a personal tragedy can stand out as such only within some
basic conviction that there ''ought to be'' a reason for whatever happens.
Rationalist philosophers and smooth preachers may be too quick to supply this, but the image of an ultimate alien force may fit the experience
of suffering less well than a model of explanation which allows the bitterness of suffering to grow with the interiority of self-opposition.

The philosopher René Le Senne speaks of degrees of suffering. There
is the ''accident,'' in which one object impedes another. There is ''frustration,'' in which a subject encounters the resistance of an object. And
there is ''conflict,'' in which a subject is divided against himself. Without analyzing this scheme closely, we can see it as suggesting grades of
interiority in suffering. An accident is suffered only so far as it frustrates
my intentions or hopes. And frustration is suffered more intensely, the
more I find myself divided in my own intentions rather than opposed
from ''outside.'' My present cold is a form of suffering, not because
bacteria are clashing with antibodies, nor even because my physical state
impedes my work, but most intimately because my intention to work is
at war with my intention to yield to the lethargy of sickness which is
''mine.''

What is indicated is that the ''otherness'' of suffering, far from
being a simply alien principle, is experienced to the extent that it is
interiorized. At the heart of all adversity is self-conflict. It is not sheer
physical loss that upsets me but the loss of something or of someone
that is truly ''part of me.'' Failure frightens me, but the *claim* that
man is a perpetual failure serves as a tranquillizer: it supports a far less
profound sense of failure than the claim that man *should* be what he is
through his self-expressions.

Death

The theme of this chapter has been that suffering is indeed a mystery,
and that the ineptness of all ''reasons'' forces us repeatedly to expand
our notion of ''reason,'' but that this serves to renew our conviction of

rationality. Mystery can be recognized as such only within the project of making sense of our life. To see what this means, and what further questions are raised, we need to look in more detail at an example of adversity. So we shall turn to death as the ultimate attack "from out-side."

Ways of Describing Death

Death is all around us. We read of it each day in the newspapers and see it on the road. We feel its horror in the intimacy of our own circle of friends. Yet, for all our familiarity with death as a natural event, how does it enter into our experience? How do we truly "suffer" it rather than merely observe it? I see death as the doctor does. I stand by as someone passes from life to death. I take part in the funeral rites and in concern for the dead. I may calculate the years that are likely to remain for me. I see my own death as an event "in" the future. But even there I am dealing only with "a case of death." My very attempt to "assist" another in dying reveals the distance between death as an event that comes to all and "my death."

The theme of mortality offers a clear example of the way in which the distinction between first- and third-person accounts is applied. My house, and even my temperament, may be described by a spectator who sets them in a class with the houses and temperaments of others. But the reduction of my own death to a case of death is a change of topic as well as of viewpoint.

We shall first examine a traditional philosophical account of death which falls in the third person. Then more recent attempts to give a first-person account of "my death" will be considered. Finally we shall draw on these attempts in order to suggest how the whole question of activity-in-passivity is summed up in the ambiguity of making something of our life and yet radically losing it.

The Death of Others

We treat death as spectators when we regard it as a purely biological event. This is perfectly legitimate. Death is an event in nature. Flowers die, dogs die, and humans die. The event is basically the same in all cases. There is a problem only in establishing the norm of death. Once we thought that the "moment of death" came when the heart stopped beating. Now we speak of irreversible chemical reactions, but the criterion is dubious and at least those who have their bodies refrigerated question it.

I can view my own death this way. And so I should, to the extent that my concern is with insurance and legacies, medicine and cemeteries. But to treat death solely as a physical event is to remove it from the categories of activity and passivity (cf. pp. 186–87). The rearrangement of chemical compounds is nothing which I ''do'' or ''suffer'': it simply occurs and is recorded by the survivors. However, if death is in any way open to a first-person account in terms of agency, then to absolutize the biological account is itself to try to *be* mortal in a certain way. This we shall consider at the end of the chapter.

Philosophers have not been content to repeat the facts of biology. Starting with older religious beliefs, they have seen death as a problem and many have posed it as a question whether anything ''survives'' death. At least since Plato, a tradition has existed which has said that man's ''body'' ceases at death but that his ''soul'' lives on, though this does not seem to have been the Biblical view.

Now such talk of ''immortality'' in terms of the ''separation of body and soul'' is as much a spectator account of death as is a purely biological version. The loss of a limb through amputation is a tragedy which is not conveyed by the surgeon's clinical account of separating one member from the body. Similarly, talk of the separation of my whole body from my ''soul'' or ''self'' (even if this makes sense) falls into the genre of clinical reports and misses the tragedy of dying. What is said is that my body dies but I do not. Reports of the ''future life'' as involving the possibility of extreme sanctions may add terror—but my concern would be about the penalties after death rather than about death itself.

This is not to say that traditional arguments for the immortality of the soul cannot be reinterpreted. But it is to say that the language of separation must be rephrased in a manner that gets away from the viewpoint of the observer and from spectator-problems about what a soul does when removed from the world and from all embodiment.

The ''separation'' account also renews the question what we mean by ''body'' and ''soul'' in any discussion of death. If my body is to be taken in the third-person as this particular thing I measure, feed, and clothe, then the account of the biologist and undertaker is enough. But much of this book has been concerned to discover a meaning for embodiment (self-opposition) and for spirituality (self-presence) that is more primitive than any report of measurement and of particular appearances. Such a meaning treats spirit and body as correlative terms (presence-in-opposition) and makes talk of one existing simply apart from the other unintelligible. It is to a first-person account of this sort that we must turn if we wish to understand what it is to *be* mortal (in oneself) rather than merely to *appear* mortal (for an observer).

MY DEATH

Such a description is of recent date in philosophy. But its antecedents go far back. The Bible does not talk of the survival of a spiritual soul but treats death rather as the close of our possibility of making something of our life. All we do in the world contributes to our basic choice, but the possibility of choosing runs up against a tragic limit. And criticism of the "separation" doctrine as irrelevant to our life of acting and suffering was not absent among early philosophers. Epicurus drew a logical conclusion: "Death does not concern us. For when we are, death is not there; and when death is there, we are no longer. Therefore, death does not concern us."

However, death does concern us. Or if we say it does not, this is because we have taken a stand of "no concern" toward it rather than because the prospect of death in no way enters into the manner we lead our life. It is interest in the way death is personally present to us that has led many philosophers in this century to write on the topic. According to them, death is not merely an event set somewhere "in" the future; "my death" belongs to the structure of my present experience. The word "my" can nowhere be applied more intimately.

In turning from a spectator- to a participant-account of death, we pass from "clock time" to "lived time." My present is not a mere "now" to be measured as it slips by but is a way in which I make myself present by collecting the facticity of my past and the possibility of my future. In such terms, my death is with me always as the limit of possibilities with which I can reckon. The experience of mortality is involved in every choice I make; a "mortal" is one for whom the field is not wide open.

If we want an image for this interpretation of death, we can find none in natural events, for example in the stopping of the rain. Whether it stops in a few minutes or goes on for ever, the present rain is the same. More fruitful hints are to be found in the realm of art. Each moment of a play or of a musical composition is structured by the conclusion which bounds it to make it a meaningful whole. The end is not an event which finally happens to come but is a fulfillment anticipated from the beginning.

Similarly, my "present of things anticipated" involves some reckoning with my possibilities as bounded and with my choices as decisive. So far as I enter into my present action, I am not merely turning out something "good enough for now." I am evaluating my life as a whole, taking a step I never have the chance to recover. I make present a life that had a beginning and faces an end.

Alternatively, we can see such descriptions in the light of our general problem of activity-in-passivity, of achievement through suffering. The death I anticipate in each act is the supreme achievement of my life. Reinterpretation is possible at each stage, but the "finality" of any particular choice foreshadows that interpretation of my life as a whole which comes with its conclusion : then alone can the biography be written. When a building has been completed, it is for the first time wholly there and can begin its life as a human dwelling. But man fulfills his life, he is wholly there, only when he loses his life.

To speak of death merely as fulfillment and achievement is one-sided. Such "edification" evaporates in the presence of anyone dying in pain or of an aged person losing his faculties. Death is equally to be seen, and experienced, as the opposite of fulfillment. It is that which makes achievement impossible, the supreme impotence, tragic helplessness and decay. It comes to us uninvited and unexpected, that absence of self-realization which has been tasted throughout our life in all our suffering and determination by forces beyond our control. Even our triumphs carry an emptiness which is a foretaste of the collapse at the end. Man is a creature who "sits in the darkness of the shadow of death."

Whether such an account of death can be given coherently is by no means sure, and some of the questions will be raised below. But the aim at least may be clear. It is to avoid treating death as a phenomenon to be observed by another and to show how we ourselves experience mortality as agents and sufferers. Attention is turned away from an event located in the future and from problems about dividing man into a part that is mortal and a part that is immortal. Instead, death becomes a structure of what we *are,* and the topic of immortality—though removed from any facile solution—becomes a question of man as a whole, inescapably agent and sufferer.

The Ambiguity of Death

If death is inseparably achievement and failure, a consistent account is not easy, and it is to be expected that philosophers who have attempted it will incline to one or the other extreme. As in other interpretations of suffering, I can tend to stress the humanity of dying as that which I "do" or the absurdity of dying as that by which I am overcome.

THE HUMANITY OF DYING

Heidegger was one of the first to write seriously on the first-person experience of death. He is certainly not to be ranked among the rationalist philosophers, but his work on this topic can be seen as an effort to "interiorize" death, to show how we inescapably take some attitude toward it which characterizes our life as a whole.

As was suggested in Chapter Four, it is impossible simply to "opt out" of choices that confront us. Once I am aware of the government's policy on some basic issue, I cannot avoid taking a stand. Even to "do nothing," to delay making up my mind or to cultivate indifference, is to adopt an attitude and express my mind. There, of course, no philosophical investigation will be sufficient to decide which policy is right or to say that evasive attitudes may not be best for the time. And if my political position must color my whole life, this needs to be shown.

However, Heidegger maintains that the attitude we take toward our death can be classified as "authentic" or "inauthentic" and that this is decisive for what we make of our life. Our "everyday" attitudes tend to trivialize the experience of mortality. They represent various ways of evading this fundamental feature of our existence as a "being-toward-death." We talk "about" death much as we might about a distant war in which we have only remote interest and for which we feel no responsibility. We console a dying person by telling him he may escape death, and we console ourselves by a complacent concern with everyday affairs that puts the radical options of a limited life safely into the background.

The details of Heidegger's description and the status of the moral alternative he poses need not concern us. What is of importance is that he views mortality as a call to decision that makes our life as a whole authentic or evasive. For him, death is "the possibility of impossibility." The tragedy of being mortal is certainly stressed. But death comes to us in the present as the possibility of· making something of our life as a whole.

THE ABSURDITY OF DYING

Sartre defines death rather as the "impossibility of possibility." The preceding account is for him "idealist" and "humanist":

> . . . Death as the end of life is interiorized and humanized. Man can no longer encounter anything but the human; there is no longer any *other side* of life, and death is a human phenomenon of life and is still life. As such it influences the entire life by a reverse flow. . . . I become responsible for *my* death as for my life.[2]

Instead, what Sartre emphasizes is the absurdity of death, the fact that it comes to us from outside as utterly nonhuman. We cannot appropriate death in any way to find a "right" way for leading our life. We are like condemned prisoners preparing ourselves for a brave performance on the scaffold and then suddenly carried off by a flu epidemic.

---

[2] *Being and Nothingness,* p. 532.

What Sartre opposes is not the effort to describe how mortality enters our present experience: "Death haunts me at the very heart of each of my projects as their inevitable reverse side." What he objects to is the claim of the philosopher to make sense of death by determining what attitudes toward it are authentic or inauthentic. Death belongs to my facticity, but I am at liberty to make any meaning of this I can manage:

> I am not "free to die," but I am a free mortal. Since death escapes my projects because it is unrealizable, I myself escape death in my very project. . . . Although there are innumerable possible attitudes with which we may confront this unrealizable which "in the bargain" is to be realized, there is no place for classifying these attitudes as authentic or inauthentic. . . .[3]

Certainly much that Sartre says is right. Death is absurd, and the attempt to "interiorize" it as a structure of my present experience should not lose sight of this. Once again, however, the question is whether we can recognize absurdity except within meaning, and whether we can talk of the invasion of an "utterly nonhuman element from outside" except within a context that is "humanist." Sartre is no less ready than Epicurus to draw the logical consequence of his position, that since death is a sheer "other," it is irrelevant to any project I make or any way I confront life. I cannot take into account what is utterly unaccountable. But if so, why all the talk about it?

THE REMAINING QUESTION

What can an analysis of questioning suggest for assessing philosophical attempts to talk about death? And what follows for the highly personal topic of "immortality," to which such attempts may be but a preliminary?

This chapter has been based on a study of the activity and passivity that are inseparably involved in being a questioner. By this standard, suspicion is thrown on any account of death, or view of immortality, which tries to separate these two elements of questioning by denying one or the other.

Some interpretations of death are suspect in that they seem to deny our agency, the possibility of the future in all we do. Radical despair would be a practical attitude that falls under this criticism; utterly to abandon hope is to deny the future, the "I can" that gives structure to my present. On a theoretical level, the same denial results from absolutizing a purely biological account of death. To say definitively that my life

---

[3] *Ibid.*, pp. 547–48.

is bounded by annihilation, by the completely nonhuman, is to say (perhaps paradoxically) that I *do* not die. The agency of dying, of facing an unknown future, is simply removed: *my* death is reduced to the death of another, recorded by an observer. But a questioner can not so easily escape from *being* mortal.

Other interpretations of death are suspect in seeming to deny the element of passivity, the lack of self-determination, that limits the way we are self-present as questioners. Here we have presumption rather than despair. A naively spiritual interpretation of the immortality of the soul would fall under this criticism so far as it suggests any simple passage of the self from embodiment in the world to an "acosmic" existence. Materiality cannot be shed, and mortality is more than a change of scenery in a play without conclusion.

Where do such comments lead? They have been negative, rejections rather than proposals. Most people, in reading philosophical accounts of death, expect to find a definite "yes" or "no" to the question of immortality. Yet any such simple answer would withdraw us from the experience of questioning in what may be its most personal form. Perhaps all the philosopher can contribute here is negative. It is the insistence that, whatever our "position" on death and immortality, we should not trivialize our experience of questioning but respect it and renew it. My death, like my life, involves both openness to the future and recognition that I do not simply control my fate but receive what comes. However I regard my death, it is "mine" only so far as it expresses both the agency and the suffering of a questioner.

12

How Do I Feel?

One of our most common greetings is the question, ''How are you?'' The reply may be an assurance that I feel fine or a recital of my latest heartaches. It is my feelings that set the tone for my day. To live as a questioner is to find oneself a creature of feeling.

This book has examined the structures of any question we ask and the variety of questions through which we make sense of our life. Indeed, the very concern to prove that questioning is inescapable prepares us for a much wider view of its varieties than the dictionary may encourage. Any way we have of going out into the world in order to find ourselves is a manner of questioning. The first cry of an infant is a question. Our very bodily existence, our most inarticulate moods and gestures, reveal us as perplexed knowers.

This is not to minimize the importance of strictly verbal questioning. It is through language that we reflect explicitly on our questioning. So it is understandable that philosophers have concentrated on questions that are put in words. However, our pride at possessing the world in words may leave us with the doubt that something has been lost in the process. Myth and ritual preceded philosophy as ways of asking ''deep'' questions. And wherever he has lived, man has shaped matter into non-practical, purely artistic forms that somehow express his feeling and his quest for what he is about.

This chapter will be concerned with feeling and with art as a basic way in which we express and possess it. The problems are great of talking in words about what escapes words. But this is a challenge offered by the previous chapter. The claim that nothing can be simply outside reason involves an acceptance that our views of what is the "right" form of reason are open to repeated revision "from within."

The Mood
of Questioning

Our moods were listed in the last chapter among the many uninvited forces we suffer. They seem to be in us yet not strictly of us. The term is vague, but we commonly oppose moods to knowledge or rationality. A person ruled by moods is looked upon as handicapped in his search for truth. His emotions and feelings confine him to a private world and need to be mastered or set aside if he is to break out to the sober realm of what holds for any dispassionate knower.

At best we might be prepared to say that some moods are a condition for knowledge but do not themselves belong to understanding. If I am in the mood for studying, then I may learn that the theorem of Pythagoras is true. But my grasp of the content of any truth in mathematics or physics is not a matter of mood. The feelings which a scientist has when he records a fact or discovers a law are irrelevant to what he discloses.

However, this common conviction of the purely intellectual nature of knowledge loses some of its force when we turn to other realms. Our feelings are involved in getting to know a person or in recognizing the qualities a poet sees in nature. And are we so certain that our way of appreciating persons or art is altogether foreign to mathematics and science? It is one thing to draw conclusions from a theorem or predict facts from a scientific law—it is quite another to see what construction line will open the way for proof of a theorem or to hit upon the law which gives meaning to a disarray of observations. Here we may appeal to an "imagination" or "creative insight" which some people have and which cannot strictly be taught. The very project of science to see the world in terms of mathematical laws springs from a mood, a way of feeling, which was not prominent in earlier ages.

If there is a mood *of* questioning, as well as a mood *for* questioning, this should not surprise us. Our moods belong to what we have described as our materiality, that limitation of a questioner to a situation from which he has to make sense of the world in some particular way. Just as I see the room from a certain angle, so my moods give me an "angle" on any interpretation, some sense for what can appear.

As elsewhere, materiality both limits my self-presence and is the arena in which I come to myself. I am ruled by my moods as by an alien force: they keep me from myself. Yet it is through my moods that I become "sensitive" to the great variety of ways in which I can overcome this estrangement and acquire a feel for things.

Long before a child discovers a world of shapes and sizes, he can identify and respond to moods as soothing or threatening, cheerful or depressing, confident or anxious. Before man could make a map of a locality, he recognized it as forbidding or luring, uncanny or familiar, energetic or peaceful. When he had as yet no adjectives to describe movement as fast or slow, he had a rich repertoire of words to reveal it as hurried, restless, furious, impulsive, restrained, or cautious.

It seems that the qualities by which we interpret the world are expressive of such moods before any thoroughly impersonal "it" is recognized and the third-person account of science becomes possible. The whispering of the wind and rustling of the curtain, the shadow darting over the floor, all belong to the vaguely personal before they are formulated as the effect of one thing on another. The personification of nature in myths is neither deliberate artifice nor sheer mistake.

The fact that mythical accounts have by and large given way to scientific ones is not lightly to be dismissed. We do need to master our moods and step out of the capricious world of feeling if we are to determine public norms of truth and falsity.

Yet the question remains whether the privacy of moods may not be mastered in forms that do not banish or lose the qualities of feeling as the anonymous world of science does. The claim of the following sections is that art is one such way of "recollecting" our feelings, of finding ourselves in them rather than merely suffering them.

The Reason for Art

To suggest that art is a way of questioning the world may appear odd, but art springs from wonder or fascination. The term "aesthetic excitement" is sometimes used, and this seems particularly appropriate for the earliest forms of artistic expression. These suggest that primitive man was thrilled by certain objects which stood out from his struggle for survival. His mind was caught by something of no practical significance and he felt the need to represent it "by itself" rather than for any evident purpose in his hard life. We may remember the strangeness that certain objects held for us as children, the fascination they exerted on us. Even the higher animals seem occasionally to exhibit such an attitude.

How are we to understand this? The very "uselessness" of art makes it hard to interpret. We explain activities most easily by saying what they are for. And it is perhaps a weakness of some of the traditional accounts of art that they have tried to impose a nonartistic purpose. This section will begin by examining two such theories which philosophers have developed. The first is that art is an imitation of what can be known without art, a surrogate or a preparation for other types of experience. The second is that art is one way of giving vent to our emotions and feelings. The parallel with two theories of language may be noticed (cf. pp. 154–56). A similar criticism will be proposed here, that such accounts miss the distinctively symbolic character of man's artistic expression. This criticism will then form the basis for a view of art as an intellectual expression of feeling.

Art as Imitation

Plato refers to the first two theories and regards each as a reason for excluding artists from the ideal state:

> We may take a poet as the counterpart of a painter. Both are engaged in productions that are of a lower grade of reality. And the resemblance goes further in their appeal to what is not the best part of the soul. Consequently we should be justified in not admitting the poet into a well ordered state. . . . Poetic imitation has a like effect on the emotions of sex and anger and on all the desires and pains and pleasures of the soul which are said to attend our every action: they are watered and nourished when by rights we should dry them up. (*Republic* 605–606)

Plato was himself a supreme artist, and ᵥthis isolated quotation scarcely does justice to his views on art. Indeed, Plato's basic approach as a philosopher could be described as aesthetic. However, this quotation certainly calls for an examination of what is meant by saying that art expresses and nourishes emotion; and Plato's first point, that art is of little value if it is concerned only with the "lower grade of reality" in representations, could be developed as a criticism of the theory that art is basically imitation.

The notion that the artist is copying what is "already there" comes easily to us when we see the painter at work before a landscape. As a philosophical interpretation of what the artist is doing, this view seems to have been predominant up to the eighteenth century. All may agree with Aristotle that "imitation is natural to man from childhood, one of his advantages over the lower animals being this, that he is the most imitative creature in the world and learns at first by imitation. And it is also natural for all to delight in works of imitation." (*Poetics* 1448b) Long after we have left childhood, our instinct to copy continues, and the pleasure that comes from imitation grows as the copy is made to approach the original.

Nevertheless, the delight of imitation—the very reason for art according to this theory—comes, as Aristotle makes clear, from its function in *learning* rather than from the mere fact of copying. Children are discovering what they do not yet know rather than repeating what they know already. This may indeed continue with maturity. But if so, the theory that art consists in imitation is certainly stated inadequately. It is not the making of a replica which accounts for the intensity and value of aesthetic experience. For this, we must look to the fascination of discovering the new rather than the technique of repeating the old.

A more serious objection is that mere imitation does not allow for the evident creativeness of the artist. The painter before the landscape is not simply "holding a mirror up to nature." No two painters would represent it in the same way, and the mark of excellence comes precisely with the individual interpretation. Yet the theory seems to suggest that the landscape is simply "there" and the painter copies it on his canvas. Is his interpretation to be explained in terms of selection? He does not reproduce indiscriminately all that is there but brings out what is most "significant." Yet the theory of imitation does not explain this significance. It suggests only that some particulars are let through and others held back—a poor sort of copy. Or does the artist improve on the original? Does he copy, not what simply is there, but what might or ideally should be there? Again, however much we may feel this is right, it is a strange notion of imitation: any "improvement" could not fail to be a falsification.

The theory of art as imitation fits in with the empiricist account of knowledge as a copy of facts that are there apart from reference to our ways of knowing. The landscape is already there as such and is then perceived by the artist and translated to colors on a canvas. However, the inadequacy of such an account is patent. Art is constructive. It does not represent but presents for the first time what is not there without it. The artist discovers what he sees only in bringing it to expression.

This is not to deny that there may be an element of sheer representation in art—not of facts "in themselves" but of what can be known apart from artistic expression. For example, Leonardo's *Last Supper* shows the twelve apostles clearly divided into four groups of three. The two groups on Christ's right represent the emotions of anger and melancholy, the two on his left stand for joyful and tranquil feelings. This division corresponds to a Renaissance classification of the temperaments and seems clearly to have been intended by Leonardo. It forms a basis from which the theme and details of the whole painting may be studied at length. Christ's right hand makes a gesture of rejection; his left hand, one of acceptance. He himself, in the center, combines all human attitudes in his own person.

If we dismiss the theory of art as imitation, we do not deny that it is one of the tasks of an interpreter to make such identifications. The music critic may draw our attention to recurrent patterns which "denote" certain feelings. Or he may simply point out bells, birds, thunder, and hoofbeats. But no mere building up of an aggregate of "themes" or "motifs" will produce a work of art. No announcer may comment a piece of music as he does a boxing match or travel film. What was said above about the *Last Supper* could well have been developed in a psychological and theological treatise. This would have given us far more information than the painting, but it is unlikely to have been a work of art. Whatever an artist "means," it is much more than that.

Art as Catharsis

The other theory to be considered is that art is a "purgation," a socially acceptable outlet for emotions which it might be dangerous to bottle up or to pour out in more direct ways. The term "catharsis," applied by Aristotle to the release of emotions offered by the drama, has been chosen. However, Aristotle may not have meant this in quite the way we are inclined to interpret it. In an age dominated by psychological theories, we tend easily to see art as a purely physical expression—or "overflow"—of feelings and desires in ways permitted by the moral censorship.

In traditional aesthetics, stress on art as expression has usually come as a reaction to "formalism," a view which concentrates on the harmony of the achieved work rather than on the activity of creating it. The emphasis on art as a way of acting is healthy. There is clearly much that responds to such a theory. It allows for the originality of art in a way that no theory of imitation could. And the idea that what art expresses is our life of emotion or passion fits in well with the theme of the preceding chapter. However, there are many ambiguities in the notion of "expression," and these must be clarified. Briefly, the theme to be developed here is that this is *symbolic* rather than *physical* expression. Through symbolic expression, emotions are transformed or intellectualized, whereas a purely physical expression leaves them much as they were, even though a new outlet is found for their discharge.

The objection to any account of art in terms of merely physical expression may be put graphically. If art were no more than this, then a concert musician could not announce his program in advance; he would have to wait and see how his mood "took" him before he could express melancholy or elation in his music.

The countersuggestion, that feelings may be intellectualized or conceived rather than merely "felt," may seem strange. Surely we can have feelings only so far as they "run over" us; the stronger they are, the greater their pressure on us and the more we "have" them. If art is the expression of emotions, can these not be present only to the extent they are physically there and "suffered"?

However, emotional pressure or disturbance is as likely to impede artistic expression as it does most theoretical or practical activities. The actor who was truly moved by his grief would not be able to carry on with the play; he would retire with a sedative. And the spectators of the play are not asked to pretend that they are on the stage enduring all the emotions and suffering the fate of the actors. If this were so, the stage would be a poor stimulus indeed, however much it might be extended into the audience and however good the sound effects. Instead, the feelings of the drama are best appreciated if the spectator remains in his seat and understands the play as he would any other meaning expressed before him. There is then nothing incongruous that the three hours should represent three years or that a satisfying dinner should still allow an understanding of the hero's tragic fate.

To try to explain art as a purely physical catharsis is really to lose the creativity of art as much as in the imitation theory. The water that flows over a dam is not thereby changed in any way. At least, it is no more "active." As the previous chapter suggested, there is no place for "being active" in any spectator account of the physical. It is only in doing art, in symbolically expressing our feelings and finding *meaning* (rather than mere relief) through our expressions, that we can allow for the notion of activity-in-passivity. This is what the theories of imitation and of catharsis both ignore.

Art as Symbolic
Expression of Feeling

Our task is to try to understand what is involved in claiming that art is emotion symbolized or brought to intellectual presence. What we can say will remain largely negative, but there could be particular reason today for renewed attempts. The prevalence of scientific thought may have much to do with a popular divorce between thought and feeling. What is not thought of things in relation to each other is held by many to be "merely emotive." Judgments of value and of beauty, metaphysical propositions, and the whole life of feeling are grouped by the philosopher Carnap with "cries like Oh, Oh!" They may perhaps be allowed to grow on their own, but the tacit verdict seems to be that they should be treated as Plato would the "desires and pains and pleasures of the soul": to refrain from watering them and allow them to dry up.

The rigid dichotomy of thought and feeling scarcely corresponds to our experience. For we find the life of reason always troubled with passion; and no activity into which we enter can be absolved of all claims to rationality. So here we shall avoid any such dichotomy and ask about the ways in which we truly "have" feelings or are present to ourselves through them.

THE AUTONOMY
AND CONTINUITY OF ART

In other words, what we shall be working toward is a view of art that makes it continuous with our other forms of self-expression. Without diluting language excessively, we should then be able to say that all our experience is in some way aesthetic. Much of our talk and many of our customs are against this. We speak of some people as "artists," and the term is denied to the great majority of us. We separate "works of art" from ordinary use and put them in galleries or collections. We forget, when we admire the beauty of ancient knives and cups in a museum, that they were originally used for eating and drinking.

A certain amount of contemporary aesthetic theory supports this separation of art from the rest of life. Perhaps in reaction to theories of imitation and expression, some theorists stress the autonomy of art. Art consists of "pure forms," neither representative nor emotive, and these in no way refer beyond the realm of beauty. Art is simply its own meaning.

What has been said in this chapter would uphold such a "purist" approach so far as it means that art cannot be translated without loss into linguistic or other nonartistic forms. Only the poet can say, in the very words of his poem, what he is saying. A commentary in ordinary prose is a poor substitute rather than an effective translation.

However, to take purism literally is to end up in the ineffable, and hence with no theory at all. There is a continuity to all forms of human expression. Language, mathematics, science, and art are all ways of existing bodily, as spirit in matter, universal in particular, intellect in sense. Though such forms cannot be translated without violence from one to the other, they have a common origin in our struggle, as questioners, to give meaning to the world in which we find ourselves. All "symbolic worlds" are extensions of the possibility of bodily activity (cf. p. 129).

The language an artist uses in talking about his own work suggests that, for all its "autonomy," it is still in continuity with our basic bodily experiences, particularly with our feeling and emotion. He speaks of life, of tempo and rhythm, of movement and rest, tension and resolution, rise and fall, tone and harmony. He is not escaping from this but possessing it more truly through the symbolic expressions of his music, sculpture or poetry. Art is not representation of what can be had in other ways but is "recollection" of what would otherwise be too diffuse, chaotic, and arbitrary to be "had" or possessed at all.

THE RECOLLECTION
OF EMOTION

This view, that art is the symbolic expression in which our feeling is brought to self-presence, may be considered under a heading supplied by Wordsworth's definition of poetry as "emotion recollected in tranquillity." Art is not sheer emotion. Feelings come and go. We may relate them to the particularities of temperament and situation. But as mere feelings they are not strictly "ours." They are not appropriated; we are affected by them without truly "having" them or "being" them (possessing ourselves through them). For this, we must not merely undergo emotion but "recollect" it.

Such a phrase presumably means more than "memory," where this is sheer reproduction of what was had before. It suggests rather an achievement of something for the first time, recollection as the "gathering together" which is an intellectual ordering of sensation. This may be what Aristotle means in his account of aesthetic pleasure: "The reason of the delight in seeing a picture is that one is at the same time learning—gathering the meaning of things." (*Poetics* 1448b). The tranquil recollection of emotion is the intellectualizing or conception of sheer feeling.

This conceiving of emotion does not mean that the feeling ceases to be such. Feeling, from being just "there" as a sheer pressure, is raised to the agency of self-presence. In acting grief, the actor retains full mastery of his material; he enters into his grief without being dominated by it. In this "stepping back" from the rush and pressure of feelings to "enact" them, we master our moods and know the world with feeling and sensitivity rather than "dispassionately."

This is not to say that art is "make-believe," an intellectual pretense of having feelings that one does not have. It is neither mere endurance nor delusion, but the fullest possible awareness of our life of feeling. Art has been said to make our feelings "transparent." The artist does not point dumbly at his own particular and private emotions; he is not stopped by their sheer opacity but makes them lucid, brings them to the light of communication. The artist works in the public world. He transforms what is otherwise too private and relative to be "said" and he opens it to his own insight and criticism as well as to that of others.

The person who simply gives himself up to daydreams in listening to music is using it to stimulate his private fancies. The appreciation of art is an act of submission to a universal "idea" which is formulated in it.

The relaxation which art affords may be likened more to discovering a mathematical proof than to sinking into an armchair.

To play music "with feeling" is not to use the music as an outlet for pressing emotions of the moment, however much our actual mood may happen to correspond to what we can find to our purpose in the sounds. Instead, we submit to the idea of music as a symbolic expression of feeling. This still allows that immaturity. or any other incapacity of feeling, may limit one's ability to understand the meaning of certain compositions and hence to render them well. An actor who has never tasted the seriousness of life may be limited in his playing of tragic roles. However, this is not necessarily so; for art is educative as well as demanding. The "recollection" of feeling deepens it and extends its range. Art helps us to understand emotions which our own situation may never have occasioned.

Nothing has been said of the distinction between art as creation and as appreciation. The omission was intentional. For if a work of art belongs, not to the private realm of physical feelings but to the public world of ideas open to understanding, then we can discuss art as we would mathematics, without constantly distinguishing between the man who first disclosed a certain proof and those who then understand it. There is much the same distinction between the creative thinker's urgent struggle for expression and the more gradual discovery of meaning by appreciation, once the expression is "there" in a book or a painting.

Similarly, no distinction has been made between the appreciation of beauty in an artefact and in nature. The mind can understand what is intelligible whether man has been responsible for it or not. The chemist employs the same techniques in analyzing a piece of rock and a piece of concrete.

However, many tensions remain. Emphasis on the similarity of art, as an intellectualizing of sense, to mathematics and any other manner of "working" matter should not blind us to the evident difference between art and other forms of symbolic expression. The following section will examine the difference by referring to some of the particular arts. Then a final section will return to the countertheme, that art is continuous with all forms of human life; even science and technology can be seen as ways of living "aesthetically."

Aesthetic Distance

Perhaps the tendency of "realism" is to make art coextensive with life, and of "romanticism" is to sharpen the distinction between the realm of art and the prosaic world of ordinary life. Nevertheless, not even the most realistic film could be classified without remainder as sociology. Aesthetic perception reveals what can come from no scientific report in terms of events that recur and are classified and counted. The separation of art from other forms of questioning has been called the "distancing" of artistic expression. We transform the commonplace into art by clearing it of its practical, everyday connections in order that it may allow the conceptualization of feeling rather than the development of other forms of knowledge.[1]

The Material for Art

Art has always had its origin in something nonartistic. It grew, perhaps, from the bodily movements of regular tasks, from natural rhythms such as breathing, from imitation of nature, and from excitement at celebrations, expressing itself in shouting, jumping, and rolling.

Art develops in close dependence upon nonartistic abilities. All articulated expression involves techniques; power of thinking is closely bound to the sensitive use of language. Similarly, all art involves craft. Art is doing; it is the making of a symbolic expression. Hence the growth of each of the arts has relied on the mastery of practical skills.

Nevertheless, a work of art appears by separating itself from the world in which it originates and the materials on which it depends empirically. It gains a context different from that of the common objects around it. It ceases to be seen as part of the network of relationships that make up the physical world and it takes on a new significance. Those who are unable to appreciate a work of art are those who remain distracted by its purely empirical or "useful" meaning.

In looking at the window, we see a rectangle in continuity with the wall. And the houses and cars we see through the window take their place in the same complex of relationships: all obey the same laws and fit into a common space and time. But in looking at the picture hanging on the wall, we enter another space and time. What the picture shows is separated from the wall in a different way from that in which the cars appear. The painting is not part of the world to which we reach out our hand or which we organize scientifically; it belongs to a world to which we have access through the pattern and rhythm of our feelings. If an archaeologist can learn from a weapon or tool how men once carried on

---

[1] The chapter on art, and this section in particular, owes much to the writings of Susanne Langer. *Feeling and Form* (New York: Scribner, 1953) can especially be recommended for the way it applies to the particular arts her account of the "nondiscursive" symbolization of feeling.

their struggle to survive, he may learn from their ornaments how it was they felt.

Transformation by the Arts

The shape of a knife may be continuous with the space of our ordinary activities and of our science. But the lines which make up its ornamentation distance us from this space and express feelings that may have little to do with hunting or eating. If the plastic arts formulate our feeling in terms of space, it is preeminently music that shows the distancing of artistic time. What a musical composition has to say is irrelevant to the twenty minutes of our everyday life that it takes. It is in this sense that we speak of aesthetic experience as "timeless." But it is closer to our primitive experience of "lived time." We make our feeling present in music by transforming a brute mood that comes upon us into a possibility of acting, of appreciating or understanding some quality of life. It may not be irrelevant that we speak of composing music and of composing our feelings: what would otherwise be an inarticulate pressure is made into a meaningful whole. The "ups" and "downs" we suffer become a rhythm that we understand and appropriate in the form of tempo and pauses, consonance and dissonance, crowding and flowing, accent, tone, and harmony.

Perhaps the art form which best combines spatial and temporal expression is one of the earliest, dancing. If language arose from the gesture, so did dancing. Pointing removes us from the instinctive level of grasping and allows us to appreciate things apart from any pressing purposes. So rhythmic gesturing distances man from particular bodily activities and gives him a sense of the meaning of his body as a whole. In stretching and balancing, whirling and leaping, he recognizes his self-possession amid the many forces in which he finds himself. The spontaneous composition of a dance offers possibilities for a more comprehensive statement of meaning than do lines or sounds by themselves. It has been said that religion was danced out before it was thought out.

It may be through dancing that language was withdrawn from its practical uses and the verbal arts were born. Understanding of what the verbal arts are doing is especially difficult because language puts us in such close touch with the world of practical concerns. The tendency is to think of the poet as first having a "message," common or exalted, and then expressing it in poetic form. But such a separation of intellectual content and artistic form is hazardous, especially if it be interpreted as a distinction between conveying information and stimulating feelings. The verbal arts distance language from its mundane uses.

Again, it must be stressed that this section needs to be complemented by the following one. There is a sense in which all expressions involve art. Everything we say, perhaps even a business letter, can convey some feeling for harmony, proportion, elegance. Yet in giving an account of art we must divide before we can unite.

The verbal arts create a space and a time of their own. What is made is "fiction," a realm resembling our ordinary world but demanding a different interpretation. The child who asks insistently for a story is asking for reality, but for a reality "through the looking glass." The fiction tells of personal histories and experiences as events transposed in imagination, renewed by the vision of the artist. The novel, most realistic of our art forms, is not concerned to record life as it is lived from day to day but rather to create, to bring to light precisely those elusive aspects which escape ordinary perception and expression. The novelist does not so much report what normally passes through his mind as try to suggest what can not otherwise get into his mind.

Words used in art are evocative of a quality of experience rather than representative of facts. The very sound of the words ceases to be indifferent and serves to express meaning. The artist explores forms of diction and imagery in trying to recapture the wonder words must have evoked at the beginning. The dictionary gives but part of the original human experience that found expression in the word. In art, the word again becomes conspicuous, fascinating, and creative.

Consummatory Experience

The previous section indicated some of the ways an artist stands back from his life of getting and spending in order to construct a symbolic world distinct from those of ordinary language and of the sciences. This section is complementary. It will explore the claim that we are all artists, that everything we do has an aesthetic dimension to it.

Surprisingly, it is the scientists today who are least disturbed by this suggestion. It is often maintained that the final criterion of truth in theoretical science is an aesthetic one. The days are gone when scientists held that there could be only one true theory for any phenomenon. If waves and particles are both "models of explanation," then we are free to adopt one or the other according to our needs or preferences. And our needs or preferences could be not merely practical but also aesthetic. Whether we are dealing with the architecture of a house or of a scientific theory, we tend to aim at a "harmony" that combines the greatest diversity of parts in the simplest system. It is for this reason of good taste or elegance, rather than for any discovery of new facts, that Copernicus succeeded Ptolemy and that Einstein has taken over from Newton.

Further, we are less embarrassed than before to speak of the ''beauty'' of a scientific theory or mathematical proof. And we are more ready to accept that each of these comes from imagination rather than from technique, from a creative leap that is similar to the vision of an artist.[2]

One philosopher who has stressed the continuity of art with all human action is John Dewey (cf. particularly his *Art as Experience*). Writing in a largely biological idiom, Dewey regards experience as man's ''interaction with his environment,'' a repeated failure and achievement of a harmonious relationship. All forms of knowledge fit into this scheme. Those experiences we term aesthetic are ''consummatory'': they are heightened because they sum up our past struggles more intensely and prepare more adequately for the future. Art is no mere prolongation of the past as routine, nor is it something capricious without roots in the past. It is a fruitful union of the stable and the novel which increases our capacity for experience in the future.

This view fits in with the analysis we have given of temporality. It also allows for Nietzsche's insistence that culture should be Dionysian as well as Apollonian. All activities consist in disclosing the form or order of experience. Yet form is not to be imposed ready-made from outside. A present consummation is a preparation for the future, and any such preparation comes as a challenge to forms merely taken from the past. Life is the pursuit of harmony, but harmony is creative rather than confining.

Those who hold that art pervades all we do often insist that it is more concerned with the quality of our ordinary experiences than with the content of some special ones. In a sense, what matters is not so much what happens to us as how we actively take whatever comes. Education is not merely gaining information but learning how to make sense of our confused experience. Languages, science, and history play their part. But so far as they are concerned with our ''feeling'' for things, all are involved in our artistic education. The artists have always had a greater influence on the shaping of a culture than have the generals and politicians. The latter bring prosperity or disaster. But it is the poets, musicians and dramatists who develop the imagination that appreciates prosperity or accepts disaster.

. [2] The various studies by Michael Polanyi give a scientist's view of the more creative side of his subject (e.g., *Personal Knowledge*, University of Chicago Press and Harper Torchbooks).

Plato may, after all, have had some reason for excluding poets from the ideal state; his own view of life was sufficiently aesthetic for him to see no need for such a class of specialists. Yet in a technological society we have a particular need for artists. Machines work well but with little feeling.

13 | Am I Free?

With Earth's first Clay They did the Last Man knead,
And there of the Last Harvest sow'd the Seed:
And the first Morning of Creation wrote
What the Last Dawn of Reckoning shall read.

Omar Khayyám expresses a theme which is to be found in all ages. From Sophocles to Tolstoy and Hardy, men have been fascinated by the thought that whatever happens has been determined by fate. It is written. Whatever will be, will be. Strangely, this is both a frightening thought and a consoling one. For some it seems to encourage heroic activity. For others it leads to renunciation or submission: and such attitudes can range from apathy to a sincere humility. The theme has been central to religious speculation, appearing as the law of *karma* in Buddhism and Hinduism, as *Kismet* in Mohammedanism, as "predestination" in Christianity. At least in the latter, the doctrine of "free will," that we are the master of our destiny, has officially triumphed; yet there has been no easy reconciliation of individual freedom with belief in an almighty and omniscient God. Since Thales and Parmenides, the rule of reason and of necessity has been interpreted by many philosophers as denying any place for freedom. Democritus finds remarkable support throughout history for his statement that "all things which were and are and will be are foreordained by necessity."

This is not the first time that the topic of determinism and freedom has appeared in these pages. With only slight changes it could have been made the central theme of the book. The discussion of computers in the second chapter could be read as a question whether all human actions can be seen as mechanical, or determined, on the model of a behaviorist psychology. The following chapter examined the way in which a scientific account tries to exclude the knowing subject by giving a report of the world in terms of objects in relation, under mathematical laws. The reminder that such an account is itself the project of a knowing, interpreting, numbering subject led to a study, in the fourth chapter, of the inescapability of subjectivity. There was a clear reference to freedom in Sartre's argument that even our attempts to avoid choosing involve choice. However, the following two chapters, in their effort to develop such hints into a method for metaphysics, adopted questioning rather than striving as a point of departure, and the idiom was one of "knowing" rather than of "willing."

Nevertheless, the emphasis throughout was on the *agency* of knowing, on our struggle to achieve a greater self-presence in and through the "otherness" of materiality and situation. This structure of activity-in-passivity became the topic of Chapter Eleven. As a subject, man does know and achieve himself through all the limitations he suffers from his temperament and history. Or, in the terms of Chapter Ten, we suffer our past only so far as it is made "present" in the light of the future as possibility: what my shyness and poverty "really are" depends on the way I interpret them as grounds for evasion or for effort in facing the future. The limitations of fate and circumstance are to be taken seriously, but they do not enable me simply to deny my freedom of self-understanding and self-realization.

However, such abstract schemes need repeated questioning. And the perennial challenge from a variety of doctrines of determinism can help to clarify and qualify our all too complacent belief that we are master of our fate.

Important and personal problems are involved. Today it has become highly questionable how far we are entitled to use "moral" language and indulge in the attitudes it expresses. If I know someone with a club foot, I may not select him for a football team but I should never think of blaming him for his misfortune. If my watch is stolen by an acquaintance, I shall take steps to recover it but shall modify my indignation on learning that he is a kleptomaniac under psychiatric care. I excuse him by saying that he could not help it. He was driven to steal by a condition for which he is not responsible; he did not do it of his own free will. However, if one of my friends has a vicious temper and insults me severely, I draw on my full vocabulary of blame and indignation. If told that "this is his character," I stand firm in my belief that he should not be this way or that he should not allow temperament to get the better of him.

A problem is apparent. It is not merely a question of where to draw the line but whether there is a line at all. Our society distinguishes between hospitals and jails. The former are not regarded as places of punishment or of exhortation. The latter represent social blame as well as self-protection. However, do not the findings and attitudes of this century prompt us to remove the distinction? Should we not destroy the jails and build more hospitals? To understand is to forgive. Do not temperamental defects and criminal behavior call for diagnosis and cure rather than blame and punishment?

Today an educator may talk to parents as though they are to blame for all the anti-social faults of their children: You are responsible for their neuroses. However, this notion leads logically much further. Parents are the children of their own parents. None is responsible and none is to be blamed. All we do has been "foreordained by necessity."

Clarence Darrow, one of the most famous of American defense attorneys, genuinely believed in such determinism and used this philosophy in a successful plea for a large number of his clients. His appeal to the jury in the celebrated trial of Leopold and Loeb in 1924 may dramatize the problem of this chapter:

> This weary old world goes on, begetting, with birth and with living and with death; and all of it is blind from the beginning to the end. I do not know what it was that made these boys do this mad act, but I do know there is a reason for it. I know they did not beget themselves. I know that any one of an infinite number of causes reaching back to the beginning might be working out in these boys' minds, whom you are asked to hang in malice and in hatred. . . .[1]

Ways of Excluding Freedom

As elsewhere in philosophy, anticipations should be moderate. No philosopher can demonstrate that the court was right to relieve Leopold and Loeb of the death penalty. Particular questions of law and psychiatry demand specialized study. The philosopher is concerned with questions about questions. And here his contribution is to clarify a highly involved question. For it is by no means evident what is the precise problem of

[1] *Attorney for the Damned: Clarence Darrow in his own Words* (copyright 1957, by Arthur Weinberg; reprinted by permission of Simon and Schuster Inc., New York), p. 37.

"freedom and determinism." Its very persistence and the concern it has aroused suggest that it cannot be explained away, though some philosophers claim to do just that. Nevertheless, it may be that advocates of freedom and those of determinism are not simply saying yes and no to the same question; or even if they confront the same statement of a question, they may do so from quite different viewpoints. Practical problems of how to treat lawbreakers and temperamental friends will remain. But a reflection on the viewpoint from which we pose such questions is a first step toward a detailed study of them.

In this section we shall consider not so much the traditional arguments for determinism as the ways of thinking which have led many people to come to conclusions which they put under this rubric. First we shall examine how the findings and project of science lead along this way. Then a reflection on the position of some philosophers who deny freedom will introduce the notion that alternative viewpoints are involved, and this will become the topic of the following section.

The Scientific Approach

Einstein, though influenced by the philosophy of Spinoza as well as by his own work, may speak for many scientists. He wrote that:

> The more a man is imbued with the ordered regularity of all events, the firmer becomes his conviction that there is no room left by the side of this ordered regularity for causes of a different nature. For him neither the rule of human nor the rule of divine will exists as an independent cause of natural events.[2]

Einstein's implication is that the very notion of science demands a constancy and predictability in nature that allows no room for the "interference" of a free agent. But before asking what sort of determinism is required by the project of science, we may look briefly at some of the particular findings of science which seem to have lessened the scope for freedom.

THE FINDINGS
OF SCIENCE

Mythical accounts of nature in terms of personal forces acting capriciously have given way to sciences which see nature in terms of events happening repeatedly in the same way according to mathematical laws.

---

[2] *Out of my Later Years* (New York: Philosophical Library, Inc., 1950), p. 28, by permission of the Estate of Albert Einstein.

The west wind is no longer a free agent, blowing where he will, but is a displacement of air predictable through the laws of meteorology.

The success of the sciences of nature has now, in many remarkable ways, passed on to the sciences of man. Pavlov's discovery of the conditioned reflex allowed a considerable extension of the stimulus-response explanation for human behavior. In far more personal realms than salivation it has become feasible to say that under what science regards as the same conditions (stimulus, cause) man reacts in the same way (response, effect). The investigations of biologists into heredity have turned the saying "like father like son" into more than a popular adage. Biochemistry has opened frightening prospects of the control of "personality" through injections, and we recognize that we are all much more the product of our chemistry than we thought.

When we turn to the influence of the environment, the rigor of science lessens, but the accumulation of statistics has sharply questioned the conviction of previous ages that people are good or bad through their own merit or fault. The correlation between crime and social conditions indicates that society can be studied with much the same techniques as nature. One does not need to be a Marxist to see the close relation between morality, or at least custom, and the "substructure" of economic and social factors.

However, it is probably depth psychology which has shown the strongest appeal toward a deterministic interpretation of man. The shock of learning that the reasons we give for our actions are so often mere "rationalizations" of primitive urges and deeply festering childhood wounds has done much to support the view that blame and exhortation are a strange substitute for diagnosis and cure. The individual "unconscious" has taken over from a cosmic fate.

Law has followed. The notion of an "irresistible impulse" has been accepted as releasing a defendant from responsibility for what he did. "Mental sickness" and "defect of reason" and "temporary insanity" are argued to remove a person from the moral realm and set him in the purely factual. The psychiatrist has become the first line of defense, and the question is a serious one whether we are not all sick rather than immoral.

THE PROJECT
OF SCIENCE

No such accumulation of findings could prove that we are completely determined. Those who have passed along the way of science to a philosophy of determinism have done so with the aim of science in mind rather than the particular facts it has revealed. The quotation from Einstein above suggests that free actions would be in competition with the "ordered regularity of all events" which scientific explanation demands. The scientist can no more incorporate free actions into his account than he can the acts of mythological beings.

Various attempts have been made to get around this difficulty. For instance, it has been insisted that the regularity of causal relationships means only that in principle a cause can be found for every event and this does not exclude that some causes are free while most are determined. But the ordered regularity which science postulates does not allow this, for the order of scientific explanations is based on the possibility of classifying events as recurrent in such a way that the *same* event will always follow the same cause. If free actions are set side by side with the events that fit readily into the account of physics, then Einstein is right that the former would be "causes of a different nature." For the common conviction of freedom is that I can act in one way or the other in identical circumstances. Magnets always attract iron, but I can take up a book or throw it away.

No scientific law can incorporate causes that in principle escape constant connection with the same effect. This is not to deny that the originally strict notion of scientific laws has been modified in various ways, notably through Heisenberg's indeterminacy principle (cf. p. 53). However, the many attempts to use this as a way of finding a loophole into which free causes can be inserted seem a strange manner of defending freedom. Quantum mechanics is no less rigorously mathematical than any other branch of science, and mathematics is as far removed from an account of why I make a decision as it is from one of what I am trying to do in painting a picture or writing a book.

The conclusion is that the mathematically ordered world of science excludes any notion of freedom. There is no place for it in any account we give of man so far as we view him as an object in constant relations to other objects. However, though this conclusion may in fact have led many to a complete denial of freedom, it does not rightly do so. As other chapters have maintained, the symbolic world of science is itself the achievement of man as a classifying and numbering subject. Science is only one of many human projects, no more privileged than the others. The scientific world is not "in itself" but only "for us." Physics is not metaphysics. And the proof or rejection of freedom is, like all "exhaustive" claims, thoroughly metaphysical.

Philosophical Approaches

Again, we are considering some of the approaches that have led to a conclusion of complete determinism rather than the many detailed arguments for it. Here we shall sample two such approaches that philosophers have followed. The first is more analytic, based on the difficulty of proving freedom or even understanding what seems to us so obvious. The second is a more metaphysical tradition which interprets freedom in such a way that choice becomes illusory or at least irrelevant.

DIFFICULTIES IN UNDERSTANDING FREEDOM

An ancient principle of philosophy, known as "Ockham's razor," is that we should slash from our talk all terms with which we find we can dispense. The contention of some philosophers today is that all talk of "free will" falls under this test. Freedom of choice may not be conclusively disproved. But no proof of it could be successful. Hence, as the scientific outlook is established in our culture, continuing talk of "free actions" needlessly retains an indigestible remnant in an otherwise coherent account.

We should of course be unhappy to see an old tradition go. However, the surgeon's knife is in the long run less painful than a continuing tumor. We talk of free acts because we suppose we experience them. But belief in freedom is no proof of its reality. And our belief has repeatedly been shattered. We find illusory freedom in compulsive and hypnotized persons, and we have often badly misinterpreted our own motives. Any proof of freedom from experience would impose the unsatisfiable demand of excluding an endless list of possible determining factors.

Our supposed experience of freedom appears most prominent when we act *against* strong desires. I say I am freely dieting because I do so in spite of my urgent craving for food. But how do I know which is my strongest desire, to have a full meal or to lose weight? In other realms, at least, that is proved strongest which wins. If I conscientiously do "right," is it not because I desire to do right? A "moral character" could come as much from heredity and environment as does a tall figure or freckles.

The above approach, whatever it is worth, remains somewhat negative. However, it is supported by an analysis of choice which declares the very notion meaningless. It is contended that the ·language of hypothetical courses of action ("could" and "could have") has meaning when applied to observable behavior and violates such meaning when applied to choices. If I "could have refused that fourth whiskey," I verifiably have the physical power to utter the word "no" after three whiskies, though I may have met someone who does not. "Could" is a power-word, and whether I apply it truly or falsely is found by observing behavior in various circumstances which are sufficiently similar for me to call them "the same." But when I apply "could" to choice and remove choice from observable behavior, I likewise remove the word "could" from all situations in which we understand its meaning. To say "I could have chosen to refuse that fourth whiskey" is meaningless. If I refer to similar occasions in support of my claim, I am reducing choice to observable behavior, on a par with "it could have rained on graduation day"—which is no denial of determinism. Or if I insist that I have in fact chosen differently in identical circumstances, I am misusing the term "in fact": we can *treat* the circumstances of behavior as "the same" (by the sort of abstraction scientists use in ordering nature as a series of "repeatable" events), but we never *find* identical circumstances for choice.

This linguistic approach invites a variety of questions. Perhaps the fundamental one is whether the notion of freedom demands power-words in its elucidation. For an act to be free, must there be an alternative course which I "could have" taken? This is a question which will arise in the more metaphysical approach that follows.

REASON AND
NECESSITY : SPINOZA

The source for this approach to the problem of freedom is the metaphysical tradition that there are "grades of reality," to which correspond grades of truth and of value (cf. pp. 116–17 and 188–89). At the lower levels a being is "dissipated," has little self-presence and is at the mercy of whatever influences bear on it. But passage up the levels of "reality" reveals highly unified persons who possess themselves in, or "return to themselves" from, their various expressions.

Some thinkers who have adopted this scheme, such as Aquinas, have claimed to incorporate choice into it, at least at the levels which represent human existence. However, there are problems. To go up the grades of reality is to pass from greater "contingency" (where things merely happen to be what they are) to greater necessity, until one comes to the supreme reality which must absolutely be what it is.

What then becomes of choice? It is difficult to reconcile this with the supreme reality (cf. theologians' problems with God's freedom to create). And though there may be room for such freedom at the lower grades, it seems to be classified as an "imperfection" which is overcome so far as we "become ourselves." Or put it this way. As reality increases, so does reason, the clear understanding of the evidence for what is so. Since there is little evidence at what number a roulette wheel will stop, I am free to think it will be a red or a black one. But the evidence that the angles of a Euclidean triangle add up to 180° is complete: I have no freedom of choice to think otherwise. As evidence grows, freedom of choice becomes irrelevant. The more I see an alternative to be irrational, the less I can seriously entertain it. Choice between alternatives is a mark of the inadequacy of knowledge, not a perfection which we should proudly claim and bitterly defend. It is perhaps to be expected that some of the most enterprising accounts of determinism come from theologians to whom such a hierarchical view is especially congenial.

This metaphysical attitude to freedom can be illustrated in Spinoza (1632–77). A Jew who was expelled from the synagogue for his speculations, he identified metaphysics with "ethics" and so entitled his principal work. For he attributed wrong action to lack of knowledge. That is, a person will act "reasonably" if he genuinely sees the reason for his actions. Do not blame people, or exhort them to "acts of will," but arouse their interest and develop their understanding. With this view, Spinoza stands in the tradition of Socrates and anticipates Freud (with whom he has often been compared).

Spinoza distinguishes various grades of knowledge. The lowest is "imagination," where we passively accept facts and merely associate them in various ways. From this we pass to "reason," where we actively integrate our knowledge and conceive it as a systematic whole; we no longer merely accept "the fact that" but we see "the reason why." Correspondingly there are stages of emotional life. There are "passive emotions," a confused and arbitrary striving in which we are at the mercy of whatever inclinations strike us at the moment; and there are "active emotions," in which we act consistently for reasons that are truly our own.

In the light of this brief account, some outlines of Spinoza's approach to the problem of freedom may appear. On one side, he denies choice ("freedom of the will") in both God and man. On the other side he still defends freedom eminently in God and to lesser degrees in man, opposing it to "external constraint":

> That is called free which exists solely by the necessity of its own nature and which acts as determined by itself alone. On the other hand, that is necessary, or rather constrained, which is determined from outside to a fixed and definite form of existence and action. (*Ethics*, Part I, Definition 7)

At the lower grades we find beings largely determined from outside. Man's claim to choose between alternatives comes from ignorance and belongs to the level of "imagination." If he could understand why he acts as he does, he would realize that he fits into the chain of causes making up nature. However, such understanding is—almost in a Freudian sense—therapeutic. In recognizing the way nature fits together rationally, we become more truly one with it and possess ourselves rather than struggling blindly. Contingency explains nothing. But reason introduces us to the realm of true necessity. To the extent that we see why our actions proceed from the necessity of *our own* nature, we accept this, and our action is determined by the agent rather than by external forces. We act necessarily but are present in what we do because we see the reason for it. Fate and freedom as "self-determination" come together.

The problems of making sense of Spinoza's view are immense. But the force of his account comes with his claim that our conviction of choosing between alternatives led traditional discussion to a false, or at best superficial, notion of freedom. To defend freedom as choice, and to oppose it simply to necessity, is—he suggests—misguided. What matters is freedom of self-determination, and this goes hand in hand with a recognition of what is reasonably and necessarily so. God "accounts for himself" in a completely rational way. The opposite of such freedom is not necessity but arbitrariness, acting "privately" without adequate reasons. And this, Spinoza holds, is the level at which we find both determination from outside and the appearance of choosing one thing or another: "impulsiveness" might be an apt translation. For Spinoza, the opposition is not between freedom and necessity but between acting for adequate reasons (which is both self-determining and necessary) and acting for inadequate reasons (which is capricious and "constrained").

In the section that follows we shall consider various ways of talking about freedom. After an introductory topic, we shall examine freedom in relation to "coercion" from outside. Then we shall investigate the notion of freedom as active self-determination. And, in the light of this, we shall return to a discussion of choice and related themes.

Ways of Talking about Freedom

It may be healthy to come down to earth from such speculative problems. So first we shall look at the way we speak of "acting for a reason." Is the determinist right to think of freedom as though this would involve causes acting "side by side" with the causes in nature? The following discussion will be related to the question of "viewpoints" and the distinction between first-person and third-person accounts.

Causes and Reasons

We say that some acts are involuntary and others are voluntary. I let out a cry of pain because a match burns my finger. I give a cry of greeting because I want to talk to a friend. However, the word "because" is used in different senses. In the first it introduces a *cause*, of the sort found in physics and physiology books. In the second it introduces a *reason*, of the sort found in history books and autobiographies.[3]

This distinction does not itself dispose of the problem of freedom. Some psychologists say that, given enough knowledge, we could reduce all reasons to causes. But the distinction is important. Failure to make it may have led to much of the confusion that covers the problem.

My cry of greeting is caused by the expulsion of air from the lungs and contraction of the vocal chords. These are caused by nerve impulses from the brain. The defender of freedom insists that at some point we reach a "free cause" (a volition, my will, myself), which was not itself caused by anything else to initiate this chain of events. The determinist finds such a notion intolerable and continues his search for causes in the subconscious, in hormones, in heredity.

If the question of freedom is correctly posed in this way, then the determinist is right. Once we start to play the game of identifying the connections of natural events from the viewpoint of a spectator, we play it to the end, i.e., indefinitely. This game allows for no "time-out," and such is any appeal to an uncaused cause, whether it be God, soul, or volition.

However, we are under no necessity to play only this game. There are others we can enjoy. And the game of reasons has very different rules. I greeted my friend because I like talking to him. On second thoughts, I wanted to get some information from him. Or I have a suspicion that I really wanted to bolster my self-esteem by pitying him. The game of reasons can also go on indefinitely. But reasons are not observed among the events of nature. There can be no mathematical relation between a reason and an event. To give a reason for any of my actions is to say what it is *for*; this is to elucidate the meaning of the action as *mine*, not to relate one observed event to another distinct from it. An action as intended (done for a reason) belongs to my subjectivity rather than to the world of events which can be numbered and repeated and thus set in causal relations. The appropriate account is in the first-person. To speak of the "same" act on another occasion is to change it to an event observed by a spectator.

A common objection to freedom states that what is predicted cannot be free. This is true, because prediction applies to a spectator account in terms of causality. But it is my actions as observed which I predict. I do not predict my actions as intended. I simply do them for a reason. I make up my mind.[4]

---

[3] For Aristotle, the distinction is between "efficient cause" and "final cause."

[4] This is not to deny that, in making up my mind or forming an intention, I

So what our language of causes and reasons suggests is that the two games represent two points of view, those from which we get a spectator account and a participant account. If we try to reduce the latter exhaustively to the former, and hence all reasons to causes (or to "rationalizations" for causes), we run into the self-contradiction we have met before. Put simply, we should inescapably be doing this for a reason. This argument will be discussed shortly.

Coercion

No one who defends freedom claims he can do everything. All admit the "constraint" or "coercion" of forces outside their own agency. I am forced to the ground by gravity if I slip, by a stronger person if I wrestle, by alcohol if I indulge excessively, by sickness if I have a heart attack. No such incidents are taken as an argument against freedom, because the forces are in competition with my physical power, not with my freedom. The prisoner is confined by the bars of his cell, but he is free to beat against them or to dream of escaping or to accept his punishment. If we say he is not free to leave his cell, what we mean is simply that he is not able to leave it. There are, strictly speaking, no *degrees* of such ability: he is either strong enough to force the bars or he is not.

Again, strictly speaking, coercive forces do not *act* against me, nor I against them. For an account of the play of forces is set in the third person, and there the notions of acting and suffering are inappropriate or are applied conventionally and analogously (cf. pp. 186–87). In the terms of such an account I am not free. But neither am I "unfree." The question of freedom is simply irrelevant. Hence we were careful above to speak of the project of science as a way of excluding free action from consideration, rather than as an argument against freedom. Freedom enters into the agency of doing science for a reason but nowhere into the scientific account of a world of causes.

Self-determination

It is only in the terms of a first-person account that freedom enters and the genuine problems about it can be stated. It is difficult to sustain such an account without lapsing into spectator language and into pseudo-problems. But we may start with the argument that has been with us since the second chapter (cf. p. 39).

take my past into account and predict what I shall do, as an observer of my own behavior. The claim is that such calculation, however reasonable, does not exhaust the notion of acting *for* a reason.

Briefly, to question or deny freedom explicitly is to affirm it implicitly. Freedom is indeed a question, but a question only as posed. In my perplexity I ask if I am free. But in the asking I implicitly affirm some authorship of, and responsibility for, my very question. Any denial of all freedom, however much evidence is adduced, is an act of denying "for a reason." The author enters into it as *his* theory, his assessment of how things really are. Whether the agency of affirming must involve choice between genuine alternatives is a subsequent problem to which we shall return; once I see an argument to be conclusive, I may have no choice to think it otherwise. But to deny what was called above the "freedom of self-determination" is to affirm it in my very agency of holding any view as mine. Freedom of self-determination is the inescapable subjectivity in all striving. It is my self-presence through all the struggles to find and express what I mean and accept. I am free so far as I am the author of my actions. And I could have no question of my freedom unless the questionable actions were in some way of my authorship.

To this some may reply "true but trivial." What is gained by the notion of freedom of self-determination? Three comments may help.

First, a limit is set to causal accounts of man, whether they come from psychologists, sociologists, advertising agents, or philosophers. All such reports are to be respected. Never before have so many people been engaged in observing and predicting human behavior, and the results are both impressive and frightening. Over great areas of our life we find that our language of reasons can be translated successfully into explanation through causes. Coercion penetrates further, and more intimately, than we thought. But any such account becomes self-destructive when it reaches the point of denying the possibility of rationally making an account.

Second, this notion of freedom does supply a context within which many of the problems discussed in this chapter can be brought together without the insoluble difficulties that come from confusing scientific and first-person questions. Accounts of human action from the viewpoint of a spectator do not provide the language or framework for posing the question of freedom. The obstacles to freedom are genuine. But they can be experienced as such only within our free agency and they can be expressed and discussed only in the first person. Indeed, the more acute our sense of losing self-possession may be, the greater our conviction of freedom, for this is the very condition without which we could not experience obstacles as such. Freedom is not one experience among many others but is the condition of any experience or desire or impulse being mine. The reality of freedom is assured without any need of excluding an endless list of possible determining factors.

Third, the notion of freedom as self-determination removes the whole dispute from the stark alternatives of freedom *or* determinism and converts it to a more fruitful and more relaxed discussion of *degrees* of subjectivity as freedom. My personal problem is never whether I am free or not: if I were not, there would be no problem for me. The question is how free I am and in what ways. Passing thoughts are scarcely mine. But if I write a book, I try with great deliberation to say what I mean and to mean what I say. I manage to attain only some degree of authorship, and it is through such limits to self-determination that I measure my freedom—not through any conflict with external forces. Cold or hot weather or the coercion of sickness may impede my ability to work, but the barrier to my freedom is the sluggishness with which I express and find my thought, the self-conflict at the heart of my own project. I want to "be myself" but discover I am not. I want to be present in my actions but realize I am painfully absent from them. To illustrate further the experience of limits *within* self-determination would be to retrace the course of the previous chapters on passivity within activity.

Choice

The term "deliberation" was used above. It commonly suggests a prolonged vacillation between alternatives. However, a deliberate act can be performed without hesitation. The question we may now ask is whether a free act even demands the consideration and rejection of an alternative. In other words, if the freedom we have proved to be inescapable is that of self-determination, does this require choice of one course *rather than* another? The question has been a recurrent one in this chapter. It underlies the problem of talk about what I "could have done." And it is at the heart of the metaphysical problems we illustrated through Spinoza.

Two suggestions may introduce the topic. The first is that choice is not one action which precedes another. I do not choose to reflect on this problem and only then begin to reflect on it. In choosing to reflect I am already reflecting, and the lengthy process that follows is a continuation of my choice—else reflection would stop. Or if I choose to change my job next month I am already organizing my life in terms of a new job. If I choose to leave my money to someone on my death, I have already made it over, contingent on death and legal processes.

The second suggestion is that there are degrees of self-presence or self-determination in choice. In the cafeteria I am scarcely present in choosing one particular spoon from a box of spoons. I am slightly more present in choosing which dessert I shall take. My choice to give myself to a certain career or to the serious study of a philosopher or to a particular woman in marriage is a decision into which I enter somewhat more fully.

However, the degrees of self-determination do not seem necessarily to correspond to other characteristics of choice. There may be more vacillation in my selection of a dessert to eat than of a philosopher to study. The number of alternative careers I consider may be less than the number of spoons from which I select. Indeed, the positive element in "choice" could perhaps remain as the serious alternatives dwindle and vanish: talk of the "only woman" may not always be romantic deception.

This is not to deny that our usual experience is one of choosing from various possibilities. However, the question whether self-determination demands the rejection of alternatives is not solved by a simple appeal to common experience or to language.

If degrees of deliberation correspond to degrees of authorship rather than to the extent of vacillation, then a higher grade of self-determination will involve a greater necessity. When books and works of art are called necessary, it is not compulsiveness that is meant but rather the clear vision of what must be. The range of possibilities (if indeed there was a range) has been narrowed down to that one which expresses the mind of the author and in which he can find what is really so. He could not do other than what he does, what is truly "his."

The philosophical defense of freedom has been tied up with a defense of choice, and understandably so, because the notion of self-determination seems empty if removed from our everyday experience of selecting among alternatives. However, freedom lies in the positive choice we make rather than in any alternative that is left by the wayside. The difficulties are not easily met of elucidating our talk of what we "could have chosen." And the notion that genuine alternatives are dispensable fits in, not only with the metaphysics of grades of reality, but also with the religious sense that we submit to a reality far greater than our own petty projects: we do not so much select one course among many as allow the expression in ourselves of what fully and necessarily is so.

Desire and Love

The suggestions above have been put forward tentatively. They show sympathy with Spinoza's effort to turn the focus of discussion away from choice between various courses and concentrate the question of freedom on the degree of self-realization we achieve, regardless of how this may be expressed in terms of rejected alternatives. To be free is to accept what is so. This becomes "mine" because I see the reason for it. Yet reason involves universality and necessity; the more adequate the reasons, the more clearly it is seen that they must apply for all.

The support for Spinoza is qualified. His view of "reason" was much less relaxed than the one proposed in recent chapters. He interpreted "seeing the reason" on a largely mathematical model, where the ignorance and facticity of self-questioning can be put in brackets. In other realms it is a more delicate problem to identify individual freedom with the acceptance of what is universal and necessary.

As an approach to this problem, it would help if we can clarify the relation between "individuality" and "universality" in acting for a reason. If I choose something, what is the "self" for which I choose? Is it purely individual or in some way universal? The following remarks will be resumed in the discussion of morality offered by the next chapter (pp. 252–54).

Throughout this book it has been claimed that I can know or want things only "for myself." It is meaningless to ask what a table or a road is "in itself." The object before me is at the moment a table because I am using it as a surface on which to write. But if I stand on it to change the electric light bulb, the "table" has become a ladder. What things are is a function of the use to which I put them, the way I want them. In this sense, all my actions are aimed at self-perfection, at the fulfillment of my intentions. What I desire is not food "in itself" but "for me": what I want is my well-being through food.

This notion, and the "reflexive" language of *self*-determination and *self*-possession which has run through this book, may suggest egoism or narcissism. That would be correct only if the "self" were my particular self, the source of all my private views and eccentricities. However, this interpretation has never been intended. Instead, it has been stressed that subjectivity should not be identified with privacy. The more metaphysical chapters have tried to discover what must be true for *any* questioning subject. Other chapters have tried to reveal what holds for anyone who engages in science or work or art or ordinary language. The "self" has always been social, in one or another of the many ways society or societies can be revealed. If a policeman stops me from using a public road as a golf course, he is not denying the thesis that things exist only "for me" and not "in themselves."

In other words, the basic distinction between "objectivity" and "subjectivity" has been between *things,* as used or desired for ends outside themselves, and *persons* who cannot altogether be reduced to such a status. A person is not merely an object for a subject but is a subject "in himself": he is the agent and source of meaning rather than an object on which meaning is conferred. He acts for reasons which are *his*. He can "make up his own mind." He can formulate intentions and carry out his policies; he sees for himself, decides for himself, and makes something of himself.

The distinction between things and persons is easier to state than to apply. To a large extent I know people as things, in terms of the roles they play and the functions they serve in my life. The policeman directing traffic is simply "for me," a means to getting my car safely across the intersection. Even my own "self-concept" is to a large extent the sum of roles into which I am cast. But the argument for subjectivity has repeatedly claimed that this cannot be all. My very embarrassment at needing to find myself through my varied appearances, through my roles and functions, is possible only in the context of some genuine, though implicit, grasp of what I am as a person "in myself" rather than merely "for another." Similarly, my knowledge of another person grows as I ask repeatedly what it is for *him* to enter, perhaps reluctantly, into the many roles through which I estimate and classify him (as an employer, citizen, husband, entertainer, etc.).

Where the emphasis was on knowledge, our basic distinction was between what it is to appear as an object and what it is to be a subject. Here, with the stress on willing, the corresponding distinction is between what it is to be *desired* or *used* as a means to another's goals and what it is to be *loved* or *respected* as a person who acts for reasons that are his. The distinction may be applied in many ways. Someone acting in a purely official capacity is a means to purposes that are mine. Some "things" (e.g., a work of art) may well merit respect as ends in themselves. We disclose the world in various ways as a realm of means and ends.

What is relevant here is that a scheme is provided for identifying individuality with universality. The table, so far as it is a mere means to particular purposes, lacks universality and necessity: I can use it as I happen to choose and you can use it as you wish. It is when we come to the individuality of what is an end in itself that we disclose true universality. In writing this paragraph I am acting, not as a means to foreign purposes, but because I think I see what is so. You may well disagree with my reasons and explain your own. But at least we are coming out of privacy and exposing ourselves to the universal by submitting to reason. We are individual in reasoning *for ourselves,* but we are acting universally in *reasoning* to what is so, in itself and for all. Philosophy is the "love of wisdom." Propaganda is the use of words for private purposes.

To sum up these remarks, freedom of self-determination is the opposite of "selfishness." It is the acceptance of what is so and of the appropriate reasoning that shows it to be so. The "self" which I determine and accept is my "true" self rather than the "private" self of my idiosyncrasies. Or the idiom of *accepting* could well be turned into that of *giving*. I give myself to what is so. The very recognition of someone as a rational being, an end in himself rather than a means for me, is a form of giving. The notion of love as both fulfillment and giving is one of man's oldest themes.

Acceptance and Rejection

The view of grades of freedom as corresponding to grades of reality and of reason is open to various objections. One is that it seems to interpret all in terms of a greater or lesser "adequacy" and to omit our basic conviction that there is falsity as well as truth, evil as well as good. The other objection is closely connected. It is that the defect of an opposite makes terms meaningless; if all is true and rational and all *my* acts are free, then such terms can be dropped from our vocabulary without loss. Similarly, it has been said that if fate governs all, then we should forget about fate.

A reply to the second objection would be that terms remain meaningful if they can be used in a comparative sense, as here suggested. But if room can be left for an opposite to freedom, then a reply is offered to both objections at once. Is this possible? It seems not, for it was remarked above that if I were not free there would be no problem of freedom.

However, starting with our consideration of skepticism in the fourth chapter, we have pointed out various possibilities of self-contradiction in agency. These were all on a highly theoretical level. The person who proposes a doctrine of total skepticism is contradicting this in his very agency of proposing the theory as true. Similarly with the doctrine of complete determinism.

The question is whether such a self-contradiction can be "lived." Can I not merely freely propose determinism but freely live "unfreedom"? Or, if the highest grade of freedom was called acceptance, can I freely "reject" my freedom?

Here one should be careful to avoid a facile moralizing. It is easy to fall to the language of a third-person account and start classifying behavior as free or unfree. Each must speak for himself. However, it does seem possible to put oneself in a state where there is a radical contradiction between what one "is" and what one "does." Apathy, degeneration, dissipation, escapism, self-hatred are terms that come to mind as ways of "freely losing oneself," or of rejecting one's true self in the name of one's private self.

If the grades of freedom cannot be interpreted in terms of self-acceptance and self-rejection, then much will be lost from our language of freedom. The image of grades of adequacy does not support very well the terminology of praise and blame in which our language is so rich. I may accuse myself of "living a lie" but scarcely of being low on a scale. And even fatalistic religious doctrines seem somehow to allow for that supreme rebellion in which the sinner "rejects fate." If the notion of choice between alternative paths has been played down in this chapter, that of self-rejection may take its place.

In any event, these suggestions would put less emphasis on one's identification of particular acts as free or unfree, and more on the "direction" of one's life. This is not to deny that the courts have the difficult task of assessing freedom in particular acts, but this should be regarded in terms of a purely third-person account of behavior. Statistically, people with such symptoms could have acted otherwise. This chapter supports the sciences of man in their project of giving as complete a causal account of behavior as possible. But it offers little support for those who would "play God." I should be prepared to accuse myself but should try to understand others. So long as the metaphysics and popular imagery of determinism are kept at bay, diagnosis and cure are worth far more than blame and exhortation.

14

Am I
Morally Bound?

Moral questions need no introduction but much clarification. As mentioned at the beginning of the opening chapter, they will be included in any list we make of the questions we find ourselves asking. Alongside the questions of fact and technique that run through our day we discover a variety of "ought" questions. Ought I to work harder or take more time for enjoyment? Ought I to go along with what "is done" or shake off my complacency and change things? The moral element can be postponed. I may for the moment rest content with a reply that it is to my profit to work hard, or simply that I want to do so. But an "ought" question reappears. Ought I to allow myself to be dominated by the profit motive? Or even, what ought I to want? Perhaps such questions are illusory. Perhaps no more is involved than in the factual questions with which we feel at home. This at least is what the present chapter will ask. It may not be trifling with words to say it is a question we ought to ask.

A completely negative answer to the question whether we are free would of course leave no place for this chapter. But even the most qualified acceptance of freedom leads on to a discussion of moral questions. If the invention of the atom bomb were as much an event of nature as the eruption of a volcano, no moral problem could appear. But the scientists and politicians engaged in this regarded it as *their* work, and many went through a crisis of conscience whether they ought to produce such a weapon. So far as I am author of my actions, I live in the realm of "ought" questions. A free act is performed for a reason, and this is not reducible to a story about causes in nature. Even Spinoza, for all his argument against the reality or importance of choosing between alternatives, would accept this; his account of the grades of what *is* real and reasonable bears the title of "Ethics" and can be interpreted as a compendious *ought* statement.

Along with particular moral questions the question of morality arises. As the first chapter suggested, it is here that "questions about questions" come home to us most dramatically. Many of the questions which philosophers ask may seem idle and academic. But our familiarity with questions of fact leads us to wonder about the status of our moral questions. Are they really as distinct as they seem from factual ones? It is a fact that the atom bomb can endanger millions of lives. It is a fact that most of us want to avoid such slaughter. It is a fact also that we want effective means of self-defense. So we may ask if our question whether we ought to produce the weapon is not reducible to a complex of such statements about the fact of technical processes and human wants. Perhaps those who made the decision did so on the basis of a calculation of likely consequences and a "sheer choice" when the limited evidence was at hand. Indeed we may wonder if the crisis of conscience belonged to any "moral realm" or could be explained by a series of biographical statements about preferences, fears, scruples, childhood influences and taboos—all in a solidly "factual realm."

Hence the problem of this chapter is about the status of moral questions. Are they really distinct from factual ones and do we all belong inescapably to a world of the "ought"? If so, in what does this consist and how do we find our way in it?

This chapter will not merely follow from the previous one but will turn back on it in much of the discussion. Freedom and morality are intimately connected themes. If we take the questions of the two chapters together, we may distinguish three possible replies:

1. I am neither free nor morally bound: what seem to be my responsible actions are revealed, sooner or later, to be merely the result of complex pressures at work on me.

2. I am free but not morally bound: through all such pressures I do act for a "reason" that is mine, but my reason is exhaustively stated as a simple "because I want—"

3. I am free and morally bound: to act for a reason involves some submission to an absolute "norm" or "law" which tells me "that I ought—"

It would seem that (1) could be omitted from consideration in this chapter as it belongs to the previous one. However, many of the problems in giving an account of morality appear to be at heart difficulties about freedom. Hence the first section will look at attempts to reduce the supposed absolute of morality (3) to the coercion of various pressures (1), with or without the intervention of a private choice that is a law to itself (2). The second section will examine the view that morality is irreducible to the battle of natural and social pressures, and that some moral law is a condition of even our most "individualistic" acting.

Social Pressures
and Private Choice

A demonstration is arranged to protest against a decision of the government. One person takes part in it because he regards the decision unjust and recognizes his obligation to oppose it. Another person remains at home because he feels the decision is unfortunate but necessary and he holds it his duty to support the government in such a case. Both claim to have acted according to their conscience; they were free to do otherwise but morally bound to do as they did.

However, a study of these two people would probably reveal many characteristics that raise questions about their claim to act for reasons of morality. The first man shows a record of protest against authority, and his relation to his parents would go a long way toward explaining this. The second man has always accepted authority readily and has shrewdly used his temperament to curry favor and improve his position. Each went predictably along the course to which the stronger pressures directed him. He may claim to have acted against his inclinations (e.g., against his desire to avoid likely sanctions), but whatever he states as his moral reason is a rationalization for a stronger pressure he fails to acknowledge.

If, however, we follow the previous chapter in defending self-determination through such pressures, it is hard to admit moral norms in our account. The more we stress a person's *self*-determination, *his* way of seeing the matter, the more difficult it becomes to interpret this as submission to a law of what is right and morally binding. If morality "binds," then is it not a further "pressure," as much a force working on us as any of the social or psychological factors to which many reduce it? If I am free to make up my own mind, then *my* reason is finally that I see things this way and I want to do them this way. The autonomy of acting freely seems as much to exclude any submission to moral norms as it does compulsion by purely social forces.

This account of the situation is weighted in such a way as to make it a problem. But it has appeared this way to many, and this section will consider (1) attempts to reduce morality to social pressures, and (2) attempts to treat freedom as an ultimate "I want" that leaves no place for acceptance of a moral law. The discussion leads to a reinterpretation of the way morality "binds," and this will become the topic of the following section.

The Influence of Society

To treat this theme adequately would be to repeat, not only much that was mentioned in the previous chapter, but a great deal of what we have learned in this century about the hidden motives of behavior. The notions have by now become common coinage, so it will be enough to indicate a few of them and raise some questions.

AUTHORITY

Whether we like to admit it or not, most of our life is spent conforming to the word of authority. Traffic would come to a standstill if we did not. So would our economic, political, and social life. Anarchism is self-defeating as a movement. We may reserve the right to break laws in minor ways on some occasions. But by and large we conform.

This, however, is not a topic on which we need dwell, for it has not usually been taken as leading far into the problem of morality. Most people regard the authority of policemen and presidents as one of many external factors which we freely accept. Morality lies in our choice to conform or protest, and the pressures we worry about (as in the example above) are those more intimate ways in which society and temperament seem to dictate or attitude toward authority, the "hidden persuaders" we shall discuss below.

Nevertheless, if authority enters so extensively into our life, the theme should not be dismissed glibly from any discussion of morality. In other fields, the acceptance of authority is a condition for advance in knowledge. No scientist could make any progress unless he simply took from his predecessors most of what he knows and the rules of working on which they have agreed. We stand on the shoulders of others. To try to judge everything for oneself is presumptuous and disruptive. Why should the same not apply to moral knowledge?

There is some truth to the analogy. Even the most critical moral judgments are not formed in a vacuum, altogether apart from the social habits, customs, and values in which an individual grows up morally.

But there are important differences. A scientist makes a relatively minor addition to a store of information, and another person could have made it as well as he did. But a moral judgment is strictly *mine* and embraces the whole of my moral knowledge in a way no scientific discovery does for its own field. Eichmann offered a morally invalid defense for his slaughter of Jews by saying he was merely carrying out the principles he took on authority or from upbringing. Scientific truths may be received, but moral principles are formed, or at least ratified, by individual judgment. Collective wisdom is a basis for each person to make his own critical moral judgments, but it does not itself supply the "ought" which each person says for himself.

Two important notes may be mentioned at this point. The first is that it is an over-simplification to view social authority as something merely apart from the individual, which he accepts or rejects. We exist socially and the voice of society is our own. Hence laws and customs are not merely imposed from outside. If I drive dangerously I am breaking a law which is an expression of my own claim that there should be safe driving conditions on the roads. This notion is difficult to apply in concrete cases and does not deny the conclusion of the previous paragraph; but the line between authority and the individual is not as sharp as suggested there.

The other note is that, in the Judaeo-Christian tradition at least, a final authority for law has been set in God. We can appeal from particular human ("positive") laws to a divine law or to "natural law" which codifies the way man is "essentially," according to the mind of his Creator. The result is that our questioning why we ought to act in a certain way comes to a halt in the answer "because God so wills it." The answer has proved much more effective, in terms of behavior, than any supplied by a philosopher. But if interpreted in this abrupt way, it is inadequate as a moral reason. If God's will is taken as arbitrary or inscrutable, then the answer no more explains why I am morally bound to follow divine prescriptions than such an answer would for the laws of respectable human authorities. Yet if, as is more likely, God is held to command for good reasons, then it is precisely these reasons which are the source of moral obligation, regardless of their social or religious authentication. Nevertheless, this account may involve the same sort of over-simplification as that discussed in the previous paragraph. And the reply that social laws are not merely imposed from outside is even more clearly applicable in regard to divine laws. Talk of what God wills is talk of what I really am or ought to be. This does not suggest why the continuing problem of what I ought to be is helped by translation into the religious idiom of what God wants me to be; but such questions belong to the following chapter.

HIDDEN PERSUADERS

The comment of Macbeth's witches, that "fair is foul and foul is fair," seems an apt summary of the conclusions of cultural anthropologists. There is scarcely a vice, according to our own standards, which has not in some culture been regarded as permissible or even as a moral and religious duty. And psychologists have shown great skill or imagination in relating the supposedly moral principles, which inform our conscience, to nonmoral events or matters of convenience in our individual and social past.

The repugnance we have for incest is absent in some cultures and seems to be the offspring of tradition. What a psychiatrist regards as childhood sexual experiences may have much to say about the strong "ought" judgments which make up a good part of our opinion and practice as an adult. And there is much to support the Marxist claim that the "morality" of a society is a complex of rules and evaluations which reflect the interests of the dominant class, often in a previous age.

However, we do not need to delve into psychiatry or anthropology to arouse the suspicion that many, if not all, of our strongest convictions may come from social pressures that are no longer present to us as such when we make our judgments of what ought to be. Modern parents are often embarrassed at their role of enforcing the standards and values of their society on children far too young to have a mind of their own. Yet it is impossible to avoid playing "Society" or "Tradition." Every word, gesture, and attitude makes an impression on the mind for which all is new. How then can we be sure that our own moral indignation or guilt is any more than the way society determines us to feel and react?

In this account, moral obligation loses its supposedly unique character. It becomes one form of the most general phenomenon of life, the way in which all organisms perpetuate and preserve themselves. Human society is not so distinct from the beehive and anthill.[1] Social approval and disapproval are as intimate a force as instinct. We live to the accompaniment of voices saying "that's right," or "that simply isn't done," or "that is immature." Courage in war is highly institutionalized: there can be less resistance on the path to heroism than to cowardice. And even the revolutionary works against his present society for the approval of some other society.

However, any pretendedly exhaustive account of our action in terms of hidden pressures is involved in the self-contradiction so often indicated in this book. Those who affirm such theories as true assert stronger motives

---

[1] For a description, in largely biological terms, of the "morality of a closed society," see the first chapter of Bergson's *The Two Sources of Morality and Religion* (Doubleday Anchor).

for themselves than can be supplied by their own theory. No claim to truth can afford to explain itself away in terms of a disturbed childhood or remote social practices. If the theory of moral relativism were itself relative to our own unsettled culture, we could simply wait for more stable times and a return to absolutism.

Two different questions, and viewpoints, are involved in a report of the *genesis* of a moral opinion and in a discussion of its *validity*. The question how I inherited my customs and inclinations is a legitimate topic for the many observers of human behavior. But the question whether I ought to accept or reform the customs, to follow or go against my inclinations, involves me in an effort to find reasons and to be reasonable rather than in a study of causes (cf. pp. 227–29). A spectator account of patterns of behavior is by no means irrelevant as I make up my mind. Yet *my* question what I should do sets me acutely in the perplexity of the agent. The reasons I give may be invalid and are always open to revision. But if I try to replace reasons with causes, validity with genesis, I do so for a reason and because I think I ought.

ACCEPTED VALUES

Nevertheless, such an argument that moral questions are irreducible to any purely factual inquiry seems empty when we face the complex decisions that make up so much of our life. The simple examples discussed in most books by moral philosophers appear singularly unhelpful. As we work toward a decision, do we not find that our concern is with difficult questions of fact? If we can sufficiently disentangle and resolve these, then does not the decision of what we "ought" to do somehow take care of itself? Or if—as is more often the case—the facts prove too involved for us, then do we not lack sufficient evidence for a "reasoned" decision, so that the one we make is much like the toss of a coin?

A glance through any newspaper would seem to support this view. Should the city build a new power plant? There are grave problems and dangers from the presently inadequate supply of electricity. There would be grave problems and dangers in the pollution of the atmosphere resulting from such a project. Arguments, all in the realm of fact, support one course; other arguments, equally factual, support the other. Experts thrash out the question which course would be best for the health and well-being of the community. Perhaps out of all this discussion it will clearly emerge which is the "right" plan. Perhaps the decision will finally be "political," based on an assessment of the less well informed opinion of the electorate. But whatever happens, questions about the unique status of "ought" judgments seem quite irrelevant.

What is suggested is that most "ought" problems are about means

rather than ends. Two doctors may disagree whether they should ampu-
tate a leg at once or try to save it. They agree, even in detail, about the
end they accept, the health and mobility of the patient. They disagree
about the best means to this. If medical books use the word "ought,"
it is in this sense of a technical adaptation of means to accepted ends.
And can this analysis not be extended far beyond the realm of simple
techniques? Are not both "hawks" and "doves" agreed about the search
for peace, at variance only in the complex means they see as best adapted
to this?

Such an account of morality could be put abstractly by saying that
an "ought" proposition is justified or falsified by its consequences, when
these are seen as means to accepted ends. "We ought to try and save the
leg" is shown to have been a wrong decision when the patient dies of
gangrene. If you reply that it is better to die with two legs than live with
one, then you are so far removed from the values of a sane society (i.e.,
ours) that you are yourself "a case for treatment": similarly, if you
prefer needless suffering or poverty to a just peace with prosperity for all.

A reply would be that the examples are loaded. The choice is not
between different means to the same state of peace but between a war for
just and lasting conditions of peace and an immediate peace that is
precarious and involves considerable injustice. Here the conflict is
between ends. Or is it? Cannot any such "ends" be reinterpreted as
alternative means toward a more general end which is accepted by all?
This end may become highly abstract in its statement. We may adopt
the slogan of "utilitarianism" (e.g., Jeremy Bentham, John Stuart
Mill) and say that the norm for judging actions is "the greatest good of
the greatest number." Or we may allow for the various ways this is
interpreted in different cultures by speaking of "the whole set of goals on
which a society is based." But moral discussion is removed from the
question of ends and is set in a factual study of means.

It will be further suggested at the end of this chapter that there is
much truth in this analysis. Perhaps it is wise to aim, as far as possible,
at keeping our language factual and our discussion in the realm of means.
However, two comments qualify this suggestion.

The first is that such a proposal leaves us with an affirmative answer
to the question whether we are morally bound. Our calculation of which
policy achieves the greatest good is made under the moral imperative
that we ought to discover and work for this goal. By reducing moral
language to one highly abstract principle we need not lessen the force
of morality in our life.

The second comment is that a supreme moral principle is a reason
for acting, not a cause or a merely imposed value. If I am to be morally
bound by it, I must see the reason for it. And the generally accepted

goals of a culture, though they usually produce social conformity, do not supply an adequate reason for conforming rather than reforming. Reform is proposed for reasons that go beyond what is at present "in possession." Health, peace, and prosperity belong to the picture most people today would make of the greatest good. But no popular vote can bridge the gap between what the majority happen to want and what I ought to work for. However, the difficulty of finding any such bridge introduces the question whether my varied decisions do, after all, involve any more than a statement of "what I want."

The Privacy of Choice

If freedom is denied, then what I call morality is reduced to some complex of social pressures. But if I am free to make my own way among the laws and customs that bear on me, how can I be bound by any "moral law"?

CHOICE AS PRIVATE TASTE

I may insist that I act for a reason, but is not the "reason" for which I act simply that *I choose* to follow this custom or accept that value? To have any moral norm imposed on my choice would be to submit to some "pressure" and thus deny my self-determination. The claim that morality is altogether "higher" and more "rational" invites renewed investigation of which earthy pressure has been sublimated in this way. The girl who says "no" for moral reasons is choosing to follow one element in her complex character; the girl who says "yes," because she likes it, is choosing less pompously to follow other elements.

Though it may seem odd that the philosophies of determinism and of "libertarianism" stand so close on this question, there is much to support such an analysis. However much we try to "weigh" our choice, what we finally do—as statesmen, generals, businessmen or consumers—seems very much a private jump in the dark. The fall of a tossed coin is both completely determined by the laws of nature and completely arbitrary from our point of view. Spinoza would agree with this identification of determination from outside and arbitrary choice. He would agree also that the account is a fair one of the way most of us perform most of our actions at the low level of reality at which we live.

Put in more contemporary terms, supposedly moral statements can be reduced to expressions of personal taste. If I say "I like tea," my statement is merely one of taste and calls for no "reason" (though I could add something about cultural causes). If I say "children ought to be polite toward their elders," I am perhaps making no more than the autobiographical statement that "I like polite children." Or if I supply reasons, then sooner or later I come to an "ought" which is a matter of taste not open to support by further reasons: I happen to like this or to have chosen it. Those who claim that such an analysis of moral language can be exhaustive propose that "ought" statements are finally imperatives or expressions of personal feeling. To "give a reason" is to give my private reason, to reveal my idiosyncrasy in making one decision rather than another.

It is embarrassing to recognize how far such a reduction goes. But there are grounds for rejecting it as exhaustive, and a consideration of some of them may lead toward an understanding of how morality can be involved in "acting for a reason," in such a way that it need no longer appear as one further pressure at work on us from outside.

ACTING FOR A REASON

On a purely linguistic level, the above analysis is suspect. In saying "complete silence ought to be observed," I am perhaps only stating an imperative which tells you what I happen to want. But if I say that it is morally wrong to cause needless suffering, I mean more than that my idiosyncrasy is to dislike this. I am not merely reporting my feelings but appealing to a universal norm. I do not say "it is my will that—" but "there is a reason why—" and all of us are obliged to submit to this reason (even though we have difficulty stating or proving it).

To give a reason is to give more than one's private ground for acting. If I ask why you did not keep an appointment and you reply that you chose to stay at home, I feel you have given me no reason but have merely appealed to freedom by restating an action as *yours*. If you reply that you had a bad cold, then I may fail to see this as an *adequate* reason, but at least we have entered the realm of discussion, of freedom as "informed" by reason. This is achieved so far as you convert your private act into a universal one: it is reasonable for all to protect health at the expense of minor appointments. The expression "private reason" is a contradiction in terms.

A reply to this would be that use of the phrase "it is reasonable" may add a note of respectability but does not change the reduction of morality to individual choice or taste. The example merely points to a very common preference for health over fidelity to appointments. Even if this accepted value happens to be found without exception, it still remains a generalization from personal choices and tastes.

The reply may be apt in this particular example. But it still does not dispose of the appeal we make, in giving reasons, to a universal norm rather than to merely accepted values or private whims. If "reason" is no more than a technique of adapting means to ends, then to "act reasonably" presupposes ends, and these may well be merely given values or common tastes. But appeal to reason in moral matters involves more than this. To identify moral obligation with "acting reasonably" is to find in reason a ground of necessity rather than a way of relating means to ends which I happen to accept. It is reasonable to go to Germany if I want to learn German; but learning German is far from being a matter of moral obligation. However, if I try to give reasons for my sense of obligation to avoid causing needless suffering, I am trying to disclose the nonhypothetical nature of a genuine moral obligation.

THE OBLIGATION
TO BE REASONABLE

Here we face squarely the difficult task of finding a metaphysical ground for morality. In acting freely I act for a reason. When this reason is questioned I supply another. Does the process go on through an indefinite series of "why" questions? If not, there are two ways in which it could be halted. The first is by discovering some particular reason or value which is unquestionable; but this is no more possible than the discovery of a particular fact that is beyond question (cf. pp. 67–68). The · second way is by revealing an inescapable structure in the very process of "acting for a reason."

If I ask "Why be honest?," I may give reasons in terms of personal and social consequences without finding any value that does not invite further questions and reasons. But if, instead of going outside the performance of being honest, I can see this as involved in my very agency of "acting for a reason" or of "being reasonable," then I reveal an inescapable ground for my moral conviction. For the challenge "Why be reasonable?" answers itself. The imperative to be reasonable cannot be avoided; any choice I make to escape from it is made for some reason. If, for example, I now propose to "act for no reason," I am doing so for a fairly obvious reason, i.e., to test or refute the claim that has just been made.

Indeliberate or coerced actions do not go against this claim as they are irrelevant to the present discussion. We are asking whether free acts must incorporate some moral norm, whether "I want" includes "I ought." If I fall to the ground when struck by a bullet or a fit, my behavior involves no freedom and no question of morality. Morality is and remains a question, but it is a question only as *asked*. In my perplexity I ask if I am morally bound. But in the asking I affirm responsibility for the way I pose my question, the way I freely enter into it and make it mine. In asking explicitly whether there is really any "ought," I implicitly affirm that I am asking as I ought. In asking explicitly whether I ought to be reasonable, I implicitly submit to the moral norm of being reasonable.

What is suggested here as a supreme moral principle shares the abstractness of other candidates considered above. Talk of "being reasonable" may seem as empty as talk of "the greatest good." But at least the principle satisfies the requirement of being one for which we can "see the reason," rather than being a statement of merely accepted goals. And the relaxed view this book has proposed of the many different ways of being reasonable encourages us to explore what it is to act for a reason in the full complexity of the decisions that face us. We speak of "good" reasons and "bad" ones. That is, the varied reasons that inform our actions may fit together or clash. If I choose to drink heavily before driving, I do so for reasons that conflict with almost all else that gives order to my purposes. Where reasons clash, I find myself under some more definite expression of the moral imperative to be reasonable. My integrity as a questioner imposes on me the "ought" of reviewing my reasons, reexamining the facts, mastering my moods, perhaps of revising accepted standards of what makes for a good reason in this particular inquiry. A questioner can in many ways violate his obligation to be reasonable, but he cannot escape from it.

The gap between such a principle and any actual dilemma is obviously great. But by interpreting rationality as an "end in itself," we do at least remove moral values from the privacy of simple acceptance and from the idiom of pressures acting on us externally. My conviction that I ought to be honest in my thinking and in my dealing with others may have much to do with the way I was brought up. Yet my very search for the reason why and how I should be honest in various complicated situations reveals the obligation at the heart of my searching rather than leaving it as a nonmoral force in my temperament and background. It is not easy to act freely in and through the pressures of circumstance; but so far as I succeed, a moral norm is disclosed as the condition of my free actions, without which they would slip from my authorship into a private chaos with neither rhyme nor reason.

Autonomy and Morality

Socrates' command to "know yourself" seems strange. If I know myself in all I do, why should this need an exhortation? But the common instruction to "be yourself" sounds even more remarkable. Surely I am myself. How can this be imposed as a law?

The problem of ignorance in knowledge, and of "otherness" at the heart of being oneself, is the theme of this book. It is only by suffering what I am not that I become what I am. The lengthy consideration of the obstacles to self-determination has fitted in with this scheme. It is through all the limitations of temperament and social situation that I possess myself and achieve the "autonomy" of saying "I will."

However, the topic of morality has added a new turn to the story. The moral law is not an obstacle to freedom, one more form of "otherness" which we struggle to appropriate. We do not receive it, as we do the slings of adversity and temperament. It belongs to our activity; it is on the side of freedom, not of pressure. And yet we submit to it in a far stronger sense than to any private inclination or social influence. The moral law is "categorical," an absolute "ought" with which we may accord or against which we can rebel but of which we cannot dispose as we will. In any act that is my own, the question "What do I want?" reveals at its heart the question "What ought I to want?" This paradox of autonomy and moral submission will be the topic of this section. We may start with a brief account of the moral philosophy of Kant, for whom this problem was central.

The Moral Law:
Kant

Chapters Five and Six presented the customary, but one-sided, version of Kant's philosophy. All we can know is *phenomena,* things as they appear to us in a variety of possible observations. Metaphysics can be established as transcendental philosophy, an analysis of the structures that belong to all *phenomena.* But reason, in its claim to go beyond this to things as they finally are "in themselves," is purely regulative. I know myself only as *phenomenon,* in the many ways I appear to myself, but never as *noumenon.*

However, as stressed on p. 111, this is a summary of the conclusions of Kant's first *Critique.* This work studies only "theoretical reason," the sort of knowledge that is involved in the sciences and in our description of behavior: i.e., what we have called a third-person account. But in Kant's second *Critique,*[2] he turns to a study of "practical reason." This is reason as it works in the realm of freedom and morality. There

---

[2] *The Critique of Practical Reason.* For a more easily readable version of his moral philosophy, see his *Foundations of the Metaphysics of Morals.*

we are not concerned with what is given to us in experience but rather with what we ought to bring about in acting ''reasonably,'' what it is to *be* reasonable.

Kant was a ''realist,'' in the nonphilosophical sense of the term. He was aware of the self-delusion in claims to be acting morally and he would have seen no problem in the many individual and social pressures discussed above. ''One need not be an enemy of virtue, but only a cool observer who does not confuse even the liveliest aspiration for the good with its reality, to be doubtful sometimes whether true virtue can really be found anywhere in the world.''[3] But this he regarded as irrelevant. There is no argument from what is observed in experience to what ought to be done. We do not go from even generally accepted values to moral obligation. Whether most people choose health over fidelity to appointments, or vice-versa, will not tell me what I ought to do when confronted with the choice. The most I can get from experience is a series of hypothetical statements; *if* I want to conform to certain accepted values and to get approval in this society, then I should act this way. But a nonhypothetical (categorical) ''ought'' must be looked for in the nature of acting for a reason rather than in any observation of how people in fact behave.

HYPOTHETICAL AND CATEGORICAL

Kant would agree with one of the conclusions of the previous chapter, that there is no place for freedom in the world of science. Such a world is intelligible so far as it is ordered according to constant connections between *phenomena*. From this point of view man is completely determined, whether by natural forces or by instincts and tendencies or even by ''values'' as a sociologist might record them. Taken merely as a *phenomenon*, as a creature of impulses and inclinations, of tastes and prejudices, man is in principle completely predictable.

However, the world of *phenomena* is also entirely relative. No object is attained as it is in itself but only as it appears to a subject. This table has no ''individuality'' apart from that which I assign it in using it for writing, or in weighing it, or in selling it for a price. Hence the necessity which I find in physics or economics or sociology is only hypothetical; it comes to light through the decision of people to organize *phenomena* according to certain intentions. So the determinisms a psychologist finds in human behavior do not tell us all about man. They tell us only how man appears to a psychologist who decides to study him

---

[3] *Foundations,* trans. L.W. Beck (Indianapolis: The Liberal Arts Press, Division of the Bobbs-Merrill Company, Inc., 1959), p. 24.

in a certain way. More probing questions arise when we turn to ourselves as psychologists or economists or philosophers. These questions are no longer about how man is related to other objects but about what it is to be a person who can interpret the world in various ways.

Here Kant claims to disclose the self as *noumenon,* no longer as the resultant of forces but as the free agent who actively makes something of his life. Kant's problem is to reveal what man is in himself, what he must be precisely as a free agent, rather than how he happens to appear as an object. His search is not for the laws of behavior but for the "laws of freedom." Whereas the former are hypothetical, the latter are categorical; they tell what I ought to do rather than what I happen observably to do, what I ought to want rather than what I in fact choose.

Hence Kant rejects as inadequate any account of morality in terms of "heteronomy" (any principle *outside* my act of deciding, such as commonly accepted values or positive laws). The only basis such norms can supply for my action is hypothetical; if I wish to be trusted I should protect my good name. A categorical norm cannot be found outside my free activity but must lie at the heart of my "autonomy." The law for which Kant is looking is that of practical reason itself: it is the law which I must implicitly affirm even in trying explicitly to ignore or deny it.

We cannot follow the details of Kant's analysis but may suggest something of his inquiry through his famous account of the "good will." When we ask what is good in itself, or without any hypothesis or qualification, we must look in the realm of intentions. Intelligence and other talents, wealth, power, health, and other gifts of fortune are good or bad depending on the intention with which they are informed. But what makes an intention good? Our common conviction is that it is our acting out of duty, regardless of any calculation of profit. This conviction, Kant holds, comes from our situation as creatures of sense, for whom duty is a struggle against desire and inclination. A purely rational being would simply "be reasonable." Hence a good person does not impose his private view on things but, by submitting to his own laws as a rational being, he attains what is really so in itself and he wills what ought to be so for all. It is the universality of acting for a reason that gives Kant his most celebrated test of morality. A consideration of this will introduce the next topic.

RESPECT FOR THE OTHER

Kant's notion is the one we considered above, that acting reasonably means coming out of the privacy of choice or impulse and submitting oneself to what ought to hold for all. In Kant's terms, this is the conversion of a private "maxim" into a universal "law." If I propose a certain course of action, I find whether it is moral by discovering whether I can formulate it as a law for all people without running into the "unreason" of a radical contradiction. His most discussed example is that to make a promise without intending to keep it is immoral because if this were turned into a universal law, then the very notion or possibility of a promise would be destroyed.[4]

The example has been much criticized and there is no need to enter the discussion here. What is important is the equivalence Kant sets between autonomy, reality, and universality. It is by acting autonomously, for reasons which I see and make my own, that I am a person "in myself" rather than merely "appearing" through a variety of roles I play. And I find what I "really" am, not by withdrawing into my particular self, but by acting in ways that can be formulated as a universal law.

This is basically the equivalence which was discussed in the previous chapter, under the heading of "desire and love" (pp. 233–35). My desire for things as means to private purposes which I impose does not take me beyond appearances; the ash-tray is defined by the purposes to which I happen to put it, as a receptacle or paper-weight or hammer. I find what is really so only where I disclose that which is no mere means to foreign purposes but can be loved or respected as an end in itself. This Kant calls "rational nature." Wherever this is located, it embraces both the individuality and the universality of reason. To be reasonable is to act for ends that are one's own and yet to submit to what is so for all, independently of private views and desires.

It is this that allows Kant to introduce the social dimension of morality. To be reasonable is to respect rational nature wherever it is found, in myself, in other selves, or in whatever belongs to the "kingdom of ends." Here alone we pass from the hypothetical to the categorical. To recognize a person and yet treat him purely as a means, as an object merely for me, is to involve myself in a radical self-contradiction.

It is not easy to say how the principle that we should respect persons as ends is to be applied. As mentioned in the previous chapter, much of our life is concerned legitimately with treating people in terms of the functions they serve. And the notion of "respect" is difficult to render precisely. But for the present discussion, the interest of Kant's moral theory is that it sees what is most truly "my own" activity as a submission to the "other." To act freely is not to do what I happen to want but is to recognize and reverence the moral law. This "ought" at the heart of all I do is no "pressure" at work on me from outside. It is not "heteronomous" but is the very law through which actions become more

---

[4] *Ibid.*, p. 40.

genuinely mine by becoming more rational and more universal. I find my true self by surrendering my private wants and allowing the expression in me of that "end in itself" to which all my questioning is a submission.

Individual and Social Morality

Some philosophers hold that all morality is social. That is, they maintain that all moral obligations come from the need to harmonize conflicting interests: where there is no such need, there is no place for morality. Thus, qualities such as humility and temperance are morally irrelevant unless they lead to social harmony. If I regularly retire to the privacy of my room and drink to excess, I am not acting immorally unless this interferes with my work among others.

To set the test for morality in one's respect for other persons might seem to lead to this conclusion. However, if this test is itself derived from the more fundamental principle of respecting rational nature as an end in itself, wherever revealed, then no such conclusion follows. The obligation applies to one's own self as much as to others. The difference is one of location, not of principle. In the example above, there could be a failure of self-respect in much the same way that I can abuse another by interfering with his opportunity to develop as a responsible person. The cultivation of one's own talents, growth in integrity, and the pursuit of truth can be as much a matter of moral obligation as the more evidently social virtues. Self-love, seeking the good in me, is far removed from selfishness, seeking my private interests.

Nevertheless, most of the moral decisions we face involve other people, and the question of acting reasonably is usually one of balancing social good and evil. Here the norm of respecting others as ends in themselves may seem at variance with the test of doing what can be made a universal law. "Respect" appears to come more often in acknowledging differences than in following rules that apply to all.

Yet there is a basic distinction between the universality of moral laws and of scientific ones. We do not know what human nature is in the way we know what sulphuric acid is. The latter is revealed by observation of recurrent facts, and what is learned can safely be applied in the same way to all instances. But man is present only as a partial achievement of what he can be and ought to be: respect for the varied experiments of self-discovery enters into the task of finding what "really" applies to all.

That is, we do not first achieve our knowledge of a person and then respect him. We come gradually to know what he is through experience informed by respect. The same applies to self-knowledge. I can tell you how I see things and decide policies for my current, highly particular self. But a lifetime of patient self-discovery is required before I can delineate in much detail my true self.

If any principle can be drawn from this for social morality, it is that we should, so far as possible, allow others to discover their own genuine interest rather than that we should hastily impose on them our own estimate of a universal rule. Our very conviction that reason is self-consistent and universal should encourage us to let others be. Even if we could know in advance what is best, we should allow others the full benefit of the arduous road along which they discover for themselves what they really want. There are no shortcuts in learning to "be oneself."

The practical problems are evident. I do not help a child far on his voyage of self-discovery if I allow him to play with explosives. But in general it is through experimenting with private interests that the universal appears. Respect for a person as an end in himself in shown by entering appreciatively into his contribution to our common effort to find what we really are.

Principles and Practice

Some philosophers feel it is their task to analyze moral language and arguments but not to derive any principles for discovering which actions are right and which are wrong. Other philosophers extend their concern to principles and arm their reader with ones of such generality that no connection with any actual decision is apparent.

It may seem that this chapter has gone along a well trodden path. What principle could be more abstract and more ineffectual than to "be reasonable"? The reader is left the full burden of discovering what counts as good or bad reasons in the tangled moral situations in which he finds himself.

So, unfortunately, he has to be. No claim has been made to supply moral principles which work out the difficult decisions each of us faces daily. The claim has been only to show that these decisions do involve a moral element. "Ought" questions are valid. They cannot be dismissed by the extensive evidence we have about the influence of nonmoral factors. Nor can we canonize freedom as a sheer "I want," where the agent is a law to himself. There is a moral law to which we respond in acting freely. And we find it at the heart of our very effort to deal reasonably with the problems we encounter.

The ambition to deduce from this law a variety of principles which can then be applied to concrete situations is misleading. Once we are convinced that we do inhabit a realm of the "ought," then we can afford to dirty our hands at once in the complexities of life. As other chapters have suggested, theory comes out of practice. What this chapter has added is a clarification that this is also moral theory, that an "ought" is to be expected in its statements.

This is not to say that our talk should be littered with moral terms. Quite the opposite. It may be wise to keep moral language at bay as long as possible. Once a moral element is assured, and it is identified with the conditions of rational inquiry, then concrete problems may well be expressed in factual rather than moral terms and the focus of attention be set on means rather than ends.

The proposal for a "factual," "pragmatic," or "utilitarian" approach to moral problems does not mean erasing the lines this chapter has tried to draw. Facts are messy and slippery. The way they are disclosed is not independent of the philosophy an investigator brings to his task. If an interpretation of the world as basically moral has any cash value, then this should appear in the moral sensitivity with which facts are revealed, even though specifically moral language is avoided.

The command to be reasonable means that we are morally obliged to give attention to finding, clarifying, and revising the reasons for whatever stand we take on serious issues. This is no invitation to be scrupulous or indecisive. Decisions have to be made, and the reasons for our actions are often painfully weak. But to investigate as far as possible and make a decision for which we cannot account "up to the hilt" is far from the privacy of prejudice or of an arbitrary leap in the dark.

15

Is There
A Final Answer?

Obviously not. We can have an adequate answer only where we are in complete control of our question. But every question remains questionable. Reflexive questions bring to light the inescapable ignorance at the heart of every direct question and its answer.

We can always impose some measure of control on our questioning. We can make questions of "existence" into questions of fact by defining a person's existence in terms of some test such as heart beat. The accident victim was still existing at noon but no longer at one o'clock. A current second-rate novelist exists but Shakespeare does not. The local bishop exists but God does not. These answers are adequate for medical or legal purposes where such purposes have controlled the question. But the answers may be inadequate for the victim's wife and are certainly so for literary critics and the bishop himself. We can redefine the question in terms of tests for literary value to allow for the continuing existence of Shakespeare. And even an unbeliever might construct tests which allow God to live and Shakespeare to pass away.

Yet such control of questions falls under the heading of *use*. Definitions are means to purposes we impose. We master or dominate questions in order to satisfy our (or society's) particular intentions. We want a world of inheritance and insurance, of scientific laws and technological achievement. There is nothing unworthy in this. But no such world yields a final answer. *Respect* for questions means allowing them their head. Questioning reveals the limited nature of every particular question and answer. The questioner may control *truths*, but he submits to *truth* as an end in itself.

What, however, of the philosopher, at least in his more metaphysical ambitions and moments? Does he not claim to settle questions in some absolute way? Have not statements about the "structures" of our life been defended in this book as a final answer rather than as a provisional reply within carefully controlled limits? Or do such statements merely serve as a spur against complacency and an incentive for renewed questioning?

To pose any alternative is to invite the question whether it is a fixed one. Perhaps it is only by making "absolute" claims to truth that we show a respect for truth which keeps us from self-satisfaction in the techniques of questioning. Absolutes are insidious. When suppressed in one guise they reappear in another. The best approach may be a sympathy which allows the relationship of absolute and relative to work itself out in its many forms.

Hence, before asking about the final answers or remaining questions of philosophy, we shall look at the forms in which absolute claims have most commonly appeared throughout history, namely in religion. Yet an assessment of any demand for allegiance to "the one truth" involves a preliminary investigation of the key term. So first we shall summarize what previous chapters have suggested about the meaning of "truths" and "truth."

What Is Truth?

So phrased, this is very much a philosopher's question. Most people spend their days asking "What is true?" rather than "What is truth?" Yet repeated problems and conflicts in answering the first question lead to the second.

When the question "What is truth?" is asked in a nonphilosophical context, the tone is likely to be one of cynicism. Truth is very much what you make it. We may try to persuade others and win converts, but there is no one truth to which all must submit. The game belongs to the man with the deepest convictions and the loudest voice. Truth is what you can get away with.

The following pages will examine the two theories of truth which have formed the basis for most philosophical discussion of this question. It will be claimed that each is valid for a certain range of questions but fails to allow for the full submission involved in questioning. So some remarks will then be added, applying the conclusions of the previous chapter to the notion of ''respect for truth.''

Correspondence

The starting-point for most discussions has been with the definition of truth as ''the correspondence of the mind to reality.'' This definition comes from the Middle Ages and can claim equivalent expressions in Plato and Aristotle. A statement we make is true if it corresponds to what is really so apart from what we say or think. Taken in a rough sense, this is almost a platitude. A glance through the window is enough to satisfy us that what the weather forecaster had in mind either corresponds or not to what the day really produces.

Such a definition can cover most of our ordinary claims to truth. But it raises a host of philosophical problems. What is meant by the three terms? Is *mind* always to be understood as an isolated statement? What, for instance, of the context of statements and the notion of language as an activity (cf. Chapter Nine)? Does *reality* consist of facts which stand out to be recorded apart from statement and context and intention? Above all, what is this mysterious relation of *correspondence*? If it is between the mind and something outside the mind, how can it be measured by the mind, as one of the terms to be compared?

A simple form of the correspondence theory can be ascribed to John Locke. But he recognized the problems. Truth is not merely a correspondence of ''ideas'' in the mind to ''qualities'' in the world, for most qualities are ''secondary,'' i.e., ''in the mind'' or thoroughly dependent on our way of knowing. That is, what the unadorned definition of truth neglects is the element of prior knowledge, the intention in our questioning. It is this which enables the questioner to be ignorant in some intelligent way and thus receive facts of a certain sort. If submission to truth meant a purely passive correspondence to facts, then nothing would register. Rainy weather is experienced as a reply to at least implicit questions about what I can do today.

This theme has been emphasized enough in these pages. ''Objects,'' ''things,'' ''facts'' hinge upon human interests and purposes. A scientist can control his questions in such a way that the world is revealed in terms of things with quantifiable properties and in terms of recurrent events. But he is constituting facts of a certain sort rather than submitting to them as already there independently of his manner of questioning. What depends on the hypotheses of specialists or the conventions of society cannot qualify as an absolute in our search for truth.

This is far from suggesting that what is ''hypothetical'' or ''conventional'' in this sense may be taken lightly. The ways the world has been formulated by history and society determine what is "really so" for most of our purposes. We ignore these norms and tests at our peril. If I drive through a light that is really red, I deserve what comes. But as a theory of truth, the notion of correspondence to particular facts satisfies only when we disregard the prior control of facts, the way in which the "reality" term of the relationship depends on the "mental" term. "Correspondence" cannot be a relationship between statements and facts, as observed by one who is not involved in the statement of facts.

Coherence

The other classical theory of truth grew out of such criticisms of the notion of correspondence. And much of our ordinary discussion puts less emphasis on appeals to fact than on the coherence of our statements or meaning. Even those people most impressed by the rule of facts may admit that these seldom settle arguments. The question "Is it so?" is not primary. For such a question presupposes that we already know what we mean by the "it" which may or may not be so. We must first ask what we mean by "straight" before we can investigate whether light travels in a straight line. If two adversaries can be brought to clarify their meaning sufficiently, they may both turn out to be right.

The philosopher recognizes this more than most. His annoying characteristic is to start discussions by saying "It all depends what you mean by—." In other words, his tendency is to absorb questions of fact in questions of meaning. And he may be led to conclude that if we could ever get our minds perfectly clear about what we mean, then there would be no "further" problem of truth. Error comes with muddle and carelessness, with inconsistent meanings. Error is removed, not by trying to go beyond statements to any facts outside all human formulations, but rather by gradually clarifying our meaning until all our statements "fit." Truth is the coherence of meanings with each other.

Though the coherence theory may sound strange when so put, there is at least one consideration which makes it attractive. The theory frees us from many of our common forms of dogmatism. Remove the notion of facts, simply out there beyond our power of reformulation, and we take away the basis for many obstinate claims to a final possession of truth, apart from the historical, social, and temperamental factors that bear so strongly on all we say and think. For no statement is true or false according as it does or does not, once and for all time, reflect a fact which is simply so. Instead, the philosopher tries to reconcile apparent differences through clarification. He steps down from his pulpit and becomes the calm interpreter of our many languages and of our varied human expressions.

However, the instinctive feeling of most people toward a pure co-herence theory of truth is a fear that it opens the way to a relativism which would remove all basis for our normal use of the terms "truth" and "falsity." Truth becomes merely a matter of degrees of adequacy. And there seems to be something radically lacking in the view that if I could sufficiently clarify my meaning I should have to be correct. Though no one likes to be wrong, we feel we have an inalienable right to be wrong, and not just confused.

Can this instinctive reaction be put on a more secure philosophical footing? The problem is whether all questions of fact can be absorbed into questions of meaning. Or does the supporter of the coherence theory find himself in a basic self-contradiction?

What, after all, is he doing? He is affirming that his theory is so, is some final answer, against the supporters of the correspondence theory or any other. They are wrong in denying that truth is just meaning. He is right in affirming that truth is only the coherence of meanings. Implicitly, then, he is saying that there is something more to truth than meaning, because his view "corresponds to reality" and others do not.

There would be a way out if the correspondence and other theories of truth could somehow be reduced to the coherence theory. This was the reply of Hegel, who tried to interpret the history of philosophy, not as a struggle between contrary claims to the one truth, but rather as a progression from less to more adequate stages of an all-comprising phi-losophical system, that of Hegel himself: "The refutation of a philosophy means only that its frontiers are crossed and its special principle reduced to one factor in a more comprehensive view."

Nevertheless, at this point some return must be made from systems and principles to fact—not the particular facts of the correspondence theory but the inescapable fact of questioning on which this book has been a commentary. However much one may be attracted by the supreme version of coherence presented by Hegel, the fact remains that we are *asking* about the nature of truth and not simply understanding it. The ignorance at the heart of every claim we make to truth renders any final coherence of all meanings unattainable—even if we can meaningfully talk about it, and even if Hegel did really mean that in talking about it.

The correspondence theory does not allow for the prior knowledge of the questioner in waiting upon facts. But the coherence theory does not adequately allow for the ignorance which makes questioning an act of total submission to a reality that we cannot master, even through the most rigorous control of the particular questions we ask and meanings we clarify. I may, if I wish, say "It all depends what I mean by—" But I first must discover what I *do* mean. And this is no mere matter of clarifying the way I happen to talk or think. I am obliged to ask what *is* the meaning I should have and to which I ought to submit. The language of this statement may turn the discussion of truth to the theme of morality raised in the last chapter.

Personal Integrity

The correspondence theory is at home in most science and in our everyday world of obvious facts. The coherence theory is at home in mathematics and in complex questions where clarification is needed and facts are elusive. However, when we look beyond the home field, inadequacies appear in each theory. Correspondence gives to particular facts a role which they are not equipped to play; we cannot offer full submission to anything over which we exercise control. Coherence, however, fails to account for this submission or acceptance which is so basic to our search for truth; the questioner is not merely tidying up his meaning but is opening himself to what is really so independently of his own intellectual mastery.

The proposal here is not for a new ''definition of truth.'' It is rather to suggest that our search for truth cannot be expressed adequately without reference to moral terms. In our ordinary language, the word ''truth'' crosses the boundary between theoretical and practical. And this is more clearly shown in religion, to which this discussion is a preliminary: ''The truth shall make you free.''

Perhaps, though, another model may introduce the topic. The term ''truth'' is sometimes applied to art. Here, no ''correspondence to reality'' is meant in the sense of a mere imitation of what is already empirically in the world, such as a cornfield or a face. The artist does not reproduce an existing object. He produces an original one. And the truth of his work is measured, not by standing·outside it and comparing it to a ''blueprint,'' but rather by discovering the adequacy of his expression to his intention. Art involves submission of the highest sort. This is not to an object but to an ''end'' which is always ahead of the artist and is grasped only through the inadequate expression he gives it in his work and vision.

Similarly, in questioning, that to which we are trying to ''correspond'' is no object already there but rather the goal or end of our inquiry. A judge does not fulfill his task by simply recording the facts as they are presented to him. That is his starting-point. His aim is to discover ''what is really so'' in a complex of deeds and intentions. He struggles to correspond to what may ever elude his adequate understanding and formulation. Questioning is correspondence to reality, and this is independent of us, not in the sense that we could have any access apart from our statement of it, but in the sense that we do not control it or make it what we will. Such independence can reside in no particular facts or set of clarified meanings. Reality is the end to which I ought to submit in all my activity of formulating questions, constituting facts, and clarifying meanings. To resume Kant's example (p. 84), I am not a passive pupil but a judge who poses questions of my making: I yield to truth so far as I *am* true to my task of responsible questioning, rather than allowing any private interests to dull my sensitivity and warp my judgment.

In other words, I disclose what *is* so by acting as I *ought.* In the realms where the correspondence and coherence theories are applicable, truth may not depend on personal integrity. At least, moral character has nothing to do with success in measuring and calculating. Here mastery is all that matters. Indeed, the techniques of controlling facts and clarifying meanings are as much involved in all forms of knowledge as is the recognition of roles and functions in understanding people. But just as more is needed to reveal what a person really is, so an attitude of respect is basic where inquiry takes us from particular truths to any "final" grasp of truth. Perhaps the problem of a "final answer" can be put by saying than any such answer could never be "grasped" but only accepted and lived.

The goal of questioning is an end in itself. It is the end of each particular questioner. In accepting it he accepts his true self and is taken out of his private self. In the self-forgetfulness by which he submits to truth, he is freed to become what he really is. The themes of freedom, morality, and truth come together. But for most people the idiom in which such themes have traditionally been put is that of religion.

The Religious Answer

Religions have normally expressed themselves in the form of answers, and of final or absolute answers. In this there is at least a change of style and temperament from that of philosophers. Questioning has usually been regarded as suspect by religious people. Yet religion may cast some light on the problem of interpreting claims to a final answer which are equally ways of renewed questioning.

The Phenomenon
of Religion

Most would say that religion is concerned with God. However, the term will be avoided in this brief introductory account of the symbolic world of religion. Our aim at first is merely descriptive, and the word "God" carries all too many polemical overtones for both believer and nonbeliever. Perhaps the word "believer" is also overloaded and incorrect, but it will nevertheless be used instead of the cumbersome term "religious man."

How does the believer make sense of his experience? If he is also member of a scientific culture, the answer would be very complex, for quite different schemes of understanding are involved. The symbols of science organize a world of things in relation to things and of events causing events, all capable of being ordered mathematically, The "same" thing and event can be identified repeatedly; nothing is unique, no happening is strictly new. But the religious account is akin to the artist's; things obtrude in an individual way and lead us to their "deeper reality" rather than to other instances linked by laws of recurrence. And as we spoke in an earlier chapter of "aesthetic distance," so here we can talk of the way the "objects" of religion are distanced from those of everyday employment.

That is, the believer "divines" a greater reality in some things than their ordinary appearance or use. What he thus sees may be called "the divine" or "the sacred." Descriptions of this must remain highly metaphorical. The sacred is frequently spoken of in terms of power, life, will, abundance, and "awefulness." It is in such terms that the believer interprets what is real rather than apparent. Whereas for the scientist reality means the order and normalcy of the world we observe, for the believer the real is that which stands out mysteriously from the common run of things. He feels himself most real when he is taken out of his everyday self in an encounter with the supreme otherness of the divine. The order and meaning in his life come, not from observation of the facts before him, but from participation in the creative activity of the sacred which draws meaning out of chaos.

The religious interpretation of experience is thus based on an opposition between the sacred and the commonplace or "profane." The sacred is attained only in the ordinary; and just as every experience is potentially aesthetic, so all objects are potentially religious. But the sacred "transcends" every object and is disclosed only in contrast to the profane. Taboos, asceticism, consecration are signs of this separation. Yet the relation has its problems. The profane is nothing before the sacred, but the latter relies for all its characteristics on its opposition to the former.

This nothingness of the profane is shown most strikingly in the transformation of the believer. Through myth and ritual he is freed from concern for his profane self and is enabled to participate in the life that really counts. In the unity of the divine he leaves behind the distractions of the everyday world and is made whole or "saved."

The sacred thus tends to nullify the profane, and this shows itself in the absolutizing tendencies of most religions. Other symbolic forms are rejected as vain or are incorporated under religious control. In primitive societies no aspect of life escapes religious determination. The events of nature, the institutions of society, the fortunes of history and of private life are all seen and "explained" as manifestations of the divine. Prayer and ritual are the appropriate response, rather than investigation and technique.

However, this very tendency to destroy or absorb the profane deprives the sacred of that opposition on which it subsists. Where the profane disappears, religion itself becomes all and hence ordinary. Nature and society offer no order of their own, so religious explanations become adequate and "normal" accounts of whatever happens. The church is a state, and prayer becomes a technique for producing commonplace benefits. Hence, by an ironic twist the sacred vanishes and the profane gains its independence.

The scheme is over-simple but suggests some interesting questions for today. Some say that ours is a time in which we have seen the final triumph of the profane. For, it is maintained, the dependence of the sacred on the profane is not reversible. We have now "come of age" and no longer think in terms of this world and any "deeper reality" beyond it. Nature and society have been desacralized. Science, technology, art, morality have won complete independence from religion. Man recognizes his autonomy. The world is his for the discoveries of his mind and the work of his hands. The society and future we have is the one we create. This independence from any reference to the sacred is called "secularity." Historically, its origins are looked for in the Renaissance (though some say, in the Bible). Philosophically, its expression is connected with the renewed sense of subjectivity that came with such figures as Descartes and Kant.

However, others hold that the distinction of sacred and profane belongs, in a variety of particular forms, to the structure of experience. Hence, the dialectic which passed from a domination in terms of the sacred to the triumph of the profane must lead to a renewal of the sacred. Secularity is no final stage but the ground for new forms of religion. If these are delayed, it is because people have not yet come to a sufficient recognition of their need: only through a deep awareness of the absence of the sacred can new forms of its presence arise.

It is not the purpose of this chapter to argue one way or the other. Our concern is with the ambiguous status of final answers and absolutizing tendencies, of which religion is a prime example. What has been argued throughout this book is that the structures of experience do involve a "metaphysical element," some valid question of a necessity and a reality beyond the world of science and ordinary concerns. Hence the conclusion would be that if secularity means contentment with the technological culture we have created, then the seeds of a radical opposition must be present in it. But whether what arises will be seen as a renewal of the experience of sacred and profane is a further question. Some might say that it could be, without insisting that it must be.

Religion and Reason

Investigations of the religious phenomenon and of the varieties of religious experience have been plentiful in this century. They strike a responsive chord in some people, as current interest suggests. But others feel this is a realm that is completely foreign to them. They have no sense of the sacred, no wish to recognize it and share in it. If religion is to play any part in their lives, they would like to be shown. And such ''showing,'' it is commonly assumed, must take the form of an argument or rational account.

This introduces the problem of the relation between the religious view of ''reality'' and that which philosophy involves. The believer stands before the absolute. Yet reason imposes absolute claims on our assent. Is this the ''same absolute?'' Or is one to be absorbed in the other? The final section will offer some comments on this question. But now we may face the rather strange spectacle of believers turning to reason to justify their belief.

It is largely within Christianity that this has come about. Partial explanations are offered in terms of missionary goals and the influence of Greek philosophy. The latter led to a result of great significance for Western culture. Rational justification or ''legitimation'' for religion could be sought in various ways. It could come as an attempt to prove the ''rightness'' of one approach to the sacred over others (as in the encounter between Elijah and the prophets of Baal: I Kings 18). Or it could come as an effort to prove the necessity of the religious experience as such; and it is this project which appeared in Christianity as the enterprise of ''proving the existence of God.''

The venture is as daring as it is ambiguous. For it claims to unite two such different traditions as the Jewish and the Greek. Sacred reality in the form of Jahweh is boldly declared to be the same as the supreme Idea, or infinite Being, or pure act, or self-thinking thought of Greek speculation. Abstract criticism of the traditional ''proofs'' is usually conducted without reference to the major cultural synthesis that is at stake. And those who find the proofs valid often forget that our religious heritage makes it easy for us to read much more into the conclusion than a purely philosophical argument warrants.

With these reminders we may now look at two of the proofs of God's existence which have some claim to be fundamental. They will first be exposed much as presented, along with some of the criticism they have provoked from the beginning. Then an attempt will be made to assess what they can be seen to achieve as proofs and what are their shortcomings as ways to the sacred.

PROOFS OF
THE EXISTENCE OF GOD

It is to Anselm of Canterbury (1033–1109) that we may first turn. The project of proving the sacred was put by him under the heading of "faith seeking understanding," and he is most commonly remembered as author of the "ontological argument," though the name comes from Kant's famous criticism of the proof. Anselm first suggested a number of arguments for the existence of God, all on the Platonic theme that grades of perfection are possible only in the light of a supreme perfection. Dissatisfied with these, he sought one argument which would make all others superfluous. The one he proposed is of remarkable simplicity and has offered philosophers one of their persistent themes of discussion.[1]

The proof can be put as follows. We have a concept of God as that greater than which nothing can be thought (the *summum cogitabile* or "supreme thinkable"). From this it immediately follows that God must exist. For if he did not, the concept would lack an obvious perfection and a greater could be thought.

The monk Gaunilo replied at once with a parody. I think of an island so beautiful that none can be thought more so. Hence it must exist. For if it did not, I could proceed to think of one that does, which would be more beautiful.

Serious replies have concentrated on two charges. The first is that existence is not a perfection or predicate. If I think of the "abominable snowman," I have an idea of a creature to which I predicate various bear-like qualities. In affirming that such a creature exists I claim that if you go to Tibet you will discover one. I may be right or wrong. But existence, though established by such tests, has nothing to do with "what" I conceive as an abominable snowman. Anselm was guilty of a serious "category mistake."

His defenders have agreed with this charge if applied to Gaunilo's parody. But they assert that the concept of God is unique. Here, and here alone, existence belongs to the essence of what is thought. Whereas we can entertain all sorts of fancies about islands which do not happen to exist, to think of God is to think of what must exist.

---

[1] Cf. A. Plantinga (ed.), *The Ontological Argument* (Doubleday Anchor, 1965).

The reply to this leads to the second charge. We can certainly talk of a completely perfect being who must exist. At least Anselm did so, and his talk springs out of a long religious tradition of rich but confusing images. However, proof is needed that we can truly think what our words utter, i.e., that the idea is coherent and "positively possible." Anselm offers no proof of God's existence: he merely tells us how he tries to use the word "God"—at least when confronted with a situation more philosophical than religious.

Some of the repeated attempts to revive the ontological argument have been in the direction of meeting this objection. For example, Descartes' version is closely connected with his (unproved) insistence that the idea of God is innate, hence inescapable. And Hegel maintained that the proofs of God's existence are ways of describing the course of all self-critical thinking. In other words, God must be thought, at least implicitly or structurally, and what we really must think must be true of reality. However, such interpretations belong to the assessment to be made shortly; they were scarcely in the mind of Anselm.

One of his most notable critics was Aquinas. In opposition to the ontological argument, which may be called *a priori*, Aquinas proposed five "ways" of proving the existence of God.[2] These are *a posteriori* in the sense that they start with an observation of basic characteristics of things in the world. With the exception of the fourth way, which is largely Platonic, they then invoke an Aristotelian notion of causality to argue to the existence of God as the ultimate cause of the world. The fifth is the "proof from design" (teleological argument), but it is the first three we shall consider here. They can conveniently be treated as one, which has been called the cosmological argument.

The proof may be summarized as follows. All things in the world are "contingent," in the sense that they could have been otherwise or not at all. That is, they are not absolutely necessary: they fail to account for themselves. But there must be an adequate reason for things being as they are, and this ultimate reason must be of such a kind as itself not to require any further reason, i.e., "outside it." This we may conceive as a "first cause," or "unmoved mover," or "necessary being." As Aquinas states his conclusion:

> It is, therefore, necessary to affirm something which is absolutely necessary, which does not have the cause of its necessity from elsewhere, but which is the cause of necessity for others; and this everybody calls God.

Objections to this argument have centered on problems in the notion

[2] *Summa Theologica*, I-2-3. For an account of these, cf. F.C. Copleston, *Aquinas* (Baltimore: Penguin Books, 1963), pp. 114–30.

of causality and on the use Aquinas makes of it. He is certainly not invoking the scientific notion of causality, by which each phenomenon in the world is related to another as much in the realm of experience. Aquinas held that there could be an infinite regress of such causes, but that the whole series would still lack an explanation for its existence. He is faithful to the Aristotelian notion of a cause as an explanation, or answer to a question, rather than as a physical event. We might put the argument as reminding us that the world invites questions about its nature and existence; these must have an answer, and the final answer is God, who "answers for himself." No reply short of this will do, for however much we expand our scientific explanations, the world as a whole remains a fact calling for explanation.

Of course, the question is in what way the notion or talk of God does constitute a final answer. Is this not merely a pious, or pompous, way of repeating the question? Do I supply a meaningful answer to my questioning by saying there must be an answer which calls for no further questioning? Or, in Kant's arid terms, is the idea of God merely regulative of my knowledge but not constitutive? This throws us back to the discussion in Chapter Six and leads to an assessment of these traditional arguments and of the whole project of proving the existence of God.

GOD AND METAPHYSICS

If we are to start by asking simply what such proofs establish, disregarding for a moment their religious context and purpose, we may notice how the ontological and cosmological arguments can be stated in a complementary fashion. The former argues that what is supremely thinkable (rational) must exist. The latter argues that what exists cannot be without a self-accounting explanation (rationality). So put, the project of proving God's existence appears as Hegel's version of the principle of sufficient reason : "What is reasonable is actual, and what is actual is reasonable." (p. 189) In other words the believer, in appealing to reason as a justification for God, seems to end by identifying God with reason. Faith seeking understanding is looking for the absolute of metaphysics.

Such an interpretation, which was that of Hegel, may be repugnant to religious thinkers. At least it offers an unperceptive approach to the wealth of experience that religion presents. However, most religious people are modest in their claims for what argument can do without faith. Hence it may be well to distinguish two steps in the quotation from Aquinas given above (p. 267). The first makes a transition from our ordinary experience (of causation, movement, contingency, etc.) to a metaphysical reality (first cause, unmoved mover, necessary being). The second step makes a transition from such metaphysical terms to properly religious ones ("and this everybody calls God," or—in the fourth and fifth way—"and this we call God").

The point of the following assessment of proofs for the existence of God is (1) that the first transition serves as a far from trivial summary of the project of metaphysics, as considered throughout this book, but (2) that the second transition involves more than philosophical argument can supply.

Terms such as "first cause" and "unmoved mover" have not appeared in these pages. Our scientific climate makes it difficult for us to return to such Aristotelian notions without supposing that they represent some supreme object. However, the term "necessity" has been present from the beginning and was used to introduce the claim of metaphysics to take us beyond the conclusions of science (cf. pp. 12–13). The rich detail of our everyday world and the impressive laws of science are possible only within certain "inescapable structures." The transition from contingent facts to their conditions of possibility is a task for philosophical argument—whatever one may think of the validity of particular proofs.

However, traditional metaphysics has claimed more than to discover the necessary structures of facts or objects or *phenomena*. It is the further transition, to *noumena* or the unconditional ground of our everyday experience, that Kant regarded as so problematic. His own proposal was that the problem is to be faced through practical reason, through our free moral activity. In this book, such a proposal has been treated as no *further* transition, because the conditions of possibility for which we have been looking are those of subjectivity, i.e., or what it is to *be* a subject rather than merely to *appear* as an object. The questioner must organize the world in temporal forms because his own manner of being is temporal. The world is unified as a field of possibility, in terms of "I can" rather than in terms of the "I think" of an uninvolved spectator.

So interpreted, the proofs of the existence of God offer no transition from a world of objects to any supreme object. The "contingency" with which they start is that of myself as a perplexed knower, not understanding what I am (cosmological argument) and not fully being what I think (ontological argument). The transition they indicate is to the ground and aim of such knowledge-in-ignorance. This is no particular being, however "supreme," but is that complete subjectivity or self-presence which is implicitly affirmed as the condition of possibility for my own limited self-presence. In Augustine's words, God is more present to me than I am to myself.[3]

---

[3] The knotty questions posed by the rival claims of traditional theism and "pantheism" are not faced in this brief account. There are many forms of religion which

Again, it should be remembered that only the "metaphysical transition" in the proofs is being considered at present. The above paragraph introduces nothing that is foreign to previous chapters. There it has been argued, for instance, that the goal of questioning must somehow be constitutive of all our limited achievements, since a purely regulative ideal is not applicable in self-knowledge as it is in making a journey or solving a technical problem. The chapters on freedom and morality have had as their theme the absolute that is implicitly affirmed in the agency of a subject. My contingency, my acceptance of a genuine "other" and my submission to absolute norms, is recognized so far as I rise to acting freely or autonomously. The more I possess myself in what I do, the more I realize that the self to which I am present is the true subject worthy of respect and reverence, rather than this capricious creature struggling for mastery.

To explore all that is necessarily involved in the agency of questioning is to investigate contingency and what is to be "concluded" from it. This is the task of metaphysics. And this it is that the proofs for the existence of God summarize in their first step. Opponents may reject such proofs because they deny the whole project of metaphysics, or because they accept it only as an analysis of the structures of *phenomena*. But it is likely that most discussion of the proofs bears more strongly on their second step, the hasty identification of some metaphysical conclusion with strictly religious topics.

Nor is the unbeliever the only one to detect a problem here. For Pascal (1623–62), the god of the philosophers falls far short of the God of Abraham, Isaac, and Jacob. And few believers base their faith on such proofs. When challenged, they tend not to give arguments for their belief but rather to give personal accounts of their decision to believe.

Can the second step be argued philosophically? That is, in addition to proving the necessity of our submission to the absolute of reason and of morality, can we prove the necessity of formulating experience in terms of the sacred, of engaging in worship and prayer and all we identify as the belief, behavior, and language of religion? The man to whom religion says little may be "lacking," in much the same way as one for whom art has no great meaning. But art does not usually make the absolute claims we find in religion. And the question is whether the demand that all should think in terms of the sacred can be matter for rational proof.

Proofs of the existence of God can be interpreted as helping one who

do not seem to invite a sharp distinction of the sacred from the "true self" coming to expression in the believer. Even in orthodox theism, allowance is made for statements such as "the love by which I love God is the love by which He loves me."

already believes to see that his faith can "fit" with a rational account of experience. Some commentators hold that this is all Aquinas intended with his five ways. And it can be argued that metaphysics and morality are "perfected" in religion. At least, most people find respect for truth and reverence for the moral law less inspiring than the worship of God. Yet others do not; and the history of religion shows interference with other values as well as their perfection. Reason and religion, questioning and faith, have more often appeared in history as rival absolutes than as two faces of the one truth. This brings us back to the problem of the status of any "final answer." The following section will therefore look at the situation, typical at least in the West, where men have been confronted with divergent claims to total acceptance.

The Remaining Question

Though the term "philosophy" no longer covers all knowledge, and detailed information about man and his world is now left to appropriate experts, something remains of the imperial role of the philosopher. Even where he has abandoned metaphysics, he still tries to tell others what they are doing without according them the privilege in return. If they usually do not retaliate, it may be because they realize how few people are moved by what philosophers have to say. The specialist can be confident of his position in a technological society. He knows how to control his questions in such a way as to get answers that work.

However, the search for more than the techniques of living is not easily suppressed. Both faith and questioning return in a variety of forms to shake us out of our complacency. Though the two present us with rival claims to allegiance, they stand together in renewing our sense of a "beyond" to all we take for granted. This brief section takes its format from their opposition, but a certain unity of purpose may stand out all the more clearly.

Faith and Questioning

Religious faith has at all times inspired the greatest dedication and self-sacrifice. The believer gives himself to God without reserve. All else in his life pales before that which counts as sacred. Holiness matters more than every gift of nature and of fortune, more than wealth, power, and even intelligence.

However, there is an ambiguity in such total submission. It is possible only within the world *as* religious. That is, we must master the world in terms of the sacred in order to submit to the sacred. Hence there arises a suspicion of questioning as a threat to our view of the world in these terms.

Yet this is too simple. There is a questioning or self-criticism at the heart of faith, and it is this which has supplied the theme for the story of religious development. The sacred escapes all forms of ordering and manipulation. It is totally other, a mystery evoking awe and evading every scheme in which we try to express it. Some religions have held that there is an infinity of names for God, but this is a manner of saying that the sacred is nameless; it is present to us only through our recognition of the futility of our efforts to comprehend it. Talk of God, or of the divine, is a final answer in the sense that it allows no search beyond religion for a further answer. But faith is not final in the sense of putting an end to questioning; belief in the mystery sets the believer and all his expressions most radically in question.

It is in this light that some look upon our present secularity as providing the opportunity for a more authentic religious experience than was previously possible. In more specifically religious times, God was "named," reduced to a function or role (such as architect, lawyer, benefactor). Today we are in a position to recognize that "every concept of God is godless." The idols of false religion have been cleared away.

Nevertheless, language is being strained by those who speak of a world without religion as religious. Those who talk of the "silence of God" may not be finding but are certainly looking. Full secularity suggests that we are not even bothering to look, that we have lost interest in any formulation of experience in terms of the sacred, present or absent. So if our current situation is to serve as the basis for a renewed faith, it could only be through experience of what we have as a serious lack, as a need which calls for faith.

Hence the dependence of faith upon questioning. Complacency with the techniques of life does represent the triumph of the profane. If the absence of the sacred is to be recognized as such, it is only through an experience of opposition within the profane that indicates some "deeper reality." That we are today aware of a variety of forms of alienation demands no comment. But it is by no means evident that these are directed toward any renewal of religion. All these remarks suggest is that the basis for such a renewal lies in the radical questioning which is the task of metaphysics. It is only if we are looking beyond the ordering of facts to their necessary ground, and beyond satisfactory answers to final answers, that we can hope to "divine" the sacred in our ordinary experience. The absolute of religion must at least be open to the absolute of reason.

Questioning and Faith

The strength and weakness of religious thought lie in the way it is bound to images. The Biblical story of the fall of man gives us a much more vivid version of our state than does a philosophical account of "self-opposition" or alienation. But the latter offers precision and proof that are lacking in the former.

Questioning involves "demythologizing," some liberation of our thought from images that hamper us in our effort to clarify what we mean and justify what we hold. Yet there is naiveté in any claim that we can so purify our thought as to come to a final statement that is not in need of further clarification. Thought requires language for its existence, and language ties thought down to the all too particular origins of words.

Many philosophers who reject metaphysics do so because they feel that the metaphysician is a victim to the allurement of language. He starts with certain "models of explanation" that particularly interest him, for professional or temperamental reasons. Aristotle was a biologist who was well served by the notion of "form" in his attempt to classify and understand living beings. For Plato the term meant the forms of geometry, art, and morality—also valid but in different ways and in different fields. Then the specialist becomes a metaphysician by an unlimited generalization which projects this model on all reality; everything must have its form or be a participation in forms. This arrogant claim to explain all reality on some particular model is at best a harmless fixation, to be met by therapy rather than by argument.

In the light of this objection, the problem of a final answer is how we can respect truth without trying to master it through the very terms in which we put our questions. Is there any model for metaphysical thinking which is self-correcting? The proposal of this book has been that we examine our very activity of questioning and accept no model outside this. For self-questioning is both self-justifying and self-revising. On this model, all metaphysical terms invite repeated questioning, yet the agency of putting them into question discloses them afresh and renews their meaning.

This is no mere sleight of hand, but it can still become a way of mastering the problem rather than of submitting to truth. The very security of this model can lead to a complacency that is far removed from the exploration of genuine questioning. For the manner of questioning, the norms of an appropriate reply, and the procedure of self-criticism can all be taken for granted. The "self-study" which an organization conducts can degenerate into a form of narcissism.

It is of interest to notice that most of what are regarded as the more important developments in the history of philosophy have come under the impetus of nonphilosophical changes. The questions of Hume and Kant are as much the result of the dramatic growth of Newtonian physics as they are of disputes within strictly philosophical circles. And it has been said that Western philosophy is a secularized retelling of the story of Western theology.

If these remarks, and this introduction to philosophy, are to close with a moral, it is that the study of philosophy is not sufficient to itself. "Outside interests" are required for philosophical thinking to be fruitful. Philosophy springs from wonder, but wonder is often best promoted by a good sound shock. Reason is an absolute, and the questioner is being unfaithful to it whenever he meekly reports that things are so rather than trying to understand why. Yet questioning is true to itself by remaining open to surprise. And the needed shock has often come from faith in a "rival absolute."

The reader intent on definite answers may feel that this discussion of religion, like that of death and immortality, has come to a tame ending. Does self-questioning lead finally to God or to atheism?

Again, however, the insistence must be that our "position" should not trivialize but respect our experience as questioners. Both theism and atheism can become final answers that close questioning with a simple "yes" or "no."

The interpretation of religion toward which this chapter has been working is one where an absolute claim, from outside the very project of philosophy, shakes us from any complacency with what we have worked out for ourselves. A final answer is a renewed question.

Index

(Language cont.)
  activity, 160–62
  atomism, 159–60
  context, 162–63, 167
  development, 156–57, 162–63, 165–67
  limited to experience, 14, 18, 85
  metaphor, 162–63, 167
  and perception, 163–65
  power-words, 224–25
  referential theory, 158
  sentences and words, 159–63
  spatiality, 165
  symbolic expression, 156–58
  temporality, 181–82
  theories of origin:
    imitation, 155
    interjection, 155–56
Leibniz, Gottfried:
  language, 160
  sufficient reason, 188–89
Leisure, 141–42, 151
Leonardo da Vinci, 207–208
Le Senne, René, 195
Linear time, 172–74
Locke, John:
  assumptions, 37–38
  ideas as objects, 34
  particularity of what exists, 114
  primary and secondary qualities, 51–52
  real and nominal essences, 61–62
  truth as correspondence, 258
  viewpoint, 35
  words and ideas, 159
Logos, 159, 190
Love and desire, 233–35, 252–54

Marx, Karl, 143–51
  alienation, 140–41, 144–46, 194
  ideological appeal, 146–47
  substructure and superstructure, 140–41, 148–50
  theory and practice, 150–51
Materiality (*see* Embodiment)
Mathematics (*see also* Number)
  influence on Descartes, 76
  influence on Plato, 60
  influence on Spinoza, 233
  and timeless truths, 170
Matters of fact, 62–63, 84, 99–100
Meaning:
  for human purposes, 38, 40
  manner of acting, 122–27, 137–38
  as noun and verb, 71, 158, 160
  and obligation, 260–61
  in suffering, 193–95

of words, 156–63
Mediation:
  meaning of term, 44
  necessity, 47
  by scientific concepts, 48, 49–50
  by symbols, 123–27
Metaphor, 162–63, 167
Metaphysics:
  ambiguity in project, 98–99
  beyond science, 12–14, 61–63, 74–75, 83–84, 97
  conflicting conclusions, 19, 101
  as fixation, 273
  general and special, 99
  immanent (*see* Transcendental philosophy)
  interpretations:
    Aquinas, 98–99
    Aristotle, 81–83, 98
    Descartes, 16–17, 75–78
    Hume, 61–63
    Kant, 83–86, 99–102, 249–51
    Plato, 59–61, 80–81
  method from questioning, 90–91 (*see also* Self-contradiction)
  natural disposition, 19
  origin of term, 13 *fn.*
  proofs of God, 265–71
  relation of meaning and truth in claims, 103–104
  revisability, 72 *fn.*, 120–21, 273–74
  transcendent (*see* Transcendent metaphysics)
Mill, John Stuart, 244
Montaigne, 87
Moods, 204–205, 208–12
Morality, 237–55
  doubts concerning, 237–40
  explained through:
    accepted values, 243–45
    authority, 240–41
    hidden persuaders, 242–43
    private choice, 245–46
  giving reasons, 246–47
  Kant:
    autonomy, 249–51
    norm of universality, 251–52
    respect for others, 252–53
  metaphysical ground:
    being reasonable, 247–48
    good and bad reasons, 248
  principles and practice, 254–55
  social, 253–54
  and temporality, 179–80, 200–201
  and truth, 261–62
Mortality (*see* Death)
Music, 208, 212, 214